Making MTSS Work

FIRST EDITION

Emily Goodman-Scott, Ph.D.
Jennifer Betters-Bubon, Ph.D.
Jacob Olsen, Ph.D.
Peg Donohue, Ph.D.

An ASCA National Model® Publication

AMERICAN SCHOOL COUNSELOR ASSOCIATION

AMERICAN SCHOOL COUNSELOR ASSOCIATION

The American School Counselor Association (ASCA) supports school counselors' efforts to help students focus on academic, career and social/emotional development so they achieve success in school and are prepared to lead fulfilling lives as responsible members of society. ASCA provides professional development, publications and other resources, research and advocacy to school counselors around the globe. For more information, visit *www.schoolcounselor.org*.

1101 King St., Suite 310, Alexandria, VA 22314
(703) 683-ASCA, (800) 306-4722, fax: (703) 997-7572
www.schoolcounselor.org

ISBN 978-1-929289-64-6

Table of Contents

Introduction

College and career readiness. Fair-share responsibilities. High caseloads. Social/emotional learning. 504 responsibilities. Mindfulness. Racial trauma. Mental health concerns. The richness of increasingly diverse schools and communities. Substance use. Restorative practices. School safety. Trauma. Social media. School counselor burnout and fatigue. The list goes on. As school counselors' responsibilities mount, we need the tools to work in an increasingly vibrant, more complex, fast-paced world. We need to work with our colleagues and stakeholders to ensure our schools meet the needs of all students and prepare them for the future. We want all students to be successful in our ever-changing world. We need to work smarter, not harder. One strategy for working efficiently, and to maximize school counselor efforts and outcomes, is to align school counseling programs with a multitiered system of supports (MTSS).

DESCRIPTION: ASCA NATIONAL MODEL

The American School Counselor Association (ASCA) calls on school counselors to meet all students needs by designing and implementing a school counseling program aligned with the ASCA National Model. Implementing an ASCA National Model school counseling program has been associated with a variety of positive student outcomes, such as higher student achievement, attendance, graduation and student retention rates; better college and career readiness; and lower student suspension, discipline and truancy rates (Burkard, Gillen, Martinez & Skytte, 2012; Carey, Harrington, Martin & Hoffman, 2012; Carey, Harrington, Martin & Stevenson, 2012).

The ASCA National Model is in its fourth edition and has existed for nearly 20 years. Specifically, the ASCA National Model is data-informed, developmentally appropriate and delivered to all students systematically, with the goal of (a) improving student outcomes,

(b) closing student achievement and opportunity gaps and (c) preparing students for post-secondary success. The ASCA National Model is composed of four quadrants:

- Define: standards that serve as the foundation of the school counseling program
- Manage: planning tools that assist in program design and implementation
- Deliver: recommendations that 80% of school counselors' time is spent directly and indirectly serving students
- Assess: tools school counselors can use to assess their program

Three domains guide the focus of a school counseling program:
- Academic
- Career
- Social/emotional

Four themes are interwoven throughout the school counseling program:
- Leadership
- Systemic change
- Advocacy
- Collaboration

EXAMPLE: **ASCA National Model (2019)**

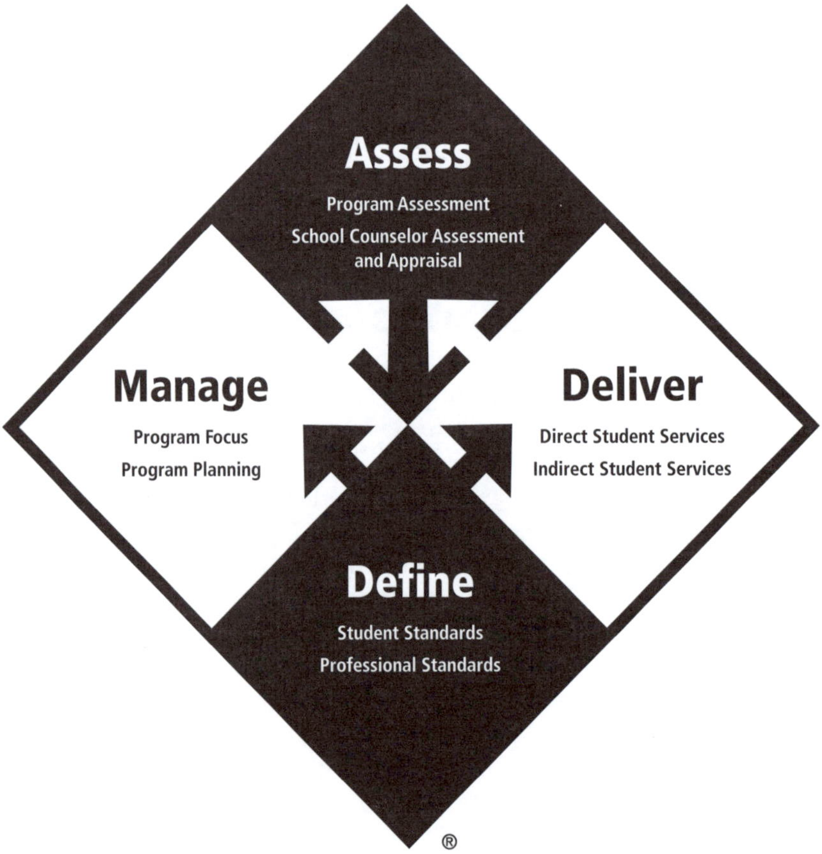

For more information, see the ASCA National Model (2019) and the ASCA National Model Implementation Guide (2019), along with the other resources listed at the end of this introduction.

ACTIVITY: Moving from Reactive to Proactive

According to the ASCA National Model, school counselors are leaders and advocates, promoting social justice and systemic change. As a result of a multitude of competing responsibilities, school counselors may find themselves reactively responding to crises and demands, rather than purposefully and proactively planning and implementing school counseling programs. How do we break this cycle, from reactive to proactive? Read the article From Doer to Leader by Young (2019) in the appendix. Next, answer these questions.

Questions for Review and Discussion

- What key points in this article stand out for you?
- In your school counseling work, are you leading or reacting?
- As a school counselor, how can you expand your circle of influence?
- Do you view yourself as a change agent? What are your leadership strengths across the five dimensions?
- Can you identify systemic barriers in your school?

One strategy for school counselors to work efficiently, improve our ability to advocate and educate key stakeholders is to embed ourselves within the system of the school, using language and initiatives familiar to building administrators and teachers. Although we know the importance and value of implementing a school counseling program, we frequently need to educate stakeholders. We need to demonstrate how our efforts align with schoolwide initiatives and priorities, using frameworks and language familiar to stakeholders and colleagues.

MTSS is one such schoolwide priority. MTSS is widely used in education; thus, our educational stakeholders and colleagues are likely familiar with this schoolwide framework. As such, school counselors must understand how to align the ASCA National Model and MTSS.

DESCRIPTION: MTSS

MTSS is an overarching framework that typically includes a continuum of prevention and intervention supports to help the whole child be successful in academics, behaviors and other dimensions such as social/emotional and mental health (Brown-Chidsey & Bickford, 2016; Goodman-Scott & Ockerman, 2019; McIntosh & Goodman, 2016). MTSS is often described as the integration of the academically focused response to intervention (RTI) and the behaviorally focused positive behavioral interventions and supports (PBIS), to comprehensively serve students across these multiple, overlapping domains.

The MTSS framework is typically composed of three tiers of prevention and intervention. All students receive Tier 1 prevention, such as core curriculum and behavioral expectations, and approximately 80% of students are successful with only this support. However, approximately 15% of students will require additional supports (e.g., small group) to be successful in school. Last, approximately 5% of students will require the most intensive supports. Thus, we often say all students receive Tier 1 supports, some students receive the additional Tier 2 supports and few students require Tier 3 supports. MTSS is driven by data, utilizes evidence-based practices, incorporates a system's approach and should be culturally sustaining based on each unique school community. We'll unpack these terms in greater detail later in the book. MTSS implementation has been associated with a plethora of positive school outcomes, such as increased attendance and achievement, as well as lower rates of discipline referrals and suspension (Childs, Kincaid, George, & Gage, 2016; Freeman, Simonsen, McCoach, Sugai, Lombardi, & Horner, 2015; Kim, McIntosh, Mercer, Nese, 2018).

Schoolwide Support Systems for Student Success

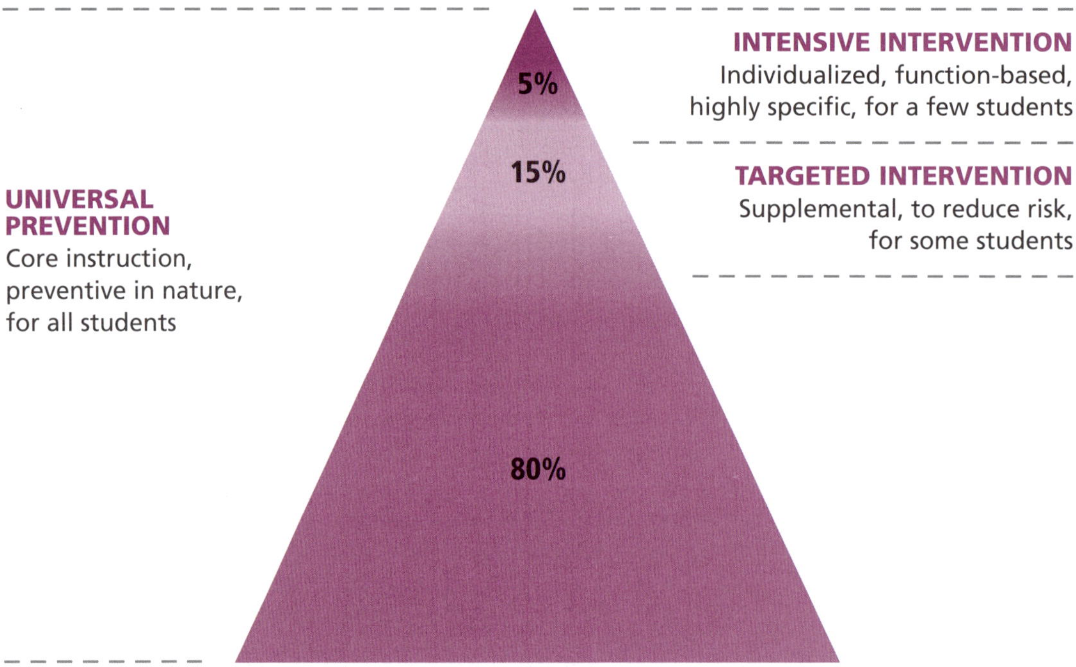

Although there are many benefits of MTSS implementation, there are also challenges (Olsen, Parikh-Foxx, Flowers & Algozzine, 2016). The literature suggests common barriers to MTSS implementation include a lack of administrator and staff buy-in, lack of district and state support and resources, as well as the time commitment, especially at the beginning. At the same time, despite these challenges, MTSS implementation comes with significant benefits. Strategies in this book will help address some of these challenges and assist in maximizing the advantages of implementation.

Overall, MTSS is implemented in every state and nearly 30% of schools across the United States. Although this framework is commonly known as MTSS, some states create their own related acronyms, such as Virginia Tiered Systems of Support and Montana Behavior Initiative. For a more comprehensive description of MTSS, see the resources at the end of this chapter.

What are Culturally Sustaining Practices?

According to Paris and Alim (2017), culturally sustaining practices "calls for schooling to be a site for sustaining the cultural ways of being of communities of color" (p. 5). Thus, rather than privileging a dominant culture, culturally sustaining schools sustain, or continue, the culture of their students, families and communities throughout their school culture and practices.

The Importance of Person-First Language

Throughout this book, we emphasize a constructive view of students. Rather than calling Ron a "Tier 3 student," we say, "Ron is a student in need of Tier 3 supports." We want to look at him across a continuum, acknowledging his strengths and areas in which he needs targeted and intensive supports. We strive to look at Ron as a whole child, including his strengths and potential and areas in which he needs more support.

The goal of this book is to help school counselors implement data-informed, culturally sustaining, systematic, evidence-based school counseling programs. We believe aligning school counseling programs with MTSS is a strategy to maximize school counselors' efficiency and effectiveness and a tool for advocacy and education, to further reinforce school counseling programs within our schools. We also believe this book can help us answer our "why." Ask yourself:

- Why did you enter the school counseling profession?
- Why have you stayed in this profession?
- What is your "why"?

Ultimately, to answer our "why," we want to be efficient and effective in implementing school counseling and MTSS alignment. In this book, we focus on aligning the ASCA National Model and MTSS (chapter one) and address this alignment through data (chapters two and three), as well as across Tier 1, 2 and 3 (chapters four, five and six, respectively). We see the books "The ASCA National Model: A Framework for School Counseling Programs," and "The School Counselor's Guide to Multitiered Systems of Support" as providing helpful background information on the "what" behind these frameworks. We intend for "Making MTSS Work" to be a practical companion to these books, describing the "how" of this alignment. As such, we suggest reading "Making MTSS Work" alongside the ASCA National Model and the Guide to MTSS. Throughout this book, we'll be referencing both books and a host of other resources, to direct readers to more comprehensive background information.

To highlight the how of this alignment, we are honored to share practical content from the field, providing key examples from exemplary schools and districts throughout the United States, specifically:

Capistrano Unified School District, Calif.: Capistrano Unified covers 200 miles and seven cities and is the largest employer in South Orange County. With more than 47,000 students and 63 schools, Capistrano has been a lead district in the MTSS implementation across

California. A special thank you to Rebecca Pianta (coordinator, counseling and student support) for her ongoing leadership and advocacy that has led to an increase in the number of school counselors in her district and has elevated school counselors into leadership roles within MTSS implementation. Her collaboration and contributions to this book are invaluable.

Culver City Unified School District, Calif.: Culver City serves more than 7,000 students across eight schools in Los Angeles County. Culver City implements MTSS at all elementary schools, Culver City Middle School and Culver City High School. A special thanks to Jeanine Lizotte (school counselor, Culver City Middle School) and Sarah Slemmons (school counselor, Culver City Middle School) for increasing the visibility of school counseling programs across the district and county and taking active leadership roles in school counseling program and MTSS alignment. Their passion for MTSS is contagious, and their contributions to this book reflect the important role school counselors play in MTSS.

Kern High School District, Calif.: Kern is located at the southern end of the San Joaquin Valley and is California's largest high school district with 18 high schools serving more than 40,000 students. Kern's MTSS implementation includes PBIS, social/emotional learning and restorative practices. In addition, school counselors have played a pivotal role in MTSS implementation across the district. A special thanks to Brian Mendiburu (director, student behavior and supports), Monica Bonillo (lead interventionist) and Cy Silver (supervising administrator, intervention and supports) for their leadership in MTSS implementation and making school counselors critical partners in MTSS implementation. Their high school perspective on school counseling and MTSS alignment is very much appreciated.

Loudoun County Public Schools, Va.: Loudoun is the third largest school district in Virginia and one of the fastest growing districts in the country, opening one to three schools every year. The district is situated in the diverse greater Washington, D.C., metro area and contains rural, suburban and urban neighborhoods. The district has more than 82,400 students and 94 schools. Loudoun County has been implementing MTSS for more than a decade, which now includes PBIS, RTI and incorporates a number of supports, including social/emotional learning, suicide prevention, academic and career planning, assigned school mental health professionals at each school, specialized reading instruction, restorative practices and bully prevention. A special thank you to Tracy Jackson, Ph.D., (district-level school counseling supervisor) and Stefanie LaPolla (district-level MTSS supervisor) for their generous collaboration and support with this book and their exemplary school counseling/MTSS alignment.

Milwaukee Public Schools, Wis.: Milwaukee Public Schools is the largest school district in Wisconsin, serving close to 75,000 students in approximately 150 schools, and one of the largest districts in the United States by enrollment. Milwaukee Public Schools' offerings include neighborhood schools, specialty schools and charter schools serving students as young as age 3 up through grade 12. Milwaukee Public Schools has utilized RTI/PBIS and initiatives of social/emotional learning, restorative practices, trauma-sensitive schools, mental health, gifted and talented, and culturally responsive teaching within this framework. Special thanks to Jon Jagemann, district discipline manager, for permission to use the website materials and to the MTSS teams for graciously sharing their ideas.

Sugar Creek Elementary School, Wis.: Sugar Creek is part of the Verona Area School District, the 28th largest district in Wisconsin. Sugar Creek's mission is to provide a safe, supportive environment where all are encouraged to experience the joy of learning and are challenged to do their best. The school of more than 500 students, including a bilingual, two-way Spanish immersion program and 70 staff members has maintained a long-standing tradition of providing a stimulating, caring environment and was the first in the Verona Area School district to implement PBIS. A special thank you to principal Todd Brunner and school counselor Miriam Brownman for their enthusiastic sharing of MTSS implementation ideas and strategies and for their continual advocacy for students and families. An additional thank you to Avery Kansteiner, former school counselor, who was instrumental in building the MTSS program.

The Stamford Public Schools, Conn.: Stamford Public Schools is the fifth largest school district in Connecticut and is located in Fairfield County, approximately 40 miles from New York City. SPS is composed of nearly 16,000 students, more than 1,500 professionals, with 38 school counselors working at the secondary level. SPS has 22 schools, including one preschool, 13 elementary schools, five middle schools, three high schools and various specialized programs, which serve students from 75 cultural backgrounds and geographic locations. SPS is making strides in aligning its districtwide school counseling program to MTSS under the thoughtful direction of their K–12 coordinator for college and career readiness/school counselor services, Rebecca Wilson, who contributed to this publication.

RESOURCES AND REFERENCES

American School Counselor Association. (2019). *The ASCA national model: A framework for school counseling programs* (4th ed.). Alexandria, VA: Author.

American School Counselor Association. (2014). *ASCA mindsets & behaviors for student success: K-12 college- and career-readiness standards for every student.* Alexandria, VA: Author.

American School Counselor Association. (2019). *ASCA national model implementation guide: Manage & assess* (2nd ed.). Alexandria, VA: Author.

Brown-Chidsey, R., & Bickford, R. (2016). *Practical handbook of multi-tiered systems of support: Building academic and behavioral success in schools.* New York, NY: Guilford Press.

Burkard, A. W., Gillen, M., Martinez, M. J., & Skytte, S. L. (2012). Implementation challenges and training needs for comprehensive school counseling programs in Wisconsin high schools. *Professional School Counseling, 16*, 136-145. doi: 10.5330/PSC.n.2012-16.136

Carey, J., Harrington, K., Martin, I., & Hoffman, D. (2012a). A statewide evaluation of the outcomes of the implementation of ASCA national model school counseling programs in rural and suburban Nebraska high schools. *Professional School Counseling, 16*, 100-107. doi: 10.5330/PSC.n.2012-16.100

Carey, J., Harrington, K., Martin, I., & Stevenson, D. (2012b). A statewide evaluation of the outcomes of the implementation of ASCA national model school counseling programs in Utah high schools. *Professional School Counseling, 16*, 89-99. doi: 10.5330/PSC.n.2012-16.89

Childs, K. E., Kincaid, D., George, H. P., & Gage, N. A. (2016). The relationship between school-wide implementation of positive behavior intervention and supports and student discipline outcomes. *Journal of Positive Behavior Interventions, 18*(8), 89-99. https://doi.org/10.1177/1098300715590398

Freeman, J., Simonsen, B., McCoach, D. B., Sugai, G., Lombardi, A., & Horner, R. (2015). Relationship between school-wide positive behavior interventions and supports and academic, attendance, and behavior outcomes in high schools. *Journal of Positive Behavior Interventions*, 1-11. https://doi.org/ 10.1177/1098300715580992

Goodman-Scott, E., Betters-Bubon, J., & Donohue, P. (Eds.). (2019). *A School Counselor's Guide to Multi-tiered Systems of Support* (1st ed.). New York City, NY: Routledge.

Goodman-Scott, E. & Ockerman, M. (2019). Integrating school counseling and MTSS. In E. Goodman-Scott, J. Betters-Bubon, & P. Donohue (Eds.), *A School Counselor's Guide to Multi-tiered Systems of Support* (1st ed. 29-61). New York City, NY: Routledge.

Kim, J., McIntosh, K., Mercer, S. H., & Nese, R. N. T. (2018). Longitudinal associations between SWPBIS fidelity of implementation and behavior and academic outcomes. *Behavioral Disorders*, 1-13. https://doi.org/10.1177/0198742917747589

McIntosh, K., & Goodman, S. (2016). *Integrated multi-tiered systems of support: Blending RTI and PBIS.* New York: Guilford.

Olsen, J., Parikh-Foxx, S., Flowers, C., and Algozzine, B. (2016). An examination of factors that relate to school counselors' knowledge and skills in multi-tiered systems of support. *Professional School Counselor, 20*(1), 159-171.

Paris, D., & Alim, H. S. (Eds.). (2017). *Culturally sustaining pedagogies: Teaching and learning for justice in a changing world.* Teachers College Press.

VOICES FROM THE FIELD REFERENCES

Throughout this book we use quotes from qualitative studies that investigated school counselors and other school staff regarding their MTSS involvement (mainly PBIS). Specifically:

Goodman-Scott, E., Hays, D. G., & Cholewa, B. (2018). "It takes a village:" A case study of Positive Behavioral Interventions and Supports implementation in an exemplary middle school. *The Urban Review, 50*(1), 97-122. doi:10.1007/s11256-017-0431-z

Goodman-Scott, E. & Grothaus, T. (2017a). RAMP and PBIS: "They definitely support one another." A phenomenological study. *Professional School Counseling, 21*(1), 119-129. doi:10.5330/1096-2409-21.1.119

Goodman-Scott, E. & Grothaus, T. (2017b). School counselors' roles in RAMP and PBIS: A phenomenological investigation. *Professional School Counseling, 21*(1), 130-141. doi:10.5330/1096-2409-21.1.130

CHAPTER 1

Aligning the ASCA National Model and MTSS

In the introduction, we relayed the importance of school counselors working efficiently, described the ASCA National Model and MTSS, suggested educating stakeholders on the school counselor's role by demonstrating the alignment of the ASCA National Model and MTSS. In this chapter, we will discuss how to align the ASCA National Model with MTSS generally, showing examples from the field. We will also discuss the school counselor's role in MTSS, as well as the MTSS team. In subsequent chapters, we will discuss the school counselor/MTSS alignment in greater detail as it relates to data and each of the three tiers.

In the last 10 years, a host of scholars have published articles describing how to align the ASCA National Model with MTSS, including RTI (Ockerman, Mason, & Hollenbeck, 2012), PBIS (Goodman-Scott, Betters-Bubon, & Donohue, 2016) and MTSS (Ziomek-Daigle, Goodman-Scott, Cavin, & Donohue, 2016). Researchers have also highlighted this alignment empirically, publishing research on the school counselor's role in MTSS; for a review of this literature, see Goodman-Scott and Ockerman (2019) and the special issue of *The Professional Counselor* edited by Sink and Ockerman (2016).

VOICES FROM THE FIELD:

"I think MTSS marries really well with the school counselor's role and our program."

VOICES FROM THE FIELD:

"School counseling and MTSS go hand-in-hand. Because of the culture we're trying to create by making sure we have a school counseling program on one side and then, on the other side, making sure we have a positive climate in our building there's most definitely an overlap. They definitely support one another."

QUESTIONS FOR REVIEW AND DISCUSSION

In the introduction we described the ASCA National Model and MTSS frameworks, mentioning their alignment and overlap. But what does that mean? What does this alignment look like? The following table shows the focus and priorities of each framework: What do you notice?

Comparing School Counseling Programs and MTSS

ASCA National Model programs	MTSS
■ Preventive	■ Preventive
■ Data-informed, guided by evidence-based practices	■ Data-informed, utilizing evidence-based practices
■ Culturally sustaining	■ Culturally sustaining
■ Utilizing a system's approach	■ Utilizing a system's approach
■ Serving all students through direct and indirect services	■ Serving all students through a tiered continuum of supports
■ Focusing on students' academic, career and social/emotional development and the interconnectedness of these domains	■ Integrating academic and behavioral development and the interconnectedness of these domains
■ Developmentally appropriate ■ School counselor roles as leaders, collaborators, advocates and systemic change agents	■ Collaborative

Goodman-Scott & Ockerman, 2019, School Counselor's Guide to MTSS

At first glance, we notice the two frameworks have similar priorities and focuses. Now, let's take a deeper dive.

ACTIVITY: School Counseling Program Examination

We will get started by examining your school counseling program.

Make a list of the following:

- What school counseling activities do you complete for all students on your caseload/schoolwide?

■ What school counseling activities do you complete for some/few students on your caseload, who have elevated needs?

By listing the activities you do for all, some and few students, you've completed the first step in aligning your school counseling program with MTSS. You've reconceptualized the activities you are already doing into the MTSS framework.

Next, look at the school counseling activities you listed above for all, some and few. Then, transfer these activities into the blank triangle: writing your responses into the tier in which they fit. Which are Tier 1 activities/activities for all? Tier 2/activities for some? Tier 3/activities for few?

ASCA National Model Aligned with MTSS

Across all Tiers,
School Counselors:

- **Define:**
- **Manage:**
- **Deliver:**
- **Assess:**
- **Incorporate ASCA Themes:**

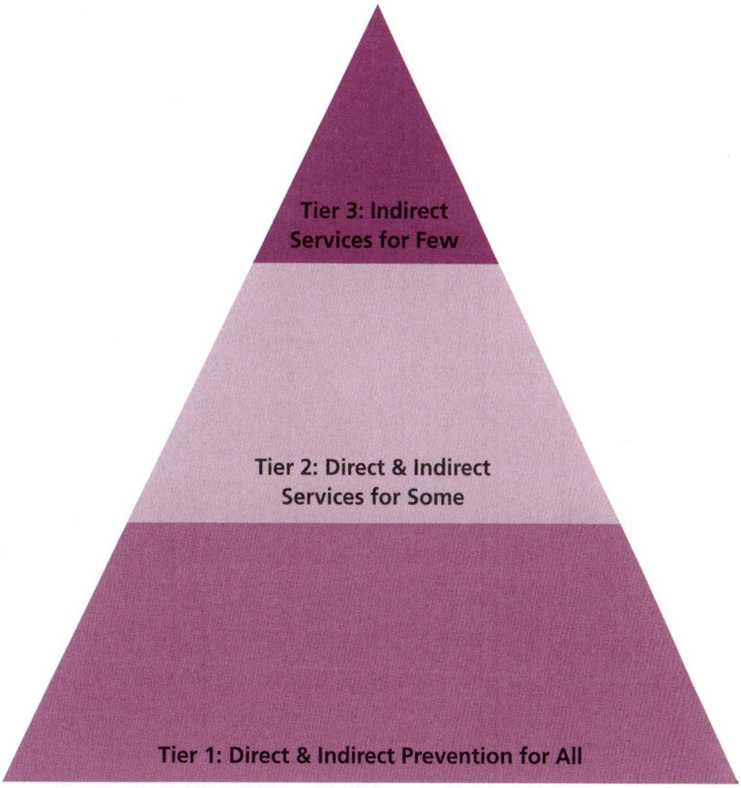

Goodman-Scott, Betters-Bubon & Donohue (2019)

Consider the remaining aspects of implementing the ASCA National Model. How do these other aspects fit in the triangle above? For instance, as you look at the triangle, how would you gather data and evaluate (as part of Manage and Assess)? How are you acting as a collaborator, leader, systemic change agent and advocate? Finally, how are you serving students' academic, career and social/emotional needs within this model?

Specifically, write your response in the blank triangle, noting the following:

- Components: Deliver, Manage, Assess, Define
- Themes: Collaboration, Leadership, Systemic Change, Advocacy
- Domains: Academic, Career, Social/Emotional

Now that you've considered how to align the ASCA National Model with MTSS, see our example (Goodman-Scott, Betters-Bubon, & Donohue, 2016; updated with content from the ASCA National Model, fourth edition).

ASCA National Model Aligned with MTSS

Across all Tiers, School Counselors:

- **Define:** MTSS and school counseling program
  - Grounded in *Mindsets & Behaviors* and professional standards
- **Manage:** MTSS and school counseling program
  - Belief, vision, mission, goals
  - Program planning tools
  - Data and action plans
- **Deliver:** prevention and intervention activities that are:
  - Culturally sustaining
  - Evidence-based
  - Focused on academic, career and social/emotional domains
- **Assess:** MTSS and school counseling program
  - Program/school counselor assessment and appraisal
- **Incorporate ASCA Themes:**
  - Collaboration
  - Leadership
  - Advocacy
  - Systemic Change

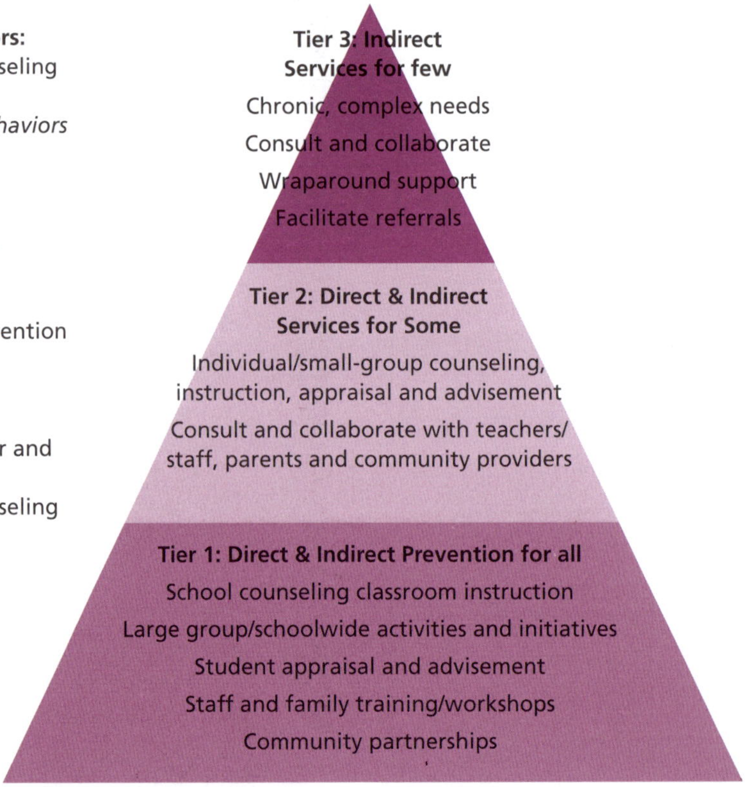

Goodman-Scott, Betters-Bubon & Donohue (2019)

To describe this image further, let's start with the four components of the ASCA National Model: Define, Manage, Deliver and Assess.

School counselors manage their school counseling program through outlining their beliefs, vision, mission and goals, as well as using data, action plans and program planning tools. They also continually assess their program. Many aspects of school counselors' use of data, and related practices (e.g., creating program goals, closing-the-gap action plans, etc.) can utilize data collected and organized by the MTSS team. Similarly, the MTSS team can use data gathered by school counselors, as well as incorporate their management and assessment strategies. Hence, when aligned, the school counseling and MTSS programs have the potential to strengthen each other.

School counselors deliver direct and indirect school counseling services. These services can be divided by tier, based on if they provide services to all, some or few students. Services are culturally sustaining and are increasingly guided by evidence-based practices. This delivery is based on how school counselors define the school counseling program, driven by the Mindsets & Behaviors and other professional standards. Hence school counselors' direct and indirect services within the three tiers are based on these standards.

Just as the ASCA National Model prioritizes three domains: academic, career and social/emotional, MTSS implementation also strives to meet the needs of the whole child. All components of the ASCA National Model are geared toward meeting students' needs across these three domains. In a similar vein, when designing and implementing a school counseling program, school counselors act as collaborators, leaders, agents of systemic change and advocates. Thus, the four themes of the ASCA National Model are also embedded throughout this alignment between the ASCA National Model and MTSS.

VOICES FROM THE FIELD:

School counselors described school counseling and MTSS as being intertwined together, helping them support the school's mission. "It's not like school counselors are over here [pointing in one direction] and we have our own agenda, and the rest of the school is doing their own thing [gesturing to another direction]. We're supporting the mission of the school."

VOICES FROM THE FIELD:

Another school counselor mentioned, "The things that MTSS teams are looking to implement, those are the things that we school counselors do."

EXAMPLES: Alignment

In addition to conceptualizing this alignment between school counseling and MTSS, let's look at examples from the field of how states, school districts and schools have put this alignment into action.

Missouri Comprehensive Guidance Program: Linking School Success with Life Success

This state-level model depicts PBIS and RTI by tier and also shows how school counseling can be described by tier.

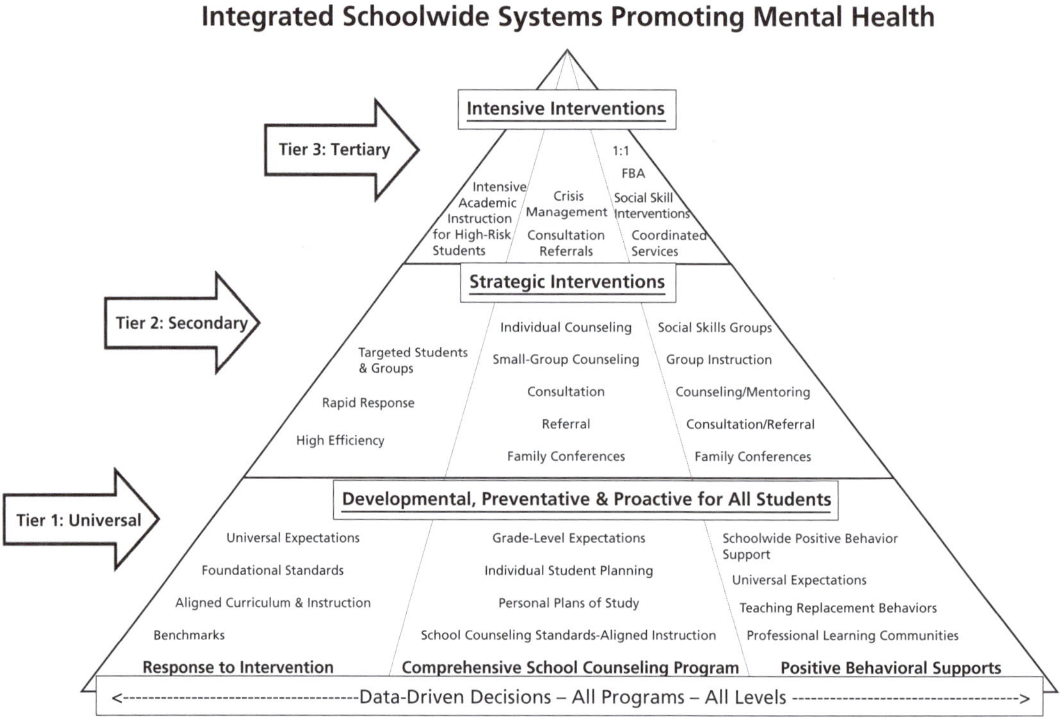

Reprinted from Missouri comprehensive guidance and counseling program: A manual for program development, implementation, evaluation and enhancement (p. 200), by the Missouri Department of Elementary and Secondary Education, the University of Missouri, and the Missouri Center for Career Education. Copyright 2011. Reprinted with permission

MTSS Continuum Map

This map from Charleston County School District is used to organize the academic, behavior and social/emotional supports schools provide for all students. Through this map, school counselors show how their work is integrated within MTSS efforts for the overall school, documenting the behavior and social/emotional supports they provide in all tiers, including core instruction, tools for differentiation, and data tracking and progress monitoring strategies. For example:

- In Tier 1, school counselors can deliver core instruction, such as using the Second Step curriculum.
- To differentiate the curriculum, school counselors might adapt lesson content, activities or lesson length to meet the academic and developmental needs of the students receiving the curriculum.

Continuum Map

Multitiered System of Supports (MTSS)	(Instructional Area: Reading, Math, Writing, Behavior, Science, Social Studies, Social/Emotional, Mental Health, Physical Health)		
Tier 1: Universal			
What school staff does for all students **(Schoolwide data reviews at least three times a year)** Provided to all students through core curriculum, differentiated instruction, ongoing screening and progress monitoring, and schoolwide student services and behavioral supports such as positive behavior support. Universal options are aimed at enhancing success and reducing barriers to learning.	**Literacy/Writing** Core: Tools for differentiation: Data Tracking/ Progress Monitoring Tool:	**Math** Core: Tools for differentiation: Data Tracking/ Progress Monitoring Tool:	**Behavior/SEL** Core: Tools for differentiation: Data Tracking/ Progress Monitoring Tool:
Tier 2: Strategic			
What school staff does for students scoring below x percentile, in the bottom 20% and top 20% of their grade, with x number of discipline referrals, failing 1-2 subjects, etc. **(Progress monitor 1-2 month; Data reviews monthly);** Options provided to remove barriers and enhance success for students who demonstrate certain risk factors that make it likely they will have increased difficulty if concerns are not addressed. Some examples might include supplemental reading instruction or short-term tutoring, enrichment, support from adult mentors and family support etc.	**Literacy/Writing** Tools for differentiation: Data Tracking/ Progress Monitoring Tool:	**Math** Tools for differentiation: Data Tracking/ Progress Monitoring Tool:	**Behavior/SEL** Tools for differentiation: Data Tracking/ Progress Monitoring Tool:
Tier 3: Intensive			
What school staff does for students scoring below x percentile and above x percentile. **(Progress monitor 1-2 week; Data reviews monthly);** Options for students who have a high likelihood of developing or who already exhibit a pattern of academic failure or high levels of social or emotional distress. Because of the intensive nature of such options, targeted interventions/ acceleration are typically needed by very few students. Examples include individualized interventions or replacement instruction, individual behavior plans and wrap-around services provided by mental health professionals.	**Literacy/Writing** Tools for differentiation: Data Tracking/ Progress Monitoring Tool:	**Math** Tools for differentiation: Data Tracking/ Progress Monitoring Tool:	**Behavior/SEL** Tools for differentiation: Data Tracking/ Progress Monitoring Tool:

*Students with identified disabilities have access to all tiered supports and may have needs that cross tiers.

- In regard to data, after identifying ASCA Mindsets & Behaviors standards to address with the classroom instruction, school counselors can use a pre-/post-test, schoolwide outcome data and teacher feedback to progress monitor the extent to which the identified Mindsets & Behaviors are being met.

Overall, the map illustrates how school counselors integrate their work with the MTSS framework at their school, how the school counseling program aligns with MTSS and how the school counselor can contribute to schoolwide and districtwide efforts to support all students.

School Counselor Services Across Levels

This example provides a view of how the school district conceptualizes school counseling activities (a) by tier, (b) across school counseling domains, (c) for K-12 schools and (d) according to Virginia standards.

School Counselor Services by Level

In this example, the school district organizes (a) school counselor activities by tier across ASCA domains and (b) lists the corresponding standards: ASCA Mindsets & Behaviors standards, Virginia standards and other student standards.

School Counseling Services By Level Adapted from Loudoun County Public Schools

Loudoun County Public Schools School Counseling Services Aligned with the Multitiered System of Supports	Grade Level			Domain	ASCA Mindsets & Behaviors	Student Standards
	ES	MS	HS			
TIER 1				ACADEMIC	M1 - M6 B-LS1; B-LS3 - B-LS8 B-SMS3; B-SMS5; B-SMS6; B-SMS8 B-SS1; B-SS7 **VA Counseling Standards** Goal: Students will acquire the academic preparation essential to choose from a variety of educational, training and employment options upon completion of secondary school. Grades K-3: EA1 - EA9 Grade 4-5: EA10 - EA14 Grades 6-8: MA1 - MA7 Grades 9-12: HA1 - HA	■ I have learned study and test-taking skills ■ I am aware of organizational techniques that can support academics ■ I am aware of future course offerings available to me ■ I have knowledge and skills necessary to improve my learning ■ I have updated my academic and career plan ■ I have reviewed my credits and know my progress toward graduation ■ I know about the PSAT, ACT and SAT testing dates and requirements for college entrance ■ I am aware of career and college opportunities ■ I am aware of college application procedures and where to locate financial aid ■ I know my educational goals and options ■ I know how to locate tutoring resources
Comprehensive School Counseling Program Foundation, Management & Accountability	✓	✓	✓			
Academic CLT Data Meetings	✓	✓	✓			
Academic and Career Plan/Portfolio	✓	✓	✓			
Academic Advising	✓	✓	✓			
Academic Program Information	✓	✓	✓			
Awards Assemblies	✓	✓	✓			
Classroom/Advisory Counseling Lessons	✓	✓	✓			
Grade Verification			✓			
Graduation Certification			✓			
Letters of Recommendation						
Parent/Guardian Information Sessions	✓	✓	✓			
Parent/Teacher/Student Conferences	✓	✓	✓			
Progress Reports	✓	✓	✓			
Senior Graduation Notification			✓			
Senior Surveys			✓			
Student Matriculation/Placement	✓	✓	✓			
Student Orientation	✓	✓	✓			
Transition Program	✓	✓	✓			
TIER 2						
Check-in/Check Out	✓	✓	✓			
Community Outreach	✓	✓	✓			
Consultation and Collaboration with Staff	✓	✓	✓			
Credit Recovery			✓			
Mentoring Programs	✓	✓	✓			
Parent/Guardian/Teacher Conferences	✓	✓	✓			
Peer Tutoring		✓	✓			
Progress Report	✓	✓	✓			
Referral to Specialty Programs		✓	✓			
Small-Group Counseling Lessons	✓	✓	✓			
Support Programs	✓	✓	✓			
TIER 3						
Academic Advising and Contracts		✓	✓			
Attendance Contracts	✓	✓	✓			
Consultation and Collaboration with Staff and Outside Resources	✓	✓	✓			
Individualized Parent/Guardian Conferences	✓	✓	✓			
Referral to Outside Resources	✓	✓	✓			
Return to Learn	✓	✓	✓			
Wraparound Services	✓	✓	✓			

Alignment With MTSS	ES	MS	HS	Domain	ASCA Mindsets & Behaviors	Student Standards
TIER 1				**COLLEGE/CAREER**	M1-M6 B-LS1; B-LS2; B-LS4; B-LS5; B-LS7; B-LS9 - 10 B-SMS1; B-SMS 3; B-SMS5;B-SMS8; B-SMS10 B-SS1, B-SS3; B-SS5; B-SS7 - 9 **VA Counseling Standards** **Goal:** Students will investigate the world of work in order to make informed career decisions. Grades K-3: EC1 - EC6 Grade 4-5: EC7 - EC10 Grades 6-8: MC1 - MC8 Grades 9-12: HC1 - HC11	■ I know my academic strength and weakness related to my broad career path ■ I have completed a career-interest inventory ■ I know how to utilize the services and information available in the career center ■ I can identify two places to explore my career interests ■ I have participated in career development experiences,such as apprenticeship/career/college fair, Job for a Day, etc. ■ I have discussed my college/career path with parent/guardian and/or school staff
Comprehensive School Counseling Program Foundation, Management & Accountability	✓	✓	✓			
Academic and Career Plan/Portfolio	✓	✓	✓			
Advanced Placement			✓			
Applications to Specialty Programs		✓	✓			
Apprenticeship Fair			✓			
ASVAB Testing			✓			
Career Interest Inventory	✓	✓	✓			
Career Day/Fair	✓	✓	✓			
College Day/Fair	✓	✓	✓			
College Entrance Examinations			✓			
College Representative Visits			✓			
Diploma Seals			✓			
Dual Enrollment			✓			
Early College Scholars			✓			
FAFSA Nights			✓			
GAP Year Fair			✓			
Job for a Day			✓			
Military Recruiter Visits			✓			
Naviance		✓	✓			
Scholarships			✓			
Service Learning/Volunteers Hours	✓	✓	✓			
Summer Enrichment Programs			✓			
Summer Jobs			✓			
Virtual Programs		✓	✓			
TIER 2						
College Field Trips		✓	✓			
Consultation with Staff	✓	✓	✓			
CTE Certification Testing			✓			
Language Proficiency Testing	✓	✓	✓			
Mentoring	✓	✓	✓			
NCAA Course Calculation			✓			
Peer Tutoring	✓	✓	✓			
Referrals to Specialty Programs		✓	✓			
Small Group Counseling	✓	✓	✓			
TIER 3						
Academic and Career Plan/Portfolio/Advising		✓	✓			
Individualized Parent/Guardian Conferences	✓	✓	✓			
Intensive Course Selection			✓			
Letters of Recommendation		✓	✓			

Alignment With MTSS	ES	MS	HS
TIER 1			
Comprehensive School Counseling Program	✓	✓	✓
Bullying Behavior Prevention and Education Lessons	✓	✓	✓
Character Education	✓	✓	✓
Classroom/Advisory Lessons	✓	✓	✓
Citizen of the Month programs	✓		
Crisis Response/Grief/Loss Information	✓	✓	✓
Parent/Guardian Information Sessions	✓	✓	✓
Parent/Guardian/Teacher/Student Conferences	✓	✓	✓
PBIS	✓	✓	✓
PEER			✓
Restorative Language/Circles	✓	✓	✓
Schoolwide SEL Programs	✓	✓	✓
SEL Transition programs		✓	✓
Self-Harm Assessments	✓	✓	✓
Signs of Suicide Presentations			✓
Sources of Strength (SOS)		✓	✓
Student Assistance Services Collaboration			✓
TIER 2			
Check-in/Check out	✓	✓	✓
Collaborate with Community Organizations	✓	✓	✓
Community Mentoring	✓	✓	✓
Consultation with Staff	✓	✓	✓
Parent/Guardian/Teacher Conferences	✓	✓	✓
Peer Mentoring			✓
Refer to PEER/Sources of Strength		✓	✓
Restorative Circles	✓	✓	✓
Short-Term Individual Counseling	✓	✓	✓
Small-Group Counseling	✓	✓	✓
Unified Mental Health Team (UMHT) Meetings		✓	✓
Weekly Progress Reports	✓	✓	✓
TIER 3			
Attendance Contracts	✓	✓	✓
Behavior Incentive Charts	✓	✓	✓
Child Protective Services Reports	✓	✓	✓
Columbia Suicide Screening Assessment	✓	✓	✓
Community Based Referrals	✓	✓	✓
Intensive long-term individual counseling	✓	✓	✓
Parent/Guardian Conferences	✓	✓	✓
Return to Learn	✓	✓	✓
Threat Assessment	✓	✓	✓
Wrap-Around Services	✓	✓	✓

Domain	ASCA Mindsets & Behaviors	Student Standards
SOCIAL/EMOTIONAL UNIFIED MENTAL HEALTH TEAM – *All Tiers* (MS & HS)	M1 - M6 B-LS1 - B-LS2; B-LS7; B-LS9 B-SMS1 - 10 B-SS2 - 9 **VA Counseling Standards** **Goal:** Students will acquire an understanding of and respect for, self and others, and the skills to be responsible citizens Grades K-3: EP1 - EP7 Grades 4-5: EP8 - EP12 Grades 6-8: MP1 - MP7 Grades 9-12: HP1 - HP4	■ I know my school counselor ■ I know how to seek support at school or in the community ■ I know how to seek help with resolving conflicts ■ I know that counseling services are available to discuss my concerns ■ I have respect for individual differences and can effectively communicate with others ■ I have record of my school and community services ■ I recognize my personal strengths and weakness that affect my success ■ I know at least one trusted adult at school ■ I have identified short- and long-term goals and developed a plan to achieve them

Please note, Tier 3 intensive supports can be for general education students, students with IEPs and other specialized populations.

District-level MTSS Pyramid of Strategies and Interventions

This school district lists services or supports by tier, as facilitated by several overlapping teams/members, including the school counselor. This is a helpful example of how school counselors implementing the ASCA National Model are integrated into MTSS supports, as one member of the MTSS team. All members bring their own expertise and specialized skills, to be part of the greater whole of supports to students and the school. This is a district-level framework, for K–12.

Based off this district-level pyramid, each school in the district created its own pyramid, listing supports by specific school and team. See the Appendix for links to examples of this pyramid from Loudoun County Public Schools at the elementary, middle and high school levels.

Adapted from Loudoun County Public Schools 2019 Multitiered System of Supports Pyramid of Strategies & Interventions

Behavioral Interventions

Tier 3: Intensive, Individual Interventions:
- Functional Behavioral Assessment and Behavior Intervention Plan
- Individual Behavior Plan/Intervention
- Restorative Conferences
- Technical MANDT

Academic Interventions

Tier 3: Intensive, Individual Interventions:
- Modified Instruction/Assessments
- Alternate Assignments
- Individualized Instruction
- Specialized Instruction (e.g., Reading, Math)

Social-Emotional Interventions

Tier 3: Intensive, Individual Interventions:
- Intensive Long-Term Individual Counseling
- Threat Assessment/Safety Plan
- Restorative Conferences
- Suicide Screening, Referral, Follow-Up
- Insight Program
- 10-Day Substance Abuse Program

Tier 3 Systems Planning and Problem-Solving Teams: Child Study, PSSST, Mental Health

Tier 2: Targeted Group Interventions: (Behavioral)
- Check-In/Check-Out
- Small Groups
- Restorative Circles
- Explicit Skill Instruction
- Relational MANDT

Tier 2: Targeted Group Interventions: (Academic)
- Targeted Evidenced-Based Strategies/Intervention
- Structured Flex/Resource
- Tutoring
- Check-In/Check-Out
- Mentoring
- Specialized Instruction (e.g., Reading, Math)

Tier 2: Targeted Group Interventions: (Social-Emotional)
- Group Counseling add Short-Term Individual Counseling
- Threat Assessment
- Restorative Circles
- Support Groups
- Tobacco Education Program

Tier 2 Systems Planning and Problem-Solving Teams: CLT, IT, SAT, Mental Health

Tier 1: Universal Strategies: (Behavioral)
- Define, Teach, Model, Reinforce Schoolwide Expectations
- Differentiation(Reteach/Model/Reassess)
- Classroom Management System(Physical Environment, Rules and Routines Procedures, Opportunities to Respond, Active Supervision, Behavior-Specific Praise, Error Correction)
- Equitable Classroom Practices
- Restorative Communication
- Relational MANDT
- PEER

Tier 1: Universal Strategies: (Academic)
- Feedback
- Differentiation (Reteach/Model/Reassess)
- Reciprocal Teaching
- Teaching Self-Verbalization
- Meta-Cognition Strategies
- Peer-Assisted Learning Strategies

Tier 1: Universal Strategies: (Social-Emotional)
- Differentiation(Reteach/Model/Reassess)
- Sources of Strength
- Classroom Counseling Lessons
- PEER
- Signs of Suicide
- Signs of Suicide Training Trusted Adults
- Substance Abuse Prevention
- Bullying Prevention (Stop-Walk-Talk & Expect Respect)
- Social/Emotional Learning (Second Step)

Tier 1 Systems Planning Teams: PBIS, RTI, School Leadership, Mental Health

Providing Coordinated Supports to Families

Not only can this alignment concept be applied to school counseling programs, but it can also support families. In this example, schools' outreach and collaboration with families provided by school staff such as social workers, family liaisons and others can be viewed within the multitiered framework, considering the level of support needed by each family.

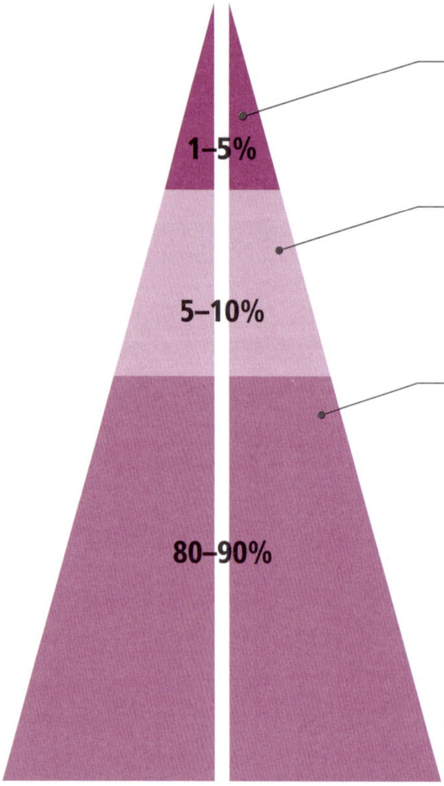

Tier 3: Intensive Individual Interventions

- Family Liaison – matched with family, needs matched with community resources
- Individual skill building sessions

Tier 2: Targeted Group Interventions

- Support groups (Military families, Newcomer group)
- Skill building sessions (Academic and behavior)

Tier 1: Universal Interventions

- Self assessments – Family engagement checklist, surveys
- Skill building series guest speaker (Topics vary-survey families)
- Newsletter, resource library, "shout outs"
- Volunteer opportunities (DOGS–Dads of Great Students)
- Teacher conferences – Goal setting, family vision, strengths discovery
- Family Fun Nights throughout the year
- School Handbook (Description, teaching matrix – promote common language between school and home)

(Adapted from Loudoun County Public Schools)

ACTIVITY: **School Counseling/MTSS Alignment**

As mentioned earlier and as illustrated by the examples, both school counseling and MTSS implementation prioritize serving the whole child, which is supported by the ASCA National Model's three domains: academic, career and social/emotional. Hatch, Duarte and DeGregorio (2018) as well as Hatch, Triplett, Duarte and Gomez (2019) have discussed aligning the three-tiered MTSS framework across the three ASCA domains and provided an in-depth focus on including the career domain within this MTSS approach.

Activity: District-level school counseling director of Henrico County Public Schools Elizabeth Parker described adapting the following activity to guide her school counseling district-level professional development, aligning the three-tiered MTSS framework across ASCA's three domains (below) (adapted from Hatch, Duarte, & DeGregorio, 2018; Hatch, Triplett, Diarte, & Gomez, 2019) (below):

Draw the following image on a piece of large paper:

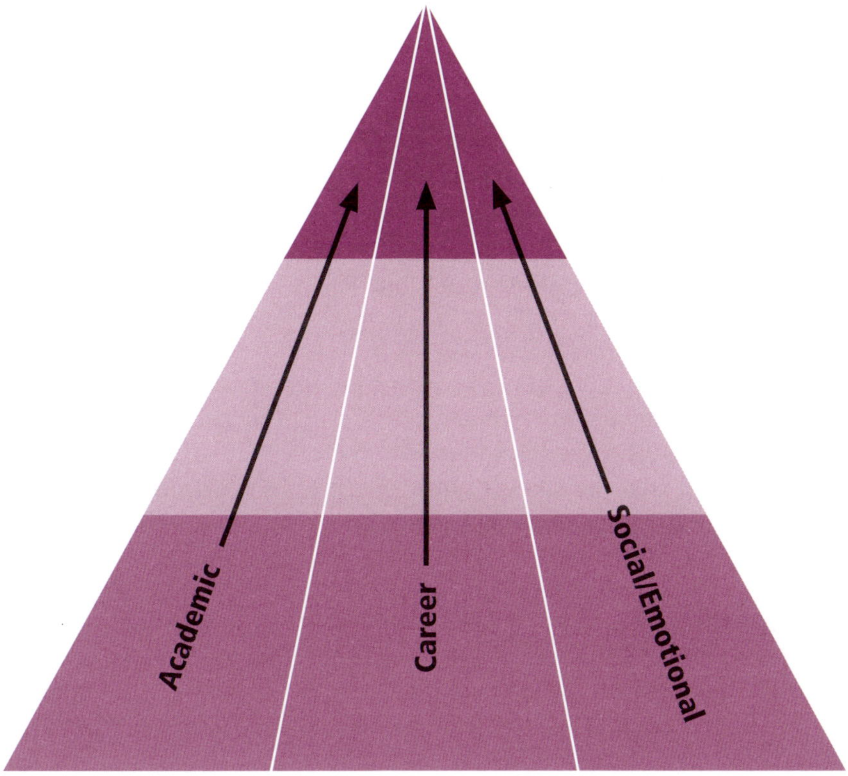

Give each school counselor/school counseling department a stack of sticky notes. For each sticky note, write one activity you conduct for all or some or few students as part of implementing the ASCA National Model. The goal is to write down a comprehensive list of school counseling activities, one per sticky note.

Next, place each sticky note on the paper within the triangle, in the corresponding tier and domain (Tier 1, 2, 3; academic, career, social/emotional), until all sticky notes with activities have been placed.

When done, review the sticky note placement and consider the following questions:

- What parts of the triangle have many sticky notes? What does this tell you about your school counseling program?
- What parts of the triangle are lacking sticky notes? What does this tell you about your school counseling program?
- What changes can you make to address your school counseling program needs as depicted by this activity?

Extension activity #1: School counseling district directors/supervisors can facilitate this activity during a district-level school counseling professional development training. Individual school counselors can tape their completed triangles on the wall (one per school) and have a gallery walk, encouraging the school counselors to review all schools' triangles. In addition to the questions above, also discuss the following:

- What did you observe in schools from across the district?
- What can you learn from other schools?
- Are there ideas/delivery you can implement in your school counseling program?

Extension activity #2: School counselors can take their completed triangle image (with sticky notes) back to their school and share with faculty and administrators (e.g., at a faculty meeting, MTSS leadership meeting, administrator meeting, etc.). When sharing the completed triangle, highlight the school counselor's role in your building, in alignment with MTSS. Also describe your school counseling program's strengths and goals.

Extension activity #3: School counselors can facilitate a version of this activity with school leadership. For instance, bring this blank image of the triangle to an MTSS team meeting. Ask the MTSS team to complete this activity, considering the activities of the school as a whole. Consider the school's strengths and needs, and create related schoolwide goals for improvement. What can you, the school counselor, do to help with these MTSS goals in your role serving students directly and indirectly through your school counseling program?

(Activity by Elizabeth Parker, Henrico County (Va.) School District)

VOICES FROM THE FIELD:

One school counselor relayed, "MTSS language became part of our school's mission and vision, and then obviously when we did our department's we used that same language."

DESCRIPTION: SCHOOL COUNSELORS' ROLES IN MTSS

According to the ASCA National Model, "MTSS mirrors the structure outlined in the ASCA National Model in which all students receive the benefits of a school counseling program (Tier 1) with targeted interventions for students who need them (Tier 2) and referrals, collaboration and consultation for and with intense interventions for a small segment of the student population (Tier 3). The MTSS approach also more clearly defines the school counselor's role in providing mental health services. School counselors provide Tier 1 support for all students, provide or coordinate Tier 2 targeted interventions for identified students and primarily collaborate and consult with Tier 3 level support" (p. xi). When outlining appropriate and inappropriate school counseling activities, school counselors should advocate for students during student review/leadership meetings; school counselors should not coordinate MTSS review boards (e.g., be the sole MTSS school leader).

Ockerman, Mason and Hollenbeck (2012) suggested school counselors act as interveners in MTSS, when they work with students directly, and supporters, when working on behalf of students, such as consulting and collaborating with stakeholders and serving on the MTSS leadership team. Relatedly, according to ASCA's position statement, The School Counselor and Multitiered System of Supports (2018; Appendix), "school counselors implement a school counseling program addressing the needs of all students. Through the review of data, school counselors identify struggling students and collaborate with other student services professionals, educators and families to provide appropriate instruction and learning supports within an MTSS. School counselors work collaboratively with other educators to remove systemic barriers for all students and implement specific learning supports that assist in academic and behavioral success" (ASCA, 2018, p. 46).

Hence, as pertinent to MTSS, school counselors directly serve students as an intervener through the Deliver component of the ASCA National Model and indirectly serve as a supporter by using data, consulting and collaborating, and sharing their expertise on the MTSS team. See subsequent chapters for an in-depth discussion of school counselors' roles in each tier.

VOICES FROM THE FIELD:

According to Loudoun County Public Schools, school counselors often serve as an MTSS internal coach in their school. In this role they facilitate a number of MTSS-related activities within their school, such as coordinating monthly MTSS meetings in collaboration with the external coach; collaborating with MTSS team members; assisting with school-based MTSS events in the school; and working with the MTSS team to present MTSS information to the staff, such as the MTSS data.

VOICES FROM THE FIELD:

"I didn't want MTSS to be seen as a school counseling program. I do want it to be seen as a schoolwide program."

EXAMPLE: Decision Tree for School Counselors

What happens when a student is referred to the school counselor? Loudoun County Public Schools created a decision tree, outlining school counselors' specific roles for serving students directly and indirectly. At the start or top of the decision tree, school counselors begin with direct supports as an intervener, including providing short-term individual or group counseling or checking-in on students. The decision tree progresses to outline interventions school counselors conduct when providing each of these three supports, as well as when to seek additional support. When soliciting extra supports, school counselors are often in the role of supporter, such as consulting and collaborating for more advanced services.

Overall, the school counselor's role in MTSS may vary somewhat by school and district. It should be explicitly outlined in each school counselor's ASCA annual administrative conference agreement, as well as annual and weekly calendars.

Proactive and Responsive Decision Tree for School Counselors

Proactive: Using effective data (discipline, attendance, academic, perception) if a student is identified as needing additional support, the school counselor chooses to:
Responsive: Student is identified by staff, parents, administration, self or other students as needing additional support. After speaking with the referral source, student and reviewing appropriate data, the school counselor chooses to:

Provide **short-term individual** counseling support for students during times of:
- A transition
- Heightened stress
- Critical change
- Other situations impeding success

Identify problem, causes, potential consequences and benefits, alternative outcomes so student can make decisions and take appropriate action.

School counselor makes parents aware of the goals of the three sessions and explains the difference between appropriate short-term counseling and inappropriate longterm therapy.

Counselor designs sessions to promote academic, career, and or social/emotional development using counseling theories and techniques effective in the school setting. Progress is communicated with parents.

Provide **short-term group** counseling support for students during times of:
- A transition
- Heightened stress
- Critical change
- Other situations impeding success

Identify problem, causes, potential consequences and benefits, alternative outcomes so students can make decisions and take appropriate action.

School counselor makes parents/families aware of the need and goals of the group. School counselor gains parent permission using Loudoun County Public Schools group permission slip.

School counselor designs group to promote academic, career and or social/emotional development using counseling theories and techniques effective in the school setting (evidence-based when possible). School counselor monitors and communicates student progress.

Provide **check-in** support for students during times of:
- A transition
- Heightened stress
- Critical change
- Other situations impeding success

Identify problem, causes, potential consequences and benefits, alternative outcomes so they can make decisions and appropriate action.

Counselor makes parents/families aware of the of the students visits (after 3-same concern) and explains the roles and limitations of a school counselor.

Counselor can continue to check in with the student as a responsive service, with goal to provide brief strategies to help student reintegrate into normal schedule.

If student continues to need support after the above strategies/Interventions:

- Consult with team MTSS (Tier 2 Kid Talk)
- Make referral to appropriate school or community resource
- Consult school social worker or school psychologist
- Continue to check in with student as needed as a responsive service
- Keep parents and teachers aware of progress and concerns
- Review academic and discipline data to identify possible need for additional support (CST)
- Attempt a different intervention or strategy above
- Record necessary data and share with problem solving team

(Adapted from Loudoun County Public Schools)

DESCRIPTION: COLLABORATION AND TEAMING

The MTSS team is a collaborative group of school-based educators, administrators and other stakeholders (e.g., family members, community members, students) who regularly meet to design, implement and evaluate MTSS implementation. Often schools appreciate having one representative from every grade or team, as well as specialists (e.g., school counselors), hourly-paid school staff and at least one building administrator who is a liaison with the school administrative team (administrative buy-in is crucial for MTSS success). Culturally sustaining practices are a priority for the MTSS team, and it's suggested that community members and families are incorporated within MTSS planning and implementation to provide input on culturally relevant practices. In fact, research has indicated that involving students in planning for Tier 1 in middle and high school is one way to make the MTSS team more effective (Flannery, Fenning, Kato, & McIntosh, 2014). In addition to MTSS teams including stakeholders from the community and families, we also suggest schools have a separate parent/community/student council that reviews and guides not only MTSS design and implementation but procedures and practices throughout the school, taking special care to ensure the cultures of all community and family members are included throughout the school.

VOICES FROM THE FIELD:

"We had a really nice, diverse group MTSS committee, and that can be helpful. Having people throughout the building helps provide more feedback about what's going on. It's helpful to get all of those points of view."

EXAMPLE: MTSS Teams

Team Structure

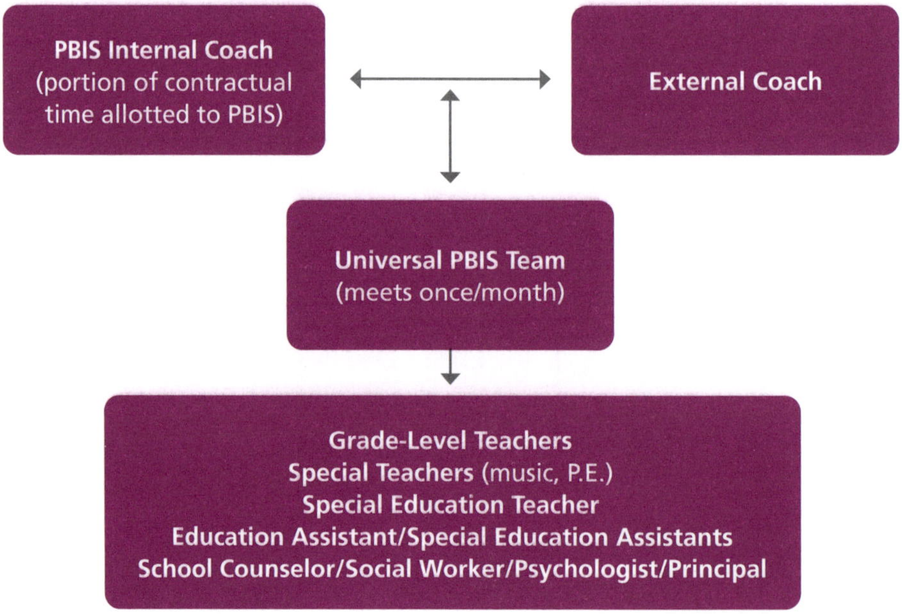

(Sugar Creek Elementary School)

Tier I PBIS Leadership Team

	Members	Team Responsibilities	Roles
Tier I	■ Administration ■ Teacher(s) ■ School Counselor(s) ■ Classified ■ Clerical ■ Campus Security ■ Special Education ■ Mental Health/ School Psychologist ■ Interventionist ■ TOSA ■ Other	■ Utilize collaborative team practices ■ Collect and organize schoolwide data ■ Review and analyze schoolwide academic/behavior/attendance data ■ Utilize continuous improvement process/unified improvement plan goal ■ Ensure implementation of district literacy, math and social emotional/behavioral plans ■ Identify professional development needs ■ Install needed resources and schedules ■ Monitor action plan integrity ■ Communicate and distribute data to appropriate teams and staff	■ Case Coordinator ■ Data Collector ■ Scribe

(Kern High School District, Calif.)

MTSS teams might differ according to tiers. Typically, there is a core MTSS team that oversees all tiers, focusing on implementation, evaluation, data, prevention, etc. That said, the core team might have additional sub-teams to focus on Tier 2 and/or Tier 3. These sub-teams may be composed of some members of the core MTSS team, as well as additional individuals with particular expertise. For instance, the Tier 2 MTSS sub-team might review data for determining the progress of students receiving Tier 2 academic and behavioral supports. These sub-teams maintain communication and integration with the larger core MTSS team.

MTSS teams are usually guided by district-level and often state-level coordinators, who provide training, coaching, resources and assist with evaluation. For instance, district-level coordinators commonly provide training to school-level MTSS teams, who then bring those trainings and resources back to their school. In addition to schoolwide trainings, MTSS team members can share essential MTSS resources through a professional learning community.

As a recap, school counselors' roles on MTSS teams include interveners and supporters, which works particularly well since they are trained to work productively and collaboratively with all school stakeholders. School counselors routinely interact with multiple colleagues each day, and they can develop strong professional alliances supporting the development of effective and efficient MTSS teams. School counselors may take a leadership role on the MTSS team, but as suggested by ASCA (2019), should not be the sole leader of MTSS efforts in their buildings.

VOICES FROM THE FIELD:

According to a school counselor, "I might be the internal MTSS/PBIS coach, but I am not doing all the work. As a school, we've been really good at working as a team."

At least one school counselor per school should be on the school's MTSS team, and similarly, MTSS team members(s) should be invited to join the school counseling advisory council to provide feedback and raise awareness. Thus, this is one strategy for maintaining open communication and collaboration between the two sets of school leaders, who both utilize a schoolwide lens. As members of the MTSS team, school counselors are encouraged to align the goals and activities of their school counseling program with the MTSS team, and vice versa.

VOICES FROM THE FIELD:

As one school counselor said, "I've sat on the MTSS committee for several years, which has been great because it gives me an opportunity to help look at the data, discuss programs and bring that information back to the school counseling department."

VOICES FROM THE FIELD:

One school counselor relayed, "MTSS language became part of our school's mission and vision and then obviously when we did the school counseling department's vision and mission statements we used that same language."

Another strategy for aligning the school counseling program with the MTSS team includes the use of data. As will be discussed in the subsequent chapters, school counselors can use student outcome data and MTSS school improvement goals generated by the MTSS team within their school counseling program (e.g., to shape annual student outcome goals, determine students for small groups, measure students' progress in small groups, etc.).

Schools are often composed of many teams or departments, such as grade-level departments, child study/student assistant teams, school counseling departments, hospitality teams, MTSS teams, administrative teams, leadership teams, crisis teams, etc. Although these teams are typically well-intentioned, staff members need to be especially purposeful in communicating and collaborating or school teams can become siloed and even redundant in their efforts.

Simply put, all school teams need to be rowing in the same direction: Working together. Communicating together. Reducing redundancies.

MTSS is a schoolwide framework and integrates school initiatives, staff and students from the entire school. As such, one strategy used in MTSS is called resource mapping. Here, MTSS teams list and describe school teams, departments, initiatives, etc., in an effort to compare goals and to consider streamlining to reduce overlap. After discovering their redundancies, a next potential step could be to address these overlaps/redundancies.

EXAMPLE: Resource Mapping

Initiative/ Committee/ Team	Purpose and Strategic Goal Supported	Measurable Outcome(s) - Data Based	Tier(s) Supported	Target Group (staff, students, community, etc.)	Staff Involved	Overlap? Modify?
PBIS	To support the PBIS framework within school, track data, plan schoolwide incentives	Discipline Disproportionality Office Referrals Climate Survey	Tier 1, 2, 3	Students	Grade-level and department representatives, school counselor, school psych, AP, dean, parent	RTI
CCC	To allow staff to bring concerns and solutions to the table			Staff and Students	Grade-level and Department representatives	Has overlapped with SLT
Sunshine	To boost morale within the school community			Staff	Grade-level representatives	Some overlap with Parent Engagement
SAT	Discuss/provide Tier 2 strategies/ support for targeted students through a referral link. Monitor interventions. Precursor to Child Study.	SAT referral Classroom Intervention Data	Tier 2	Students	Grade-level teachers, admin, counselors	Overlaps with PBIS Tier 2 supports
SLT	Meeting place for all areas to be represented so they can discuss schoolwide initiatives			Staff and Students	Grade-level and department representatives and administration	Has overlapped with CCC
Parent Engagement team	To plan events that engage families and staff			Community	Grade-level representative, Reading Team	Some overlap with Sunshine team
RTI team	Use the information we gain from MTSS-RTI trainings,to adapt and support various systems at school and to build and provide resources for teachers		All tiers	Staff and Students	Representation from grade-levels, SPED, administration	PBIS

(Adapted from Loudoun County Public Schools)

ACTIVITY: Resource Map

School counselors, along with their school leadership team, complete a resource map. Be sure to include key administrators, and consider the integration of the school counseling program and school counseling domains as noted in the blank resource map below.

What staff committees, teams or initiatives exist in your school? List one per line (e.g., Leadership Team, MTSS, Hospitality, Equity, etc.)	What are the goals and purpose of each?	Do they look at data/focus on outcomes? If so, which?	What tiers do they support?	What is the target group? (e.g., all teachers, seventh-grade students, students with disabilities, etc.)	What staff are involved?	Do these teams relate to students' academic, career or social/emotional development? Is the school counseling department involved in this team? Should it be (according to ASCA's appropriate/inappropriate responsibilities?)	Outcome: Continue overlap? Modify? What are next steps to increase staff collaboration and streamline school efforts?
1.							
2.							
3.							
4.							
5.							
6.							

Goodman-Scott (2020)

Overall, making changes to systems can take time and persistence. Thus, engaging in resource mapping requires deliberate communication, as well as buy-in from key school leaders.

Effective school counselors know their resources in the school, district and in the community. One way to capture the full spectrum of stakeholders internally and externally is to regularly update a resource list. This may be done in conjunction with your district and other professionals in your building, such as school social workers. School counselors can use this list within their school counseling program (e.g., referring students to long-term outside counseling), as well as to make recommendations to the MTSS team for resources they may need.

ACTIVITY: Resource List

Complete the following resource list, and consider updating it at least annually. We suggest adding resources that are most pertinent to your population and community, such as translation services, food banks, domestic violence shelters, temporary housing, a community LGBTQ+ center, and so forth.

Internal Resources	External Resources
School counselor(s):	Mental health agency(ies):
School psychologist(s):	Social services/Department of Children and Families:
School social worker(s):	Intensive in-home mental health care agencies:
Other mental health provider(s) employed by school:	Social work agencies:
School resource officer(s):	Mental health professionals (licensed professional counselors, social workers, psychologists and family therapists):
Literacy interventionist(s):	Consulting pediatrician(s):
Numeracy interventionists(s):	Financial assistance for families:
Behavioral interventionist(s):	Parent education resources:
Other(s):	Other(s):

ACTIVITY: Self-assessment

As you are now at the end of the first chapter of this book, we suggest you take this self-assessment as a pre-test (Sugai, La Salle, Everett, & Feinberg, 2019).

School Counseling and MTSS Self-Assessment	Self-Rating 5 high.....1 low
1. I am a member and active participant in schoolwide MTSS leadership team (Tier 1).	5 4 3 2 1
2. I am a member and active participant in targeted or indicated MTSS teams (Tier 2/3).	5 4 3 2 1
3. My school counseling practices and systems are aligned with and integrated into MTSS practices and systems.	5 4 3 2 1
4. MTSS practices and systems are aligned with and integrated into my school counseling practices and systems.	5 4 3 2 1
5. I am active participant in MTSS professional development activities.	5 4 3 2 1
6. I directly train and coach others in becoming fluent users of school counseling program and MTSS practices and systems.	5 4 3 2 1
7. I collect and develop descriptions, displays and demonstrate examples of effective school counseling program and MTSS practices and systems.	5 4 3 2 1
8. I align and integrate school counseling program and MTSS schoolwide funding and policies.	5 4 3 2 1
9. I collect and disseminate school counseling program data within MTSS decision making.	5 4 3 2 1
10. I consider MTSS data (e.g., universal screening and progress monitoring) when collecting and analyzing school counseling program data.	5 4 3 2 1
11. I regularly assess the implementation fidelity of my school counseling practices and systems.	5 4 3 2 1
12. My decision making emphasizes the use of evidenced practices and data-based decision making.	5 4 3 2 1
13. I actively recruit and prepare others on school counseling program practices and systems within MTSS.	5 4 3 2 1

George Sugai, La Salle, Everett, & Feinberg (2019) A School Counselor's Guide to MTSS

Based on your results of this self-assessment:

- What are your professional strengths and the strengths of your school counseling program?
- In what areas could you and your school counseling program could use more support?

REFERENCES AND RESOURCES

American School Counselor Association. (2018). *The school counselor and multitiered systems of support.* American School Counselor Association Position Statement. Retrieved from https://www.schoolcounselor.org/asca/media/asca/PositionStatements/PS_MultitieredSupportSystem.pdf

Betters-Bubon, J. (2014, March). The Role of School Counselors in Multitier Models of Support (e.g., RTI, PBIS): Ideas and Implementation Strategies [webinar]. In American School Counselor Association (ASCA) webinar series.

Flannery, K. B., Fenning, P., Kato, M. M., & McIntosh, K. (2014). Effects of school-wide positive behavioral interventions and supports and fidelity of implementation on problem behavior in high schools. *School Psychology Quarterly, 29*(2), 111.

Goodman-Scott, E. & Ockerman, M. (2019). Integrating school counseling and MTSS. In E. Goodman-Scott, J. Betters-Bubon, & P. Donohue (Eds.), *A School Counselor's Guide to Multi-tiered Systems of Support* (1st ed. 29-61). New York City, NY: Routledge.

Goodman-Scott, E., Betters-Bubon, J., & Donohue, P. (2016). Aligning comprehensive school counseling programs and positive behavioral interventions and supports to maximize school counselors' efforts. *Professional School Counseling, 19*, 57-67.

Ockerman, M. S., Mason, E. C. M., & Hollenbeck, A. F. (2012). Integrating RTI with school counseling programs: Being a proactive professional school counselor. *Journal of School Counseling, 10*(15). Retrieved from tp://jsc.montana.edu/articles/v10n15.pdf

Sugai, G., La Salle, T., Everett, S., & Feinberg, A. B. (2019). Multi-tiered Systems of Support: The what, why, and how for school counselors. In E. Goodman-Scott, J. Betters-Bubon, & P. Donohue (Eds.), *A School Counselor's Guide to Multi-tiered Systems of Support* (1st ed. 1-28). New York City, NY: Routledge.

Ziomek-Daigle, J., Goodman-Scott, E., Cavin, J., & Donohue, P. (2016). Integrating a multi-tiered system of supports with comprehensive school counseling programs. *The Professional Counselor, 6*(3), 220-232. doi:10.15241/jzd.6.3.220

The Professional Counselor Special Issue: School Counselors and a Multi-Tiered System of Supports: Cultivating Systemic Change and Equitable Outcomes. 2016: Volume 6(3). Editors: Sink, C. & Ockerman, M.

CHAPTER 2

Beginning Strategies for Using Data Program Alignment

For close to two decades, school counselors have asked and been asked this question: How are students different as a result of your school counseling program? Although there are many resources to help school counselors examine data within their program, this chapter focuses the alignment of school counseling programs, specifically the ASCA National Model and MTSS, through the use of data. In this chapter, we will provide (a) an overview of data (b) how school counselors can align and strengthen school counseling programs and MTSS implementation through the use of data and (c) examples of how to use data within an integrated school counseling/MTSS program process.

ACTIVITY: Data Literacy

Before diving in, take a few minutes to answer the following questions, using the 1–5 scale. What is your data literacy? 1=Never 2=Rarely 3=Sometimes 4=Often 5=Always

1.	Do you collect data within your school counseling program?	5 4 3 2 1
2.	Do you analyze the data you collect?	
3.	Do you examine school data to make decisions about your programs and interventions?	5 4 3 2 1
4.	Do you examine school data to determine inequities in systems, policies and/or practices	5 4 3 2 1
5.	Do you know the different types of data (e.g., participation, Mindsets & Behaviors and outcome data)?	5 4 3 2 1
6.	Do you share data findings with stakeholders (administrators, teachers, parents, students and community members)?	5 4 3 2 1
7.	Do you consider yourself to be a data expert?	5 4 3 2 1
8.	Do you find yourself saying the following: "the data is amazing" or "the data has been fabulous"?	5 4 3 2 1
9.	Do you find yourself thinking: "I like data, but it makes me nervous" or "I want to like data, but I need more information"?	5 4 3 2 1
10.	Do you wish you had more time to examine and analyze data?	5 4 3 2 1

Adapted from Young & Kaffenberger's (2018) Making DATA Work

Reflection

What do you notice about your answers? Are data collection and analysis a strength? Do you wish you had more time to collect data? Do you feel like you need additional information about data so you can more successfully analyze the data you collect? Do you wish to use data to better advocate for changes in systems and practices in addition to student needs?

This purpose of this chapter is to improve your data literacy so you may say something like the school counselor below:

VOICES FROM THE FIELD:

"It's all data-based. I know what to do from things that are happening, the referrals and because I'm gathering that data. I can be more specific. It gives you more of a pulse of what's going on in the school. Everything I do is somehow affected by knowing that data."

Before we dive into types of data, complete the activity below:

ACTIVITY: Data Types

Examine the triangle. What types of data do you currently collect across each tier? Specifically:

- What types of data do you collect for students requiring Tier 1, Tier 2 and Tier 3 supports in your school?
- What do you notice about the data you collect?

Description: Data Overview

Why do we focus so much on data? Data helps school counselors move from the vague to the specific and allows us to refine our programs and interventions to better help students succeed. The examples below show how specific data can guide our understanding and set measurable goals:

VAGUE	SPECIFIC
Ninth-graders are unmotivated this school year.	57% of ninth-grade students do not believe what they are learning in school is important to their future careers.
Fifth-graders have problems with fighting on the playground.	7% of fifth-grade students have three or more disciplinary reports for fighting after the first month of school.
Seventh-graders have the worst attendance.	83% of seventh-graders have an attendance rate of 93% or better.

As you can see in the description above, data helps define programs and interventions. An example of how this works can be found from Sugar Creek Elementary School, which was experiencing discipline issues on one bus route. At the beginning of one school year, the MTSS Tier 1 team, which was co-led by the school counselor, was concerned about behavior reports on one of the school buses. The contracted school bus driver was reporting, through written bus reports to the administration, a number of behavioral infractions on the rides to and from school.

The team examined root causes, comparing the bus report data between this bus and others and spoke with students, parents and the bus driver. As a result, the team discovered several important points. First, this bus route included many students who received free and reduced lunch and were in racial and ethnic minority groups, traveling to and from an urban neighborhood 10 miles away from the suburban school. Second, the bus was overcrowded and had two to three times the number of students as on the other bus routes. Thus, the behavior problem was less about student behavior and more about inequitable and biases systems, such as the distribution of school resources. The principal advocated, sharing the data with the superintendent. Because the school as a whole had embraced MTSS and documenting specific data and equitable decisions, leaders at the district level added an additional bus route for students. Bus referrals from the current bus and the new bus decreased immediately.

As we've seen in this example, school counselors, in concert with the MTSS teams, can use data to move from vague concerns (e.g., bus behavior reports) to specific data (e.g., better understanding the root cause), which can guide action to be more effective and appropriate. Specifically, the MTSS team examined the root causes of behavioral reports, comparing multiple data points and talking with students, families and bus drivers. In the end, the principal advocated for systemic change, and the outcome was more equitable practice for students.

All too common in education, when we see an increase in student behaviors perceived as negative (e.g., referrals or absences), we are quick to intervene at the student level (e.g., meeting with the student/family, calling home, etc.). However, it's crucial to have an accurate understanding of the problem. In other words, we engage in root-cause analysis (Taylor & Burgess, 2019), which includes examining the school as a system, including procedures and practices put in place by the school staff (e.g., school rules, student consequences), as well as organizational resources (e.g., bus overcrowding for traditionally underserved student populations) and even staff biases.

Considering the root cause can help know whether we intervene at the systems level, the staff level, or student level. How do we determine the root cause?:

- Gather data from multiple sources (e.g., different stakeholders; perception and outcome data)
- Asking why (e.g., Why is this concern happening?)
- Asking what (e.g., What are potential causes? What trends do you notice?)
- Then, determining the level of intervention (e.g., systems, staff or student level)

After gathering data that shows an area of concern we conduct a root-cause analysis: (a) gather more data, (b) examine existing school systems and practices that could have contributed to concern, then (c) make changes to the school systems and/or practices.

For additional information on data and root-cause analysis see Taylor and Burgess (2019) and Young and Kaffenberger (2018).

DATA: TYPES

Now that we've explored an overview of data, let's take a look at data that is often used within school counseling programs and MTSS.

Participation Data	**Mindsets & Behaviors Data**	**Outcome Data**	**Supplemental Data**
Who, What, Where, When/How Long	*Student Skills, Knowledge and Attitudes*	*Achievement, Attendance, Discipline*	*Universal Screening, Surveys*

Participation Data: Participation data includes general information on activity types and focus, who took part and the length of time. This is used in both school counseling program and MTSS frameworks.

Examples:

- 88% of parents attended junior academic planning conferences with their child.
- 95% of seventh-grade students received classroom instruction on goal setting.
- 100% of students participated in the focus and motivation classroom instruction.

Mindsets & Behaviors Data: This data is specific to the ASCA National Model and includes assessments of how students change in knowledge, skills and attitudes as a result of programs and interventions. This data is grounded in research-based standards and outlines key noncognitive factors, including knowledge, attitudes and skills, that lead to student success. The 35 Mindsets & Behaviors can be aligned with other academic and school initiatives and measured across time to determine program impact. For additional information, see the ASCA National Model.

Examples:

- After SEL lessons on building positive friendships, 80% of students indicate they know how to be assertive if they see or hear someone being mean around them.
- After lessons on goal setting, 90% of ninth-graders are able to write a SMART goal.
- Upon receiving instruction on career types and goals, 88% of 11th-grade students strongly agree that postsecondary planning is important.

Outcome Data: The outcome data is often the data most prized within schools and districts and includes achievement, attendance and discipline data. Specifically, school staff track achievement data, such as graduation rates, college-going rates, test scores and GPAs; attendance data, such as the percentage of days students are present in school; and discipline data, such as office discipline referrals. All three types of data are utilized within school counseling program and MTSS planning.

Examples:

- After a small-group intervention, identified ninth-graders increased their GPA from 2.0 to 2.75 between first and final marking period.
- During the 2019–20 school year, the number of office discipline referrals for physical aggression decreased by 40% across the school.
- The overall middle school attendance rate for grades six, seven and eight is 94.5%.

Following are some common types of outcome data by school level:

- Elementary school: Reading level, attendance, standardized test scores, discipline referrals
- Middle school: GPA, attendance, standardized test scores, discipline referrals
- High school: Credits earned, on track for graduation, GPA, graduation rate, dropout rate, discipline referrals

Many high school counselors have questions about how they can use data within their complex programs. For additional information, see Flannery, McGrath, Kato and Horner (2019) and Martinez, Kern, Hershfeldt, George, White, Flannery and Freeman (2019).

VOICES FROM THE FIELD:

"I looked at their state standardized test score scores, and I can prove that prior to interventions scores were really low. Now I can say, 'Their scores have increased.'"

Because data drives decision making across all tiers, it's important to note that many types of outcome data are based on staff perception (e.g., grades, discipline referrals). Unless implicit bias and culturally sustaining tenants are addressed staffwide, data used for MTSS can perpetuate disproportionality rather than lead to equitable outcomes. In other words, in considering root cause, we must continually look back to the data and examine if there are concerns at the system level, staff level, student level, or if there is a need to gather more data.

Supplemental data: Supplemental data is gleaned from parents/students/staff and through universal screening. Common examples are surveys, such as bullying, school safety, school climate, etc. This data is used in both school counseling program and MTSS frameworks.

Examples:

- 80% of parents indicated ninth-grade registration and career planning conferences were helpful in determining their child's future choices.
- On the annual bullying survey, 30% of fourth-grade students indicated they had experienced bullying.
- 95% of seventh- and eighth-graders indicated they had an adult with whom they were connected.

VOICES FROM THE FIELD:

"Identify barriers to student learning, because MTSS is a part of that, and that's what we are here to do, and that's how we support it as well. It's systemic change for the entire building and for us."

Schools have a number of options when choosing to gather supplemental data from stakeholders. School staff may select common school climate items in a Google form for ease of use. Others use existing surveys, including The School Climate Survey (La Salle, McIntosh, & Eliason, 2018; for elementary and middle/high school students, parents and school personnel; for more information on this survey, see the resources at the end of this chapter).

For additional readings on supplemental data and on school climate surveys see Olsen, Preston, Algozzine, Algozzine and Cusumano (2016) and Olsen, Parsons, Vezzuto, Rochman, and Bender (2019).

Universal screening is another type of supplemental data. Just as we regularly screen students to identify deficits in literacy, numeracy, vision and hearing, mental health screening helps school-based teams support students in a timely and efficient manner. We can identify students needing intervention by systematically screening every student for universal mental health concerns, particularly when these concerns are barriers to students' learning and healthy development. As a member of the MTSS team, school counselors can play important leadership and supportive roles in this screening process across all levels, based on the school and district procedures.

The following eight steps from the University of Maryland can help your school's planning:

1. **Gather a team:** Include all school based mental-health providers (e.g., school counselor, school psychologist, school social workers, administration, teachers).
2. **Clarify goals:** For example, what behaviors or needs should we screen students for?
3. **Establish resources and logistics:** Consider cost, time, personnel involved, etc.
4. **Identify an appropriate screener:** Select based on school and community needs.
5. **Secure parent permission:** This can be passive or active permission.
6. **Collect data, administer and follow up:**
   - Who will complete (e.g., teachers, parents or through student self-report)?
   - When and how often will it be done (e.g., homeroom, advisory, English), yearly in October?
   - How will it be done (e.g., electronic or handwritten)?
7. **Create a plan for intervention follow-up and data analysis:**
   - If more than 20% of students in a classroom, grade level or school are found to be "elevated" or "highly elevated," a Tier 1 intervention should be planned.
   - If less than 20% are identified, small-group (Tier 2) and intensive (Tier 3) interventions are designed.
8. **Plan for continual improvement.**

(National Center for School Mental Health [NCSMH], 2020).

Because engaging in universal screening is a timely process, start slowly in collaboration with multiple stakeholders. For more information, see recent school counseling research on universal screening (e.g., Donohue, Goodman-Scott & Betters-Bubon, 2016; Erikson & Abel, 2013), as well as cross-disciplinary universal screening research (Lane, Menzies, Oakes & Kalberg, 2011; NCSMH, 2020; Splett, et al., 2018). Also, for practical information for school counselors, see The Case for Universal Mental Health Screening in Schools (Goodman-Scott, Donohue, & Betters-Bubon, 2019) in the Appendix.

VOICES FROM THE FIELD:

"Participating in the universal screening measure Signs of Suicide with our eighth-grade cohort was invaluable. Of the 275 students screened, 14 risk assessments were completed, several of which were with students who were not on the school counseling team's radar. During the process, we made important connections we likely would have missed otherwise."

Overall, by looking at the different data types, including participation, Mindsets & Behaviors, outcome and supplemental data, it's easy to see how much overlap exists between data used in school counseling program and MTSS frameworks.

Data	School Counseling	MTSS
Participation	X	X
Mindsets & Behaviors pre-/post-test data	X	
Outcome: GPA	X	X
Outcome: Graduation rates	X	X
Outcome: Advanced Placement exam	X	X
Outcome: State/national tests (e.g., ACT, SAT, achievement tests)	X	X
Outcome: Suspension/expulsion	X	X
Outcome: Discipline data	X	X
Supplemental: School climate survey	X	X
Supplemental: MTSS fidelity data		X

With a better understanding of school counseling program and MTSS data, let's revisit the activity you completed earlier in the chapter.

ACTIVITY REVISITED: Data Types

Examine the triangle you completed earlier in the chapter. Now that you know about different types of data, how can you add these types of data to the triangle image? Label the types of data you collect for All, for Some and for Few. What do you notice about the types of data you collect? How can you expand on this data to include multiple voices and experiences?

Now that we've looked at data common in both school counseling programs and MTSS, let's look at additional sources of data specifically collected as part of MTSS implementation and how to use this data in your school counseling program.

MTSS DATA

Although both school counseling programs and MTSS teams examine discipline data, let's take a closer look at how discipline data is often collected within MTSS. MTSS teams regularly examine discipline outcomes such as suspensions and expulsions. In addition, discipline referrals are a common strategy to monitoring discipline needs and interventions, as this data helps school staff know the specifics: where, when and what happens in the school building. MTSS teams meet weekly or bimonthly to discuss discipline referral data and determine subsequent universal (Tier 1) and tiered (Tier 2 and 3) interventions. To obtain this data, the MTSS team uses systematized office discipline forms, completed by school staff, that outline established and defined behavior. Following are two sample office discipline forms from pbis.org.

Office Referral Form

Name: ______________________	**Location**
Date: __________ Time: __________	☐ Classroom ☐ Hallway
Teacher: ______________________	☐ Playground ☐ Cafeteria
Grade: K 1 2 3 4 5	☐ Bathroom ☐ Library
Referring Staff: ______________________	☐ Other ______________

Minor Problem Behavior	Major Problem Behavior	Possible Motivation
☐ Defiance	☐ Defiance	Get
☐ Disruption	☐ Disruption	☐ Peer Attention
☐ Disrespect	☐ Disrespect	☐ Adult Attention
☐ Physical Contact	☐ Abusive Language	☐ Item/Activity
☐ Tardy	☐ Harassment	
☐ Inappropriate Language	☐ Fighting	Avoid
☐ Property Misuse	☐ Electronic/Tech. Violation	☐ Peer Attention
☐ Dress Code	☐ Property Damage	☐ Adult Attention
☐ Electronic/Tech. Violation	☐ Lying/ Cheating	☐ Item/Activity
☐ Other ______________	☐ Dress Code	
	☐ Inappropriate Display of Affection	
	☐ Other ______________	

Action Taken	
☐ Time Out/Detention	☐ In-School Suspension (______hours/days)
☐ Conference with Student	☐ Out-of-School Suspension (______hours/days)
☐ Loss of Privileges	☐ Action Pending
☐ Parent Contact	☐ Other ______________
☐ Individualized Instruction	

Others involved in incident:

☐ None ☐ Teacher ☐ Substitute ☐ Unknown

☐ Peers ☐ Staff ☐ Other ______________

Other Comments:

☐ I need to talk to the students' teacher ☐ I need to talk to the administrator

Parent Signature: ______________________ Date: ______________

Major Office Discipline Referral Form

Name:________________________________ Grade:______ Date: ______________

Referring Staff:______________________ Time of incident: ______________________

Others involved: ☐ No One ☐ Peers ☐ Teacher ☐ Staff ☐ Substitute ☐ Unknown

Check 1-2 behaviors as applicable. Circle the primary behavior.

Major Problem Behavior	**Location**	**Perceived Motivation**
☐ Defiance/Disrespect	☐ Classrooms	☐ Attention from peers
☐ Physical Aggression	☐ Hall	☐ Attention from adults
☐ Disruption	☐ Playground	☐ Obtain item/activity
☐ Abusive Language	☐ Cafeteria	☐ Avoid peers
☐ Tardy	☐ Bathroom	☐ Avoid adults
☐ Harassment	☐ Bus Loading Zone	☐ Avoid work/activity
☐ Fighting	☐ Commons	☐ Don't know
☐ Electronic Violation	☐ Don't know	☐ Other: ______________
☐ Dress Code	☐ Other: ______________	
☐ Other: ______________		

**Please avoid using "don't know" or "other" whenever possible. Thanks. ~PBIS Team*

Action(s) Taken:

☐ Time Out/Detention ☐ Conference w/ student ☐ In-School Susp. _______ days

☐ Loss of Privilege(s): ______________________________ ☐ Out-of-School Susp. _______ days

☐ Parent Contact ☐ Other: ______________________________

What happened? ____

____

FOLLOW UP AGREEMENT

Name:________________________________ **Date:** ______________

1. What rule(s) did you break? (Circle) ☐ Be Safe ☐ Be Respectful ☐ Be Responsible

2. What will you do differently next time? (Continue on back as needed)

____

____

____

Student Signature:______________________ **Adult Signature:** ______________________

You will note the discipline referral forms contain specific information, including time of day, location, etc. This allows MTSS teams to report on "The Big 5," which includes a breakdown of discipline referrals by location, time of day, student, type of infraction and grade level. This form systematizes information that can be readily input into data systems. Discipline referrals are most effective (a) when staff members know the form's purpose, (b) when at least 80% of staff are consistent about reporting incidents, (c) when completion leads to intervention and (d) when behaviors are defined (e.g., teacher managed versus office managed.

Culturally sustaining principles are critical. When creating discipline referral forms and processes, teams must have culturally sustaining systems in place. As you will note in the previous chapter on alignment, MTSS teams should be representative so multiple voices have input in the creation of MTSS forms. In addition, systems, including a clear T-chart, or plan for how to utilize discipline referrals, must also be in place. Further staff may need additional training on vulnerable decision points – those discipline situations prone to bias, including implicit bias – to ensure discipline referrals are effective and do not lead to disproportionality. Leverson, Smith, McIntosh, Rose and Pinkelman (2019) have created a comprehensive guide to assist teams in this work. In addition, we suggest reading: Bubon, Brunner and Kansteiner (2017); Betters-Bubon, Kortemeier and Smith-Durkin (2019); Girvan, Gion, McIntosh and Smolkowski (2017); and McIntosh, Girvan, Horner, Smolkowski and Sugai (2018).

EXAMPLES: Office Discipline Referrals

By Location

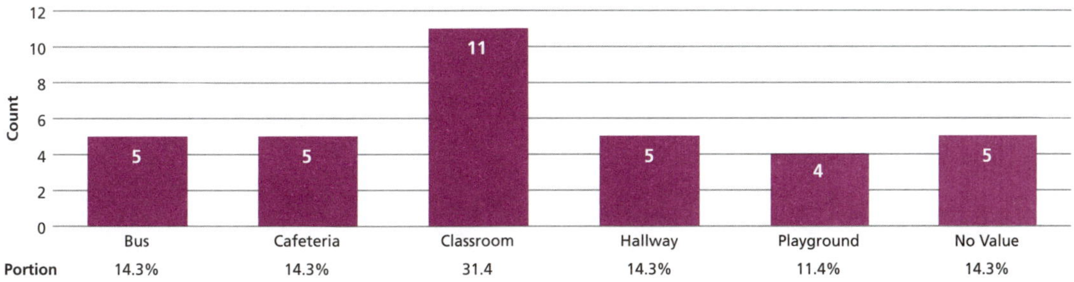

By Student

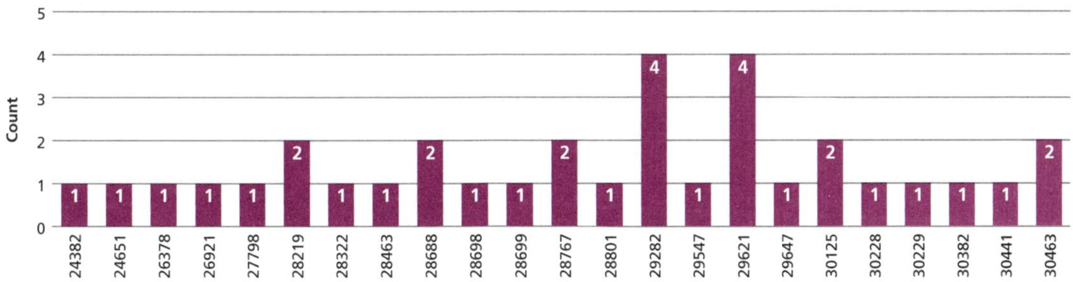

By Time/Day of the Week

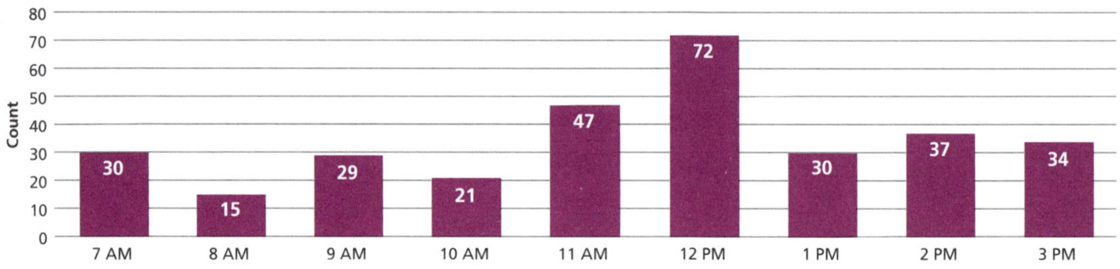

By Type of Infraction

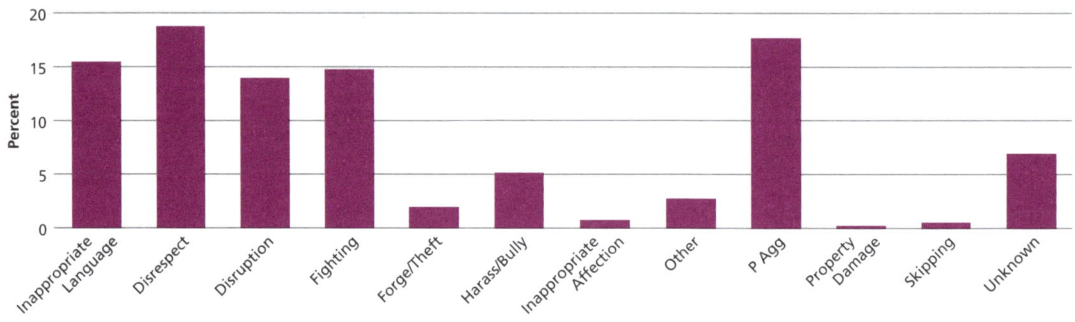

By Grade Level

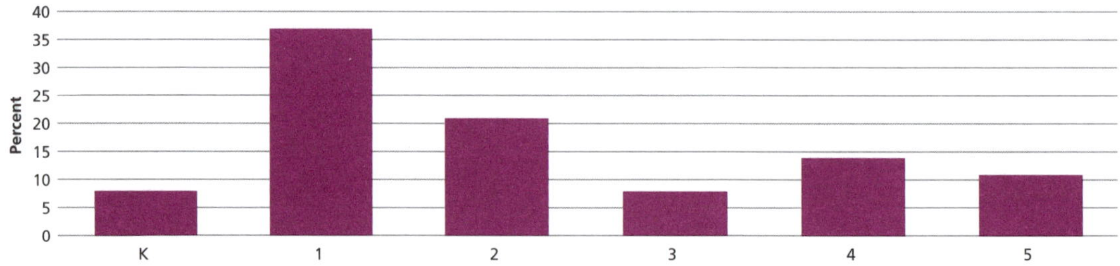

Disaggregated by subgroup (race/ethnicity; socioeconomic status, disability status)

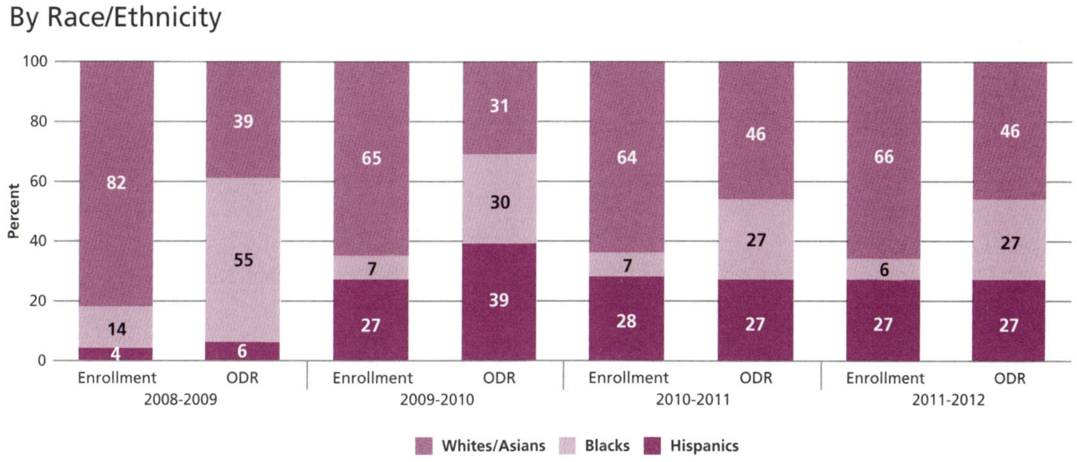

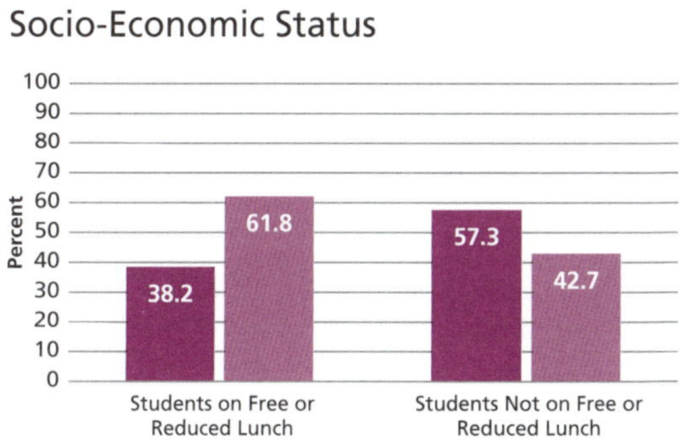

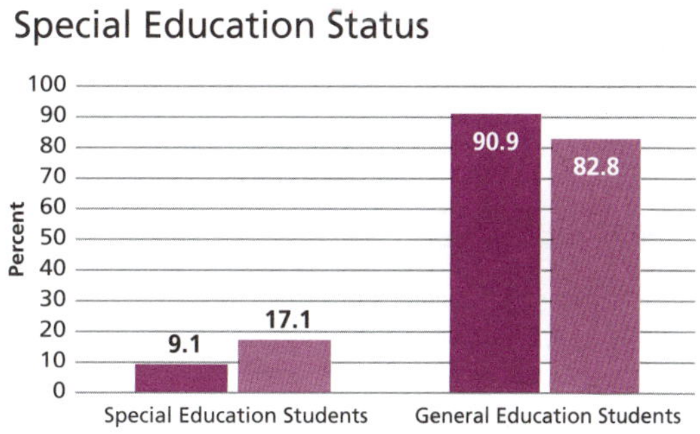

Percent of student population
Percent of office referrals

VOICES FROM THE FIELD:

According to a school counselor, "[Several] students reported that they were impacted by racial and cultural bullying. ... It was a disproportionately high number of Hispanic and African American students. ... we might have to work on racial, cultural understanding and respect and awareness."

By breaking down data by time, location and type and disaggregating across different subgroups, MTSS teams have a better understanding of where and for whom systemic supports are needed. Also, as mentioned earlier, this data helps us move from vague data to the more specific, allowing us to better understand root cause. As a result, both Tier 1 universal strategies and Tier 2/3 interventions can help us better understand and then better meet student and staff needs.

The goal of aligning the ASCA National Model and MTSS is to work smarter, not harder. Let's recap what we know:

- School counselors value using outcome data to guide their student outcome goals and assess the effectiveness of their school counseling program.
- The MTSS team is a school-based leadership team that collects and analyzes schoolwide outcome data.
- School counselors are often on the MTSS team.

Thus, consider: how can the MTSS and school counseling program efforts be coordinated. Answer these questions:

- How can school counselors use MTSS data sources within their school counseling program?
- What are the benefits of using discipline referrals as a data source?
- What are the potential negatives of using discipline referrals as a data source?
- Take another look at the discipline referral data disaggregated by subgroup. Given your role as a systemic change agent, what data stands out? How might you intervene?
- What other sources of data can you, as a school counselor, analyze in addition to discipline referrals to create a complete picture?
- What could you learn by bringing together a focus group of students, teachers or parents to discuss discipline referrals at your school?
- Share discipline referral data with school counseling advisory group and your school's parent/community/student advisory council to discuss trends and potential interventions.

VOICES FROM THE FIELD:

"MTSS is all about student outcome data. So, having that experience is what helped me digest the direction in which the school counseling department was going in terms of data collection."

DESCRIPTION: ALIGNMENT OF SCHOOL COUNSELING PROGRAM DATA AND MTSS DATA

As you've seen, there is tremendous overlap between school counseling program and MTSS data, as both frameworks monitor student success by achievement, attendance and discipline data. Hence, aligning the ASCA National Model and MTSS helps us be efficient and effective.

Both school counseling programs and MTSS use data to ensure programs and interventions are effective. Thus, school counselors can be even more effective when they integrate MTSS data within their school counseling program, as it provides additional data to use for prevention and intervention. Likewise, school counselors can incorporate Mindsets & Behaviors pre-/post-data to help them understand student outcomes. For example, school counselors can examine MTSS data to form small groups and measure change in student attitudes, skills and knowledge.

Goodman-Scott and Grothaus (2017) interviewed school counselors at RAMP schools who had successful MTSS implementation. What could we learn from school counselors who had RAMP-level ASCA National Model and MTSS implementation? One of the strongest themes was data. These school counselors tended to love data. They used MTSS data in their school counseling program and shared their school counseling data with the MTSS team to coordinate efforts, strengthening both.

VOICES FROM THE FIELD:

"RAMP helped me take MTSS data and know even better what to do with it because I've already gone through it."

VOICES FROM THE FIELD:

"When I did my end-of-year data presentation to staff, I integrated my school counseling program results with our schoolwide MTSS data, including discipline referrals. I didn't single handedly make schoolwide discipline referrals decline, but our school counseling program and MTSS alignment contributed to a schoolwide goal."

Thus, school counseling program and MTSS data can be used together provide a complete picture of needs and interventions within a system. Consider the example below:

Example:

During the first week of January, 95% of fourth-grade students received one classroom lesson on anger/emotion regulation. The week after the lessons, at the monthly MTSS meeting, team members, including the school counselor, reviewed schoolwide student outcome data. This data, prepared by the school counselor and a teacher leader, showed an increase in the number of discipline referrals related to physical aggression among fourth- and fifth-grade boys. What might be going on? It might be that (a) there are systems/policies, procedures or practices within the school/grade level that led to an inequity in learning, (b) the school counseling lessons were not effective, or weren't taught in culturally sustaining ways or (c) there might be a gap in students' knowledge vs. skills and, thus, a subset of students may need reteaching. Thus, there is a need for additional data: conducting a root-cause analysis.

As a member of the team, the school counselor helped examine the root cause behind the change in behavior. The team met to examine the systems/policies, procedures and practices that may have contributed to the change in behavior. Because only boys were reported as exhibiting the behavior, they discussed what was normative within male peer groups and the potential staff biases that might exist in discipline referral patterns. The school counselor examined the classroom lessons to ensure the teacher allowed for various ways of engagement and demonstration of learning and provided teachers with professional development on engaging boys in learning. The teachers attempted multiple strategies. When the behavior referrals continued, the school counselor intervened on the student level. The school counselor constructed a pre-/post-test, measuring student knowledge, attitudes and skills related to anger/emotion regulation (e.g., Mindsets & Behavior data) before and after the next school counseling lesson. Upon analysis, with a subset of the MTSS team, the school counselor noted that although some fourth- and fifth-graders have the attitudes that controlling their anger is important, they lacked the skills.

Next, the school counselor implemented a small-group intervention focused on anger management/emotion regulation skill development with the specific students in need. After the group ended, the school counselor collected additional Mindsets & Behaviors data, examined discipline referrals with the MTSS team, reported the results to the MTSS team and then to all staff at a staff meeting.

Questions for Review and Discussion:

In looking at the example above, the school counselor used both MTSS outcome data and Mindsets & Behaviors data to generate interventions for staff as well as referrals for small-group counseling/Tier 2 supports and then continued to monitor this data, to determine students' progress and potential areas for staff development.

- How are you like the school counselor in the above scenario? How often do you intervene with staff? With students?
- Who can you partner with in the building to assess outcome data? Who can you consult and collaborate with to determine the level of your interventions?
- How can you use MTSS data in your school counseling program to improve your activities and interventions? How can you use MTSS data to ensure you are engaging in culturally sustaining practice?

VOICES FROM THE FIELD:

According to staff, they appreciated that their school data trends were shared schoolwide at MTSS team meetings, grade-level meetings, monthly staff meetings and parent conferences. One school counselor mentioned that being informed of data trends increased her awareness of school issues: "Due to the data shared school counselors know reading is an issue. What can we do to help students read?"

For additional readings on data and data alignment, see Taylor and Burgess (2019) and Young and Kaffenberger (2018).

ACTIVITY: School Data Summary

Now that you understand about the alignment between school counseling program and MTSS data sources, let's see how to better use data in your school counseling role. Complete the school data summary, from the ASCA National Model (2019). Additional questions related to MTSS are included in callout boxes to help you think more about alignment of data and practice.

School Data Summary Template

Create your school's data story by reviewing the school improvement plan, school data reports, other data resources (e.g., student behavior surveys, climate surveys, school engagement surveys, etc.).

1. Identify who in the building can help you. Who is your data expert; who can help you interpret the data?

↓

Given the MTSS data team's expertise, how could they assist accessing and interpreting data?

2. Identify the school improvement plan goals.
   - In which areas can the school counseling program support the work?
   - List those goals:

↓

What schoolwide improvement goals are the focus of the MTSS team? How can the school counseling student outcome goal support or be aligned with the MTSS goal?

3. Review available school data reports for previous years to identify trends.

For example:

Is there a subgroup that historically underperforms on standardized achievement benchmarks?

Is there a grade level that historically has the most absences?

Is there a subgroup that historically receives the majority of discipline referrals?

- What is working well according to your school data reports?
  - Achievement
  - Attendance
  - Discipline
- Highlight possible areas of need according to your school data reports.
  - Achievement
  - Attendance
  - Discipline

↓

Consider how the MTSS team addresses data; how can you partner and work together to have an impact on data?

4. Compare your school's data with district and state data or other comparable data points.

5. Identify what else you need to know.

6. Identify and prioritize data points you will address through your school counseling program.

Data Points	How Addressed Through the School Counseling Program
1.	1.
2.	2.
3.	3.
4.	4.
5.	5.

Reflection:

After completing the school data summary, reflect on your answers:

- What overlap do you see between MTSS and school counseling program data?
  - How can MTSS data inform school counseling programs?
  - How can school counseling program data inform MTSS?
- What data do teams in your school (e.g., MTSS, leadership, school counseling, equity, etc.) already collect?
- Who are the other data experts in your school? How can you collaborate with them to co-construct data goals?

In addition to reviewing the school data summary, let's look at how to apply this practically by examining an example loosely based on the work of a school counseling team from Loudoun County, Va.

A middle school counseling team in Loudoun County Public Schools completed the school data summary as part of their school counseling program and also to integrate their work with MTSS.

1. As members of the MTSS team, the school counselors coordinated their work with data experts who serve on the MTSS team.
2. The school counselors and MTSS team examined the schoolwide school improvement and noted the following goal:

   Instructional staff will use a variety of evidence from diagnostic, formative and performance-based assessments to support the personalization of instruction, course placement, purposeful grouping and a system of tiered interventions. The essential action associated with this goal was: Utilize specific research-based instructional practices to increase achievement levels in mathematics for all subgroups with specific attention toward English-language learners (ELL).

3. The MTSS team, which included a school counselor, examined and disaggregated data to determine how to best to have a positive impact on the school improvement plan.

4. The team compared this disaggregated data with other schools and noted that their school had an inequity (e.g., lower scores) for eighth-grade ELL students in math. Subsequently, the MTSS team set a schoolwide SMART goal:

   By June 2019, at least 80% of identified eighth-grade students who are ELL level 3-4.5 and failed their math 7 SOL will (a) increase their math 8 or algebra SOL score by 30 points or (b) pass their math 8 or algebra SOL.

5. Individuals on the MTSS team identified possible root causes and subsequent interventions, including study groups co-facilitated with ELL teachers and eighth-grade math teacher, as well as a homework club.
6. As MTSS team members and to purposefully align school counseling goals with the school improvement plan, the school counselors identified and prioritized data points they wished to address (e.g., students who were ELL level 3-4.5 who failed math) and thus developed a student outcome goal and associated interventions they facilitated as part of the school counseling program.
   - Student outcome goal: By the end of the academic year, 50% of eighth-grade students with an F in math 8 or Algebra SOL will increase their grade to passing.
   - School counseling plan to close the gap, which included:
     - Small-group instruction: The school counselors implement small-group instruction to address ASCA Mindsets & Behaviors related to the MTSS SMART goal. In this case, the school counselors created groups focused on the following Mindsets & Behaviors standards: Use time-management, organizational and study skills (B-LS.3); demonstrate perseverance to achieve long- and short-term goals (B-SMS.5); demonstrate ability to overcome barriers to learning (B-SMS.6).
     - Individual advisement: School counselors included individual advisement to support the identified students to develop SMART goals related to their math achievement short- and long-term goals and problem solve barriers to reaching their goals.

The MTSS team met mid-semester to discuss strategies and action steps. School counselors were able to share data from their small-group counseling (pre-/post-data change in Mindsets & Behaviors), teachers were able to share academic math data, and all were able to create plans to move forward in creating additional goals to meet the school improvement plan. They created a list of things to add, change and a goal for the next quarter.

In conclusion, using the ASCA school data summary as a guide can help school counselors (a) collaborate with the MTSS team surrounding data collection and analysis, particularly the use of student outcome data and (b) ensure the school counseling student outcome goal is aligned with the schoolwide improvement goal.

Questions for Review and Discussion

- How can you, as a school counselor, be more involved with school improvement goals?
- How can the school improvement goals guide the school counseling program goal (e.g., student outcome goal)?
- How can school improvement goals be inclusive of all students in the school community?
- How can school improvement goals evaluate systems/practices and policies to ensure equitable results for all students and families?
- What MTSS data sources will you use as you develop your school counseling goals?
- What activities are you doing to impact students that might relate to the goals?

In sum, using the ASCA school data summary as a guide can help school counselors (a) collaborate with the MTSS team surrounding data collection and analysis, particularly the use of student outcome data, and (b) ensure the school counseling student outcome goal was aligned with the schoolwide improvement goal.

DESCRIPTION: DATA ORGANIZATION AND REPORTS

Because schools have many different types of data systems and ways to collect/organize data, school counselors will need to develop ways to organize their data. ASCA results reports (closing the gap and Mindsets & Behaviors reports) may be helpful to ensure data is collected and reported in response to activities and interventions. Other common data systems include:

- Microsoft Excel: a quick Google search will reveal ready-made templates for data collection and analysis
- Schoolwide information system
- School data systems (Infinite Campus, PowerSchool, etc.)
- MTSS specific data systems (Panorama, Intellispark, etc.)

The final case study highlights an integrated and aligned program, and specifically focuses on how the school counselors can have an impact on practice across both Tier 1 and Tier 2 of the MTSS system through their school counseling program.

CASE STUDY: OFFICE DISCIPLINE REFERRAL AFFECTING UNIVERSAL PRACTICE: ELEMENTARY SCHOOL

An elementary school counselor and the MTSS team noted a high number of discipline referrals for physical aggression in 2016–2017. (Case study from Sarah Bazemore, then from Henrico Public Schools, Va.)

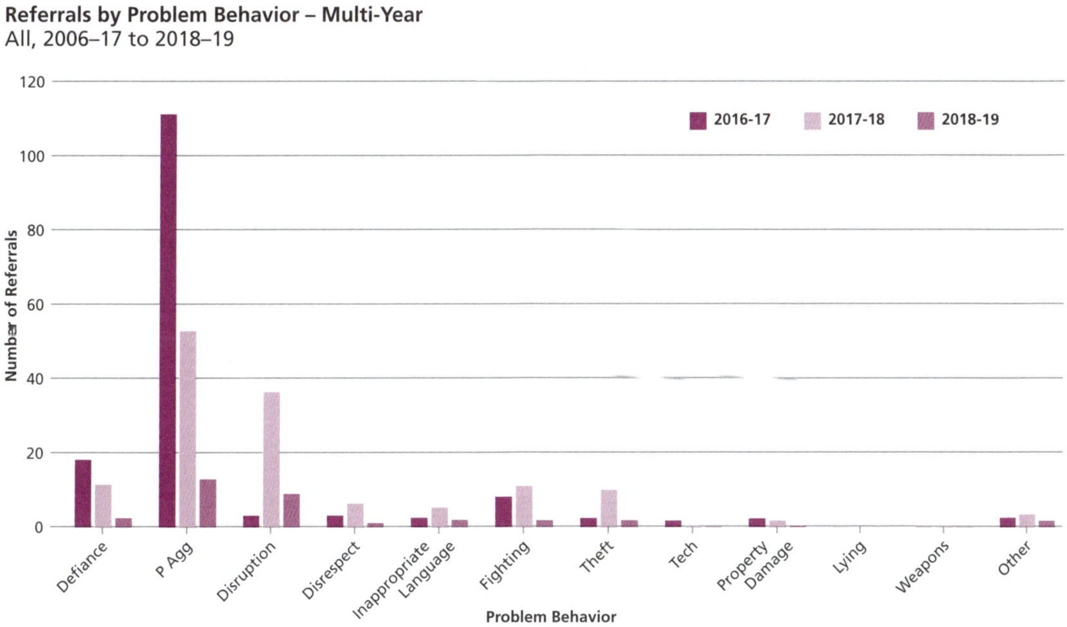

After seeing this outcome data, the school counselor gathered supplemental data (e.g., teacher surveys and student interviews). As a result of both the outcome and supplemental data, though an integrated approach, the school counselor worked with the MTSS team to coordinate Tier 1 supports focused on emotional regulation and related social skills. Thus, the school counselor created resources for teachers, aligning teachers' classroom lessons to Mindsets & Behaviors while the MTSS team created visuals and shared language.

Specifically, through the school counseling curriculum, the school counselor and the classroom teachers taught lessons to meet the emotional regulation standards (e.g., I understand the functions of my upstairs and downstairs brain and how they affect my ability to regulate my emotions). The school staff were heavily trained and prepared to incorporate this content in their classrooms. Thus, teachers were able to successfully respond and reinforce skills when students were experiencing uncomfortable emotions (e.g., offer specific praise when students implemented calming strategies, apologize respectfully, handle a conflict peacefully, etc.). Even the school administrators had these related visuals in their office and would refer to them when talking through concerns with students. The concepts became a part of the school culture, infused throughout the building. Truly the success of this school counseling-led initiative largely came from focusing on changing the behavior of the adults in the building, which then trickled down to shaping students' behaviors.

After the universal lessons, the school counselor disseminated data in a results report noting school counseling data (see next page).

RESULTS REPORT: Emotional Regulation Lessons (Schoolwide)

Grade Level	Lesson Topics	Projected Start/End	ASCA Domain & Mindsets & Behaviors Standard(s)
K-5 **Process Data** 855-873 Students (depending on year)	Lesson #1: I can understand that everyone feels uncomfortable emotions. I can recognize how anger looks and feels. Lesson #2: I can identify my personal triggers. Lesson #3: I can identify ways to calm down and control uncomfortable emotions. Lesson #4: I can manage my conflicts peacefully. Lesson #5: I can apologize meaningfully (4 parts)	Lessons are in their third year of implementation! 2018-2019 Dates School Counseling Intro Lessons First two weeks of October 5 Teacher Taught Lessons During month of January Emotional Regulation Video February	B-SMS 2: Demonstrate self-discipline and self-control B-SMS 7: Demonstrate effective coping skills when faced with a problem B-SMS 9: Demonstrate personal safety skills B-SS 1: Use effective oral and written communication skills and listening skills B-SS 2: Create positive and supportive relationships with other students B-SS 3: Create relationships with adults that support success B-SS 8: Demonstrate advocacy skills and ability to assert self, when necessary B-SS 9: Demonstrate social maturity and behaviors appropriate to the situation and environments

Student Outcome Data

Office Referrals for physical aggression decreased dramatically after implementation of this curriculum.

Average number of office referrals for physical aggression in 2016-2017 school year was 11.2 per month. In 2017-2018 school year the average dropped to 5.4 per month. In 2018-2019, as of March, the average number of office referrals per month is 1.8.

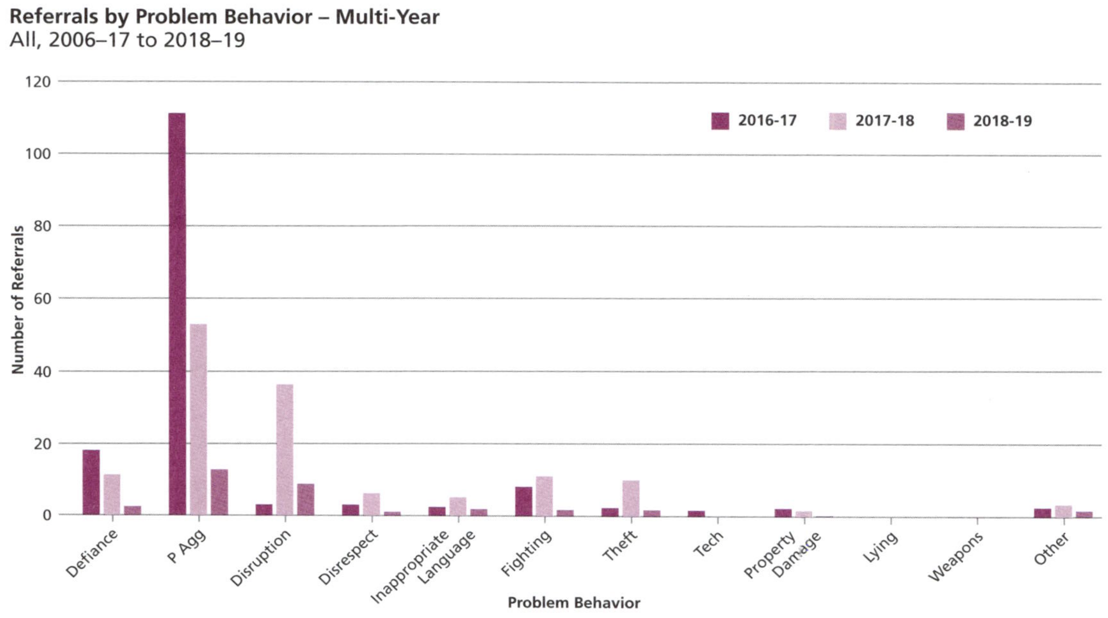

Perception Data	
Teacher feedback from survey: "The apology lesson has made it much easier to guide students through apologies and they have been very open to it. Also some of my students have been asking for times to talk out their problems instead of letting them escalate." -Shannon, 3rd Grade Teacher "I've noticed empathy toward understanding other's anger/ frustration." -Tom, 4th Grade Teacher "The students really responded well to the "iceberg" lessons. They also really liked discussing additional ways of handling anger in a "clean" way (like squishing a stress ball)." -Christie, 4th Grade Teacher "Yes, I have witnessed the kind and unkind anger problem solving and the correct way to say I'm sorry. I have one child in particular that has been able to problem solve because of our morning meeting discussions." -David, 5th Grade Teacher	"The lessons are great, and I love the fact that you supply them and we don't have to think them up! I also appreciate the follow-up that's available when you both come into the classroom. Thanks for all you do! It's so helpful to have a schoolwide program that everyone follows. This is evident just in the improvement we've seen in student behavior at assemblies over the last few years. We're very fortunate to have you!" -Cheryl, 2nd Grade Teacher "I have seen so much progress in controlling emotions in my class!" -Chloe, Kindergarten Teacher "I have seen a student use kind anger choices. He walked away from an argument at recess that he was very upset about. He took some time to himself before he went back to the game to work out the problem." -Kim, 3rd Grade Teacher

(By Sarah Bazemore, Virginia)

Questions for Review and Discussion

- What do you notice about the school counselor's role in responding to data at the Tier 1 level?
- What services did the school counselor perform? Consider the school counselor's role as intervener directly serving students,and as supporter, providing indirect services.
- Were the interventions culturally sustaining and inclusive of all learners?
- How did the school counselor align the school counseling program with the MTSS goals? How did the school counseling program assist in MTSS implementation?

After the school counseling lessons, the school counselor examined data to determine which students were not successful. She facilitated Tier 2 small groups, based on data and teacher referral, for students who needed additional practice with emotional regulation. She integrated pre-/post-tests to assess change in knowledge, attitudes and skills and shared results with stakeholders. Finally, the school counselor and a special education teacher formed Tier 3 groups for students who needed additional teaching.

Throughout this case study, the school counselor (a) used a system's approach, changing the practices of the school staff, (b) used data and (c) worked alongside the MTSS team to create prevention and intervention activities to have a positive impact on student outcomes at Tier 1, 2 and 3. The school counselor served as an intervener, leading classroom lessons (Tier 1) and conducting small groups (Tier 2). As a supporter, the school counselor also created content for school staff that they used to teach and reinforce content throughout the school, both in teaching classroom lessons (Tier 1) and small group and individual work with students (Tier 2). The school counselor worked smarter and not harder, aligning goals and data to impact student outcomes.

Questions for Review and Discussion

- What data can you utilize to plan your Tier 1 lessons? Your Tier 2 supports?
- How can you use data to align your school counseling program with the school's needs?
- How can you utilize the ASCA National Model results reports to share you results?

This chapter provided an overview of different types of data, discussed how to align data across school counseling and MTSS frameworks and demonstrated several examples of this alignment from the field. You should now be able to see that aligning school counseling data with MTSS data while working alongside other professionals in the school (e.g., the MTSS team) can help you meet the needs of students and families.

REFERENCES AND RESOURCES

Betters-Bubon, J., Brunner, T., & Kansteiner, A. (2016). Success for all? The role of the school counselor in creating and sustaining culturally responsive PBIS programs. *The Professional Counselor,* 6(3), 263-277.

Betters-Bubon, J. Kortemeier, H., & Smith-Durkin, S. (2019). Culturally responsive MTSS: Advocating for equity for every student. In E. Goodman-Scott, J. Betters-Bubon, & P. Donohue (Eds.), *A School Counselor's Guide to Multi-tiered Systems of Support* (pp. 298-329). New York City, NY: Routledge.

Dimmitt, C., Carey, J. C., & Hatch, T. (2007). *Evidence-based school counseling: Making a difference with data-driven practices*. Thousand Oaks, CA: Corwin Press.

Donohue, P. (2019). Universal screening to support MTSS. In Goodman-Scott, E., Betters-Bubon, J., & Donohue P., (Eds.). *The School Counselor's Guide to Multi-Tiered Systems of Support*. (pp. 189-221). New York, New York: Routledge.

Donohue, P., Goodman-Scott, E., & Betters-Bubon, J. (2015). Using universal screening for early identification of students at risk: A case example from the field. *Professional School Counseling, 19*(1), 133.

Erickson, A., & Abel, N. R. (2013). A high school counselor's leadership in providing school-wide screenings for depression and enhancing suicide awareness. *Professional School Counseling, 16*(5), 2156759X1201600501.

Flannery, K. B., McGrath, K. M., Horner, R. H. (September, 2019). *Using outcome data to implement Multi-tiered Behavior of Support (PBIS) in high schools*. Eugene, OR: OSEP TA Center on PBIS, University of Oregon. Retrieved from www.pbis.org

Girvan, E. J., Gion, C., McIntosh, K., & Smolkowski, K. (2017). The relative contribution of subjective office referrals to racial disproportionality in school discipline. *School Psychology Quarterly, 32*, 392-404. doi:10.1037/spq0000178

McIntosh, K., Girvan, E. J., Horner, R. H., Smolkowski, K., & Sugai, G. (2018). *A 5-point intervention approach for enhancing equity in school discipline*. OSEP Technical Assistance Center on Positive Behavioral Interventions and Supports.

Martinez S., Kern L., Hershfeldt P., George H. P., White A., Flannery B., Freeman J. (September, 2019). *High School PBIS Implementation: Student Voice*. Eugene, OR: OSEP TA Center on PBIS, University of Oregon. Retrieved from www.pbis.org

Lane, K. L., Menzies, H. M., Oakes, W. P., & Kalberg, J. R. (2011). *Systematic screenings of behavior to support instruction: From preschool to high school*. Guilford Press.

La Salle, T. P., McIntosh, K., & Eliason, B. M. (2018). *School climate survey suite administration manual*. Eugene, OR: OSEP Technical Assistance Center on Positive Behavioral Interventions and Supports. University of Oregon. LINK:. Retrieved from https://assets-global.website-files.com/5d3725188825e071f1670246/5dd46215547220c4077341d3_School%20Climate%20Survey%20Suite%20Manual.pdf

Leverson, M., Smith, K., McIntosh, K., Rose, J., & Pinkelman, S. (2019). *PBIS cultural responsiveness field guide: Resources for trainers and coaches*. OSEP Technical Assistance Center on Positive Behavioral Interventions and Supports. www.pbis.org.

National Center for School Mental Health (NCSMH, 2020). *School Mental Health Quality Guide: Screening*. NCSMH, University of Maryland School of Medicine.

Splett, J.W. et al. (2018). Comparison of universal mental health screening to student already receiving intervention in a Multitiered System of Support. *Behavioral Disorders, 43*, 344-356.

Olsen, J., Preston, A. I., Algozzine, B., Algozzine, K., & Cusumano, D. (2016). A review and analysis of selected school climate measures. *The Clearing House: A Journal of Educational Strategies, Issues and Ideas, 91*(2), 47-58.

Olsen, J., Parsons, J., Vezzuto, L., Rochman, D., & Bender, L. (2019). School conditions and climate validity and reliability technical design group: School conditions and climate survey analysis summary. Orange County Department of Education.

Taylor, J. & Burgess, M. (2019). Using data in MTSS to demonstrate how school counselors make a difference. In E. Goodman-Scott, J. Betters-Bubon, & P. Donohue (Eds.), *A School Counselor's Guide to Multi-tiered Systems of Support* (p.246-266). New York City, NY: Routledge.

Swain-Bradway, J., Gulbrandson, K., Galston, A., & McIntosh, K. (2019). *Do Wisconsin schools implementing an integrated academic and behavior support framework improve equity in academic and school discipline outcomes?* OSEP Technical Assistance Center on Positive Behavioral Interventions and Supports. www.pbis.org https://assets-global.websitefiles.com/5d3725188825e071f1670246/5d82aa7feb813389e04fabad_Wisconsin%20Integrated%20Academic%20and%20Behavior%20Support%20Framework.pdf

U.S. Department of Education (2020). Ed School Climate Survey (EDSCLS) Washington, DC. Retrieved from https://safesupportivelearning.ed.gov/edscls/data-interpretation

Young, A. & Kaffenberger, C. (2018). *Making DATA Work.* Alexandria, VA: American School Counselor Association.

CHAPTER 3

Advanced Process for Using Data

In the last chapter, we provided an overview of data and how school counselors can align and strengthen culturally sustaining school counseling programs and MTSS implementation through data use. In this chapter, we provide a more in-depth overview of (a) the cyclical process of how and why school counselors use data, (b) how school counselors can create culturally sustaining practices and systems that guide interventions and (c) how aligning school counseling programs and MTSS creates systemic change. Throughout this chapter, we will provide strategies and examples to bring the alignment process to life.

DESCRIPTION: HOW AND WHY SCHOOL COUNSELORS USE DATA TO CREATE SYSTEMIC CHANGE

As you read in chapter 2, data is used to inform school counseling programs and MTSS. Further, school counselors can more easily accomplish program goals when they work in tandem with MTSS teams. In "Making Data Work" (2018), the authors outlined a cyclical model of "How and Why School Counselors Use Data," highlighting the importance of school counselors using data within school counseling programs. Within their model, Young and Kaffenberger defined a seven-step process for school counselors, to show how their data use affects student outcomes (e.g., achievement, behavior, etc.). Specifically, Figure 3.1 (following page) outlines this process, starting with the mission and vision and ending with systemic change throughout the school and district culture.

Figure 3.1

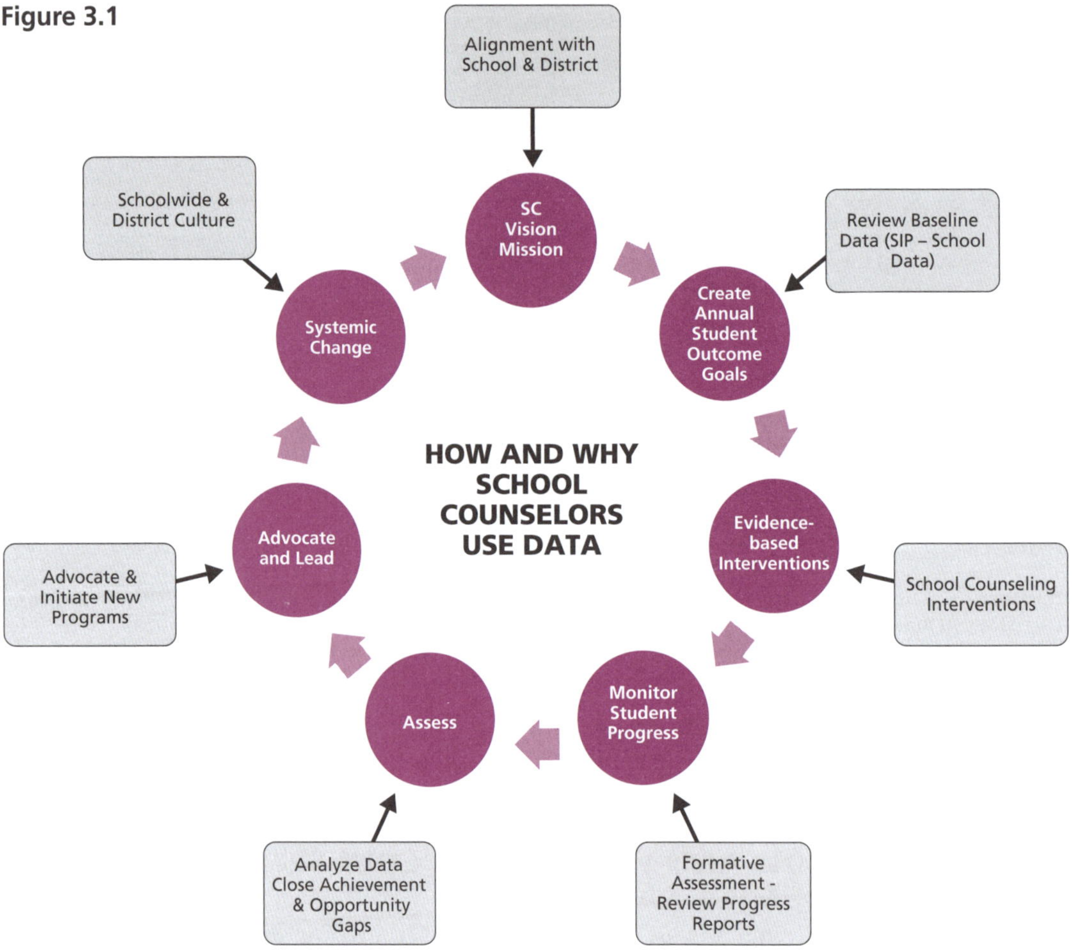

Young & Kaffenberger (2018)

Young and Kaffenberger's (2018) model aligns with content we've discussed previously in this book. For example, as noted in chapter 2, school counselors align their program mission/vision with the school and district mission to create program goals. Similarly, as described in chapters 4, 5 and 6 (Tiers 1, 2 and 3), school counselors use culturally sustaining, evidenced-based interventions within and across tiers to have an impact on and monitor student progress. Finally, as discussed throughout this book, school counselors use data to evaluate programs to have an impact on achievement and opportunity gaps. Thus, school counselors use data to examine systems to ensure they are working for all learners in an inclusive, positive and culturally sustaining school environment.

DESCRIPTION: MTSS DATA, SYSTEMS AND PRACTICES

Within the MTSS framework, a similar process exists in which school teams have an impact on student outcomes through an intentional focus on data, systems and practices across Tiers 1, 2 and 3 (Sugai, & Horner, 2009). For instance, at each tier:

- Data is used to identify needs (e.g., system, staff, student) and monitor progress (e.g., participation, outcome data).

- Systems are designed to support and guide staff (e.g., policies, procedures, protocol, resource allocation and opportunities to assist with implementation).
- Practices are supports and interventions, designed and implemented by school staff, to support students (e.g., evidence-based interventions).

The three elements interact and inform school goals and objectives to achieve desired academic, behavioral and social/emotional outcomes within systems. As you can see from the figure below, there is overlap between the three elements, and each contributes in unique ways to student outcomes.

Figure 3.2

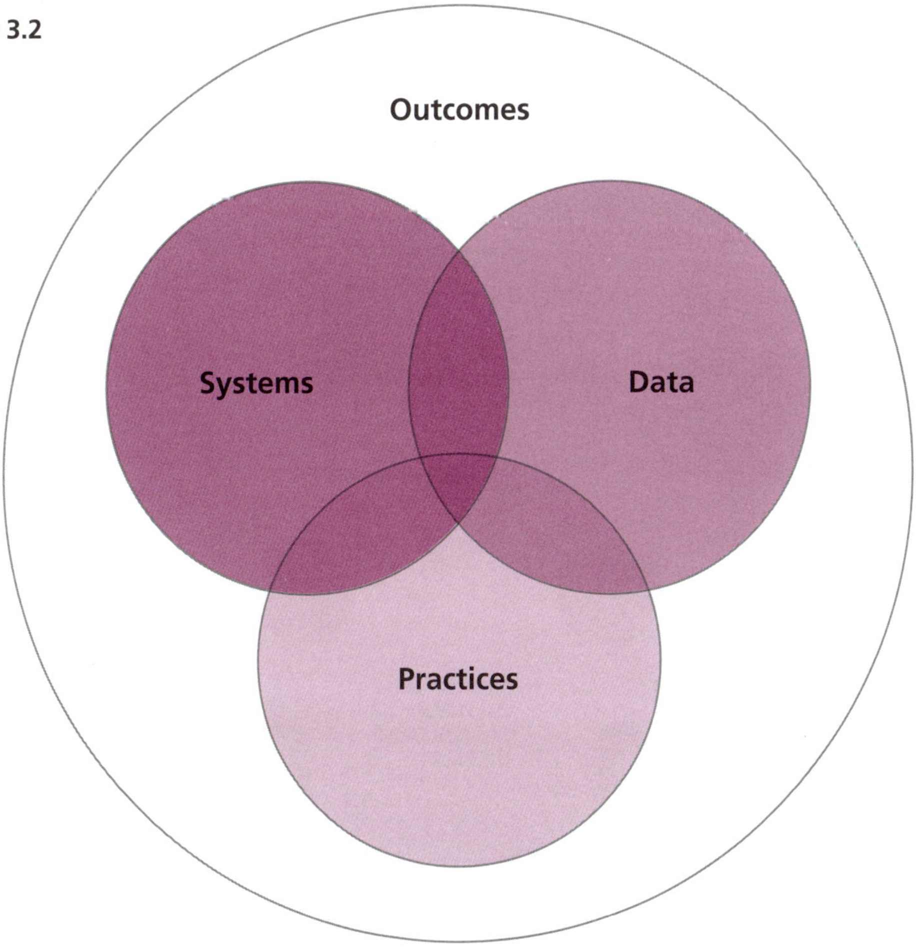

DESCRIPTION: ALIGNMENT AND INTEGRATION

To fulfill our goal of aligning school counseling programs and MTSS goals and practices, we used Young and Kaffenberger's (2018) "How and Why School Counselors Use Data" cycle and embedded MTSS tenants (data, systems and practices). Thus, as a summary to the book, we highlight an ongoing and cyclical process of how school counselors can integrate school/district and MTSS priorities within their school counseling program.

The image below outlines each of Young and Kaffenberger's (2018) seven steps, recognizing that school counselors work as leaders and advocates by aligning their school counseling program with MTSS initiatives and activities. The additions in the dark pink boxes show how school counselors can embed culturally sustaining MTSS tenants into their role designing and implementing a school counseling program. Through school counseling program/MTSS integration, school counselors can more readily identify systemic barriers and create change within and across systems (Figure 3.3). Of note, through this process, we suggest that school counselors do more than label their activities within the MTSS tiers; rather we suggest they take an integrative approach to aligning their program and collaborating with MTSS teams. Further, we encourage school counselors to use data to determine inequitable systems and then move to changing current practices. As we have emphasized throughout this book, this ensures that school counselors work smarter not harder, when implementing a school counseling program, such as the ASCA National Model.

Figure 3.3

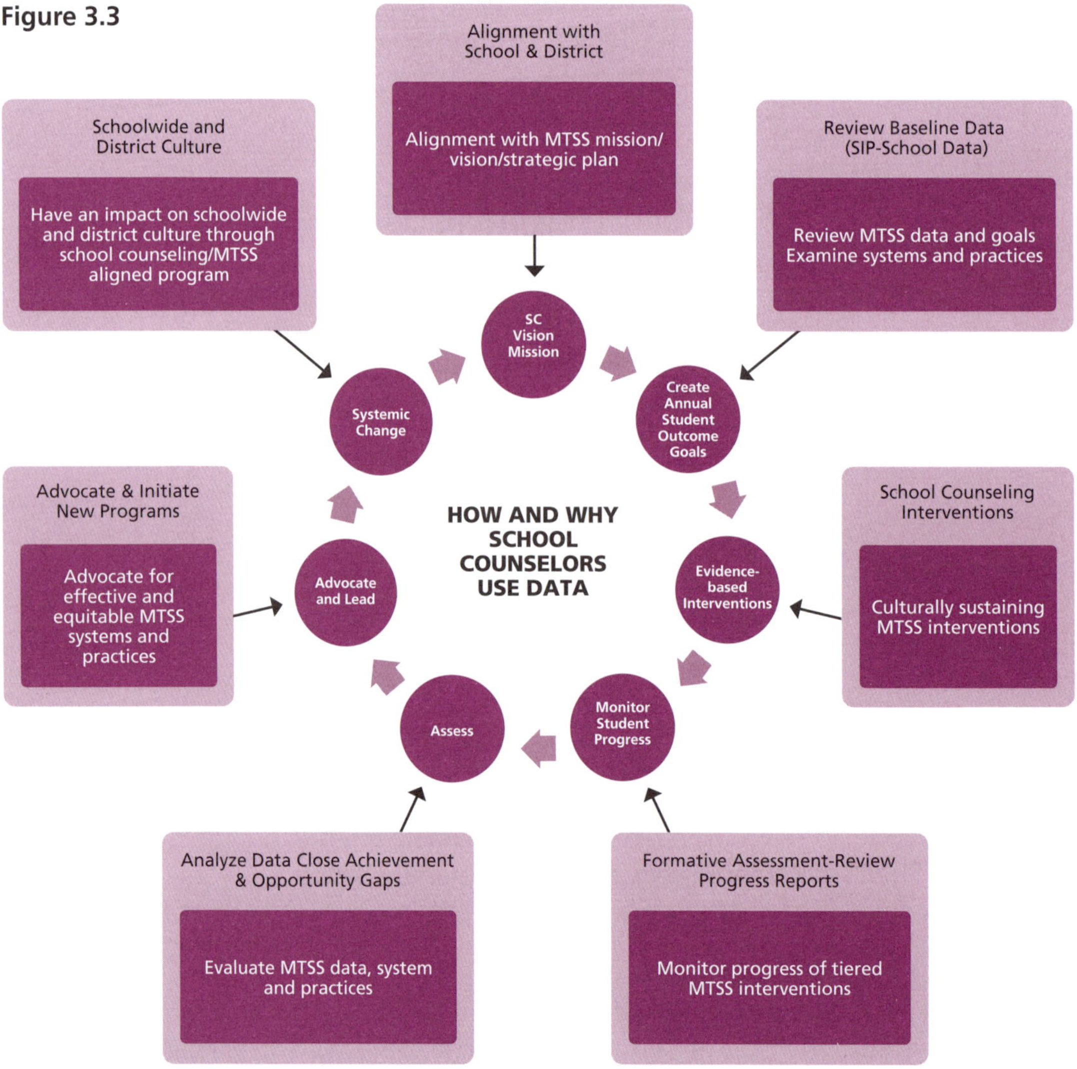

Adapted from Young & Kaffenberger (2018)

VOICES FROM THE FIELD:

"Identifying those barriers to student learning, because MTSS is a part of that, and that's what we are here to do, and that's how we support it as well. It's systemic change for the entire building and for us."

Case study: To bring the previous model to light, let's look at an extended case study, loosely based on the work of the Sugar Creek Elementary School counselor and MTSS team. Throughout this example the student services members, including the school counselor, the school psychologist and the school social worker, collaborate to provide supports and interventions in collaboration with the MTSS team. The school has been implementing MTSS since 2009 and has engaged in multiple trainings related to school counseling programming and MTSS over the years. Each of the seven steps from the aligned cyclical process (Figure 3.3) is outlined subsequently.

DESCRIPTION: STEPS 1 AND 2: ALIGNING MISSION, VISION AND GOALS

Steps 1 and 2 focus on alignment between the school counseling mission/vision and program goals with those of the school and district. School counseling programs aligned with MTSS will include intentional integration between the school counseling and the MTSS team missions/visions. First, the school, MTSS and school counseling mission statements should align, as shown below:

School Mission	MTSS Mission	School Counseling Mission
The community of students, families and staff at Sugar Creek Elementary School strives to provide a safe, supportive environment where all are encouraged to experience the joy of learning and are challenged to do their best.	The mission of the MTSS team is to create systems to support all staff. These systems guide positive practices to support all students both academically and social emotionally.	The school counseling program at Sugar Creek Elementary School advocates for equity, access and student success for all. Maximum effort is given to ensure students feel safe to learn learn and grow in academic, career and social/emotional areas.

As shared in chapter 2, school counselors review data and school improvement plans, along with current systems and practices, to create their program goals. As school counseling programs and MTSS can share similar data to align actions and goals, school counselors can work in concert with the MTSS teams to have an impact on the same school goals. In fact, when true alignment is present in a school, everything is integrated. Thus, it may be difficult to determine a school goal vs. an MTSS goal vs. a school counseling goal.

Case Example: The Sugar Creek Elementary School counselor met with the principal prior to the start of the school year. Together, they examined the school improvement plan goals. These school goals direct the work of the MTSS team and the school counseling program:

- **School Behavior SMART Goal:** All learners will (a) meet 95% of total attendance hours required by the state, (b) reduce the percentage of students missing four days or more, and (c) 25% of elementary school students will have four or fewer absences during the upcoming school year.
  - **School strategies:** Use the existing school leaders and teams present in the building, including the MTSS team and the school counselors, to have an impact on the goal.
  - **MTSS team strategies:** The MTSS team uses the school behavior SMART goal to create universal activities to have an impact on attendance. The team first conducts a data root-cause analysis to assess disproportionality and determine potential systemic barriers for school attendance. For example, team members talk with students and note the inconsistency in the public transportation. Some students have to take multiple bus transfers to get to school on time, and often buses are late or full. As they work to change systemic barriers, they also want to intervene for students who are lacking motivation when it comes to school attendance. Thus, the school counselor worked on both the system (e.g., public transportation) as well as with students (e.g., motivation). Specifically, the school counselor, who serves as a co-leader of the MTSS team, helps plan lessons to be delivered during advisory on the rationale behind school, relating it to students' future goals. Teachers teach these lessons once a week for the first month of school. The MTSS Tier 2 team, which includes the school counselor, monitors individual student data weekly to identify students for increased intervention.
  - **School counselor strategies:** As a member of both the MTSS Tier 1 and 2 teams, the school counselor acts as a liaison, aligning MTSS goals and interventions with the school counseling program. The school counseling program actively addresses the school-level attendance goal in tandem with MTSS efforts. To align goals, the school counselor disaggregated the school attendance data from the prior year, noting that 33% (n = 55) of students had four or more days absent. The school counselor then used the ASCA annual student outcome goal plan template to create an attendance-related SMART goal. The school counselor intentionally tracks attendance data and intervenes with small-group counseling for students with two or more absences. Thus, the school counseling program's focus has a direct impact on a schoolwide SMART goal in tandem with the MTSS team's work on this schoolwide goal.

VOICES FROM THE FIELD:

"You can to choose an area of data you want to focus on in the school counseling program. For example, student GPA, attendance or disciplinary records. It's the same data that we're using for MTSS."

Questions for Review and Discussion

- How does your school counseling program mission/vision statement align with the school and MTSS team?
- How can you align your school counseling goal to both MTSS and the schoolwide improvement plan? How can you align your goals to include work on systems and practices?
- What overlap do you see in the work of the MTSS team and your school counseling program?
- How do you decide what goals to prioritize? Which voices do you include in the process? How do your data decisions have an impact on equitable outcomes for students?

DESCRIPTION: STEPS 3 AND 4: ALIGNING EVIDENCE-BASED INTERVENTIONS AND PROGRESS MONITORING

With aligned goals, school counselors and MTSS teams can work together to analyze data and coordinate interventions, as outlined in steps 3 and 4 of Figure 3.3. A critical component of successful school counseling/MTSS programs includes the use of evidence-based interventions, along with continuous monitoring, to determine the effectiveness of interventions. Further interventions are focused on the student, staff and system levels. As you read in chapter 2, too often in schools we aim all interventions toward students. In integrated programs, we engage in root-cause analysis to determine where to intervene. Further, in truly aligned programs, it may be difficult to differentiate school counseling compared to MTSS supports.

Case Example: The Sugar Creek Elementary School counselor, school psychologist, school social worker and other MTSS team members created the following visual to outline MTSS systems across tiers, with recognition that coordinating the school counseling program with MTSS has the greatest impact. This image is based on Figure 2: data, systems and practices.

Figure 3.4: What do MTSS Systems Look Like: Integrating School Counseling, Psychology and Social Work

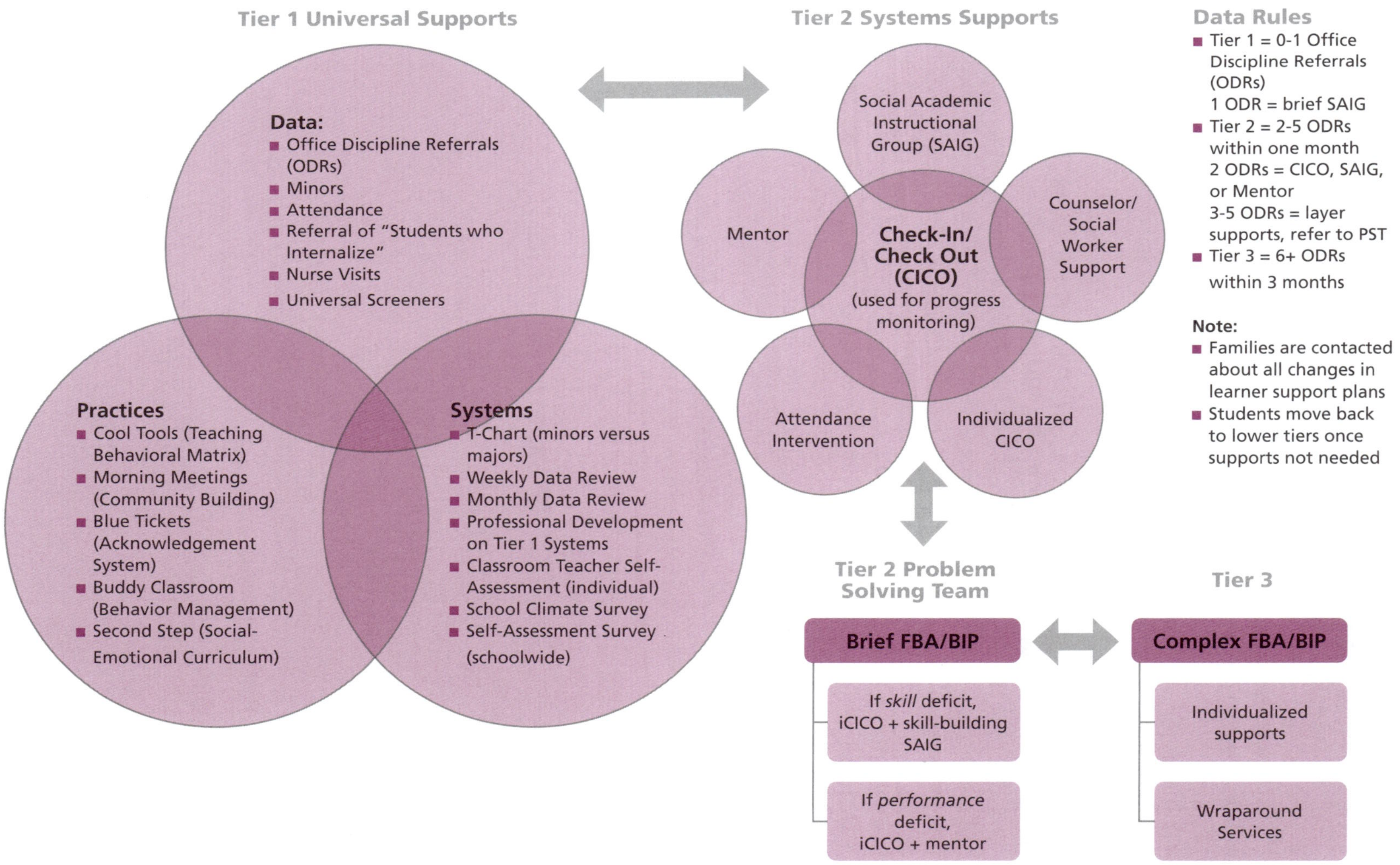

Tier 1 Universal Supports

Data:

- Office Discipline Referrals (ODRs)
- Minors (logged in Google form)
- Periodic referral of "internalizers" by Teachers
- Attendance Data
- Nurse Visit Data
- Universal Screener (to be implemented soon)

Practices:

- Cool Tools (1-3/month, delivered by classroom teachers)
- Morning Meeting (daily)
- Blue Tickets (universal acknowledgement system)
- Community Gatherings (monthly)
- Common language (Four Expectations, Above the Line, Behavioral Matrix, DeBug Steps)
- Positive teaching strategies tool box: Nurtured Heart, Love & Logic, Restorative Practices, Nonviolent Crisis Intervention, Responsive Classroom
- Second Step

Systems:

- Weekly Data Review (to plan student supports)
- Monthly Data Review (to plan schoolwide supports)
- Data rules for enrollment in Tier 2 interventions
- PBIS School Committee
- T-chart of behaviors (major vs. minor)
- Professional development delivered by School Counselors on Tier 1 practices
- Regular sharing of student behavior data to support sustainable practice
- Classroom Teacher Self-Assessment for teachers to assess their fidelity to Tier 1 practices
- School Climate Survey
- Self-Assessment Survey (PBIS) to assess schoolwide fidelity

Tier 2 Systems Supports

Data:

- Reviewed weekly by Tier 2 Team
- Check-In/Check-Out (CICO) progress monitoring data

Systems:

- Parent and Teacher Education on Tier 2 Supports
- CICO Fidelity Checklist

Practices:

- Attendance Intervention: family letters and meetings
- Mentoring: individualized attention and building relationships
  - Basic: 15 minutes per week for six weeks
- Check-In/Check-Out (CICO)
  - Basic: Primary entry intervention, successful for 70% of participants; greeter in morning, feedback throughout the day, greeter in the afternoon prior to the end of the school day
    - May also be Recess Plan or Bus Plan
    - Graduation after 20 data points of meeting goal (80% average)
  - Intensive: CICO w/ individualized features (iCICO)
    - Modification of time, location, goal, or greeter to support performance
- Social Academic Instructional Group (SAIG) (can be 1 kid!)
  - Basic: single re-teaching of Tier 1 materials
    - review of the Recess Behavioral Matrix
    - review of DeBug Steps
    - review of Calm Down Steps
  - Intensive: multiple sessions of reteaching Tier 1 materials
    - reteaching entire unit of Second Step
- School Counselor / Social Worker support:
  - Individual: Intensive social problem solving, bullying cases, wellbeing check-ins, etc.
  - Group: Family change group, Restorative circles, etc.

Tier 2 Problem Solving Team (PST)

Data:

- If Tier 2 supports are not being successful, teacher and counselor fill out Brief Functional Behavior Assessment (Brief FBA)

Practices:

- bFBA
- Partner Meeting
- Begin MTSS (Multi-Tiered Systems of Support) documentation
- Parent invited to meetings

Systems:

- Teacher meets with PST (Problem-Solving Team) to create Brief Behavior Intervention Plan (Brief BIP)
  - Individualized CICO + Mentor if FBA reveals that there is a skill deficit OR
  - Individualized CICO + Skill Building SAIG if FBA reveals that there is a performance deficit

Tier 3: Wraparound

- Complex FBA/BIP completed with Psychologist and needed supports provided by various staff members
- Wrap around services provided with Social Worker

The Practice of PBIS

At each Tier:

- **Data** is used to identify needs and monitor outcomes
- **Practices** support *students*
- **Systems** support *staff*
- The three elements interact to achieve desired academic and behavioral outcomes

Let's unpack Figure 3.4 further. First, note the outline of school counseling program and MTSS processes within Tiers 1, 2 and 3. Specifically, the first part includes a visual of the MTSS intervention process while the second part lists these interventions and supports across each tier. Because the flowchart was created and modified as part of MTSS training, the team specifies data, practices and systems across tiers. Let's take a look at the school counseling program alignment, as well as the MTSS processes. Within Tier 1:

- **Data** is used to identify needs (student, staff and system) and monitor progress. At Sugar Creek, the school counselor and MTSS team monitor office discipline referrals, attendance, nurse visits and students with internalizing behaviors.
- **Systems** support and guide staff. The school counseling program and MTSS systems include those that guide staff behavior (e.g., T-chart; see chapter 4), those that guide teams (e.g., data review times) and fidelity of implementation measures.
- **Culturally sustaining practices** support students. The school counseling program and MTSS practices include the evidence-based Second Step curriculum, an acknowledgement system, morning meetings and a behavioral matrix.

Questions for further reflection

Using Figure 3.4 flowchart, reflect on the following:

- What do you notice about the data, systems and practices outlined in Tier 1?
- What do you notice about the data, systems and practices outlined in Tier 2/3?

Case Example. Let's examine how aligning school counseling program and MTSS activities/interventions and progress monitoring works within and across Tiers 1, 2 and 3 at Sugar Creek Elementary School. As with previous examples, note that in some cases staff members intervene at the student level while other times they intervene at the systems or staff level.

Tier 1: The alignment between the school counseling program and MTSS works seamlessly when the MTSS team regularly reviews office discipline referrals and other supplemental data and when school counselors are active members on the MTSS team. MTSS teams review school-level "big five" data (e.g., office discipline referrals by location, type, etc.) and other data at least monthly to plan schoolwide actions. This data serves as a progress monitoring tool on overall school climate and health. What does this look like when alignment is in place? School counselors use MTSS data to (a) perform a root-cause analysis, (b) examine systems (e.g., policies and procedures), (c) plan school counseling program universal activities/interventions and (d) help coordinate MTSS universal activities/interventions.

Tier 1 Example: An elementary school counselor from Sugar Creek Elementary School, who is a member/leader of the MTSS team, shared with staff that (1) a third of all discipline referrals from the previous month had occurred on a Friday, and a third of them from the previous month happened on the playground. During the MTSS team meeting, the team did a quick root-cause analysis to ensure the discipline referrals were not specific to a group of students or staff members or a time of day. They then intervened at the student level. First, the school counselor created a mindfulness lesson for teachers to deliver to all students (Tier 1). This lesson included the creation of Friday calm-down centers in an open room in the school. Teachers would sign up for a 30-minute slot to participate in a variety of mindfulness and calming activities with their students. When staff looked at the data the next month, the number of discipline referrals that occurred on Fridays had been drastically reduced. This lesson also encouraged teachers to complete a mindfulness activity with their students prior to learners going out to recess, which led to fewer fights and instances of physical aggression. Finally, the school counselor continued to monitor office discipline referral data and re-teach the playground expectations and calm-down skills to students who were referred to the office.

In this example, the school counselor often acts as supporter as a member of the MTSS team that analyzes data and creates these schoolwide initiatives. In addition, a school counselor might also consult and collaborate with a particular teacher whose students need extra practice with emotional regulation and mindfulness strategies. As an intervener, the school counselor may join the teacher during the morning meeting or in the Friday calm-down centers to co-teach lessons. Thus, the school counselor is working as both an intervener and supporter to deliver school counseling program services aligned and integrated within the MTSS efforts.

Tier 2: With aligned goals, the school counselor and MTSS team can also work together to analyze data and coordinate Tier 2 supports and interventions. The MTSS Tier 2 team meets weekly or biweekly to review student-level behavioral and academic data and to organize interventions to support students needing additional skills practice. Similar to Tier 1, school counselors can act as interveners with students who need additional skill support and practice. Let's continue with the example above from Sugar Creek Elementary School to see Tier 2 alignment.

Tier 2 Example. The Sugar Creek Elementary School student services team/Tier 2 team set aside 30 minutes each week to align and monitor interventions. The school has MTSS Tier 1 and 2 systems in place. This team uses its weekly 30 minutes to (1) review individual student behavior data (e.g., which students qualify for Tier 2 support), (2) progress monitor Tier 2 students already utilizing check in/check out, (3) review student data on the number of and reason for nurse visits and (4) ask teachers for referrals for internalizing students. The primary intervention the Tier 2 team assigns first is check in/check out. When determining students for check in/check out, the MTSS Tier 2 team first creates a list of students who will move into the check in/check out intervention. Next, they review check in/check out data for students already receiving this intervention. Thus, they progress monitor and track individual student check in/check out data. At one of these weekly meetings, the student service/Tier 2 team noted check in/check out wasn't an effective support for two students. The school counselor offers to support these students by leading a brief social and academic instructional group grounded in the Tier 1 Second Step social/emotional curriculum, which was chosen after using a pre-/post-test measuring Mindsets & Behaviors. The team added the students to a tiered intervention poster and continued to use the daily report card to monitor student behavior. When the team members met the next week, they examined data for next steps.

What is Check In/Check Out? Check in/check out is an intervention that provides students with a positive adult contact at the start and end of each day along with continual behavioral feedback from teachers throughout the day on a daily report card. Research has noted the effectiveness with individual students, particularly those who respond to adult attention (Maggin, Zurheide, Pickett, & Baillie, 2015). For additional information on check in/check out, see chapter 5 and the following resources listed at the end of this chapter: Conley, Kittelman, Massar, & McIntosh, 2018; NEPBIS (2018); Olsen, 2019).

In addition to check in/check out, the team has a list of other interventions that are options for students, including a mentor program, an attendance intervention, short-term school counselor/social work support and a specialized check in/check out program (see chapter 5 for evidence-based examples). These interventions are implemented when students are not successful in check in/check out. Throughout the Tier 2 process, the MTSS team uses a tiered intervention poster (see below) to track those who are receiving Tier 2 interventions.

Tiered Intervention Poster

- One poster for each grade level team
- Group and individual supports
- Use at team meetings to summarize interventions
- Can put names or student initials of referrals in gray zone or "loading dock"
- Could organize intervention type or by student
- Once intervention done, take off poster

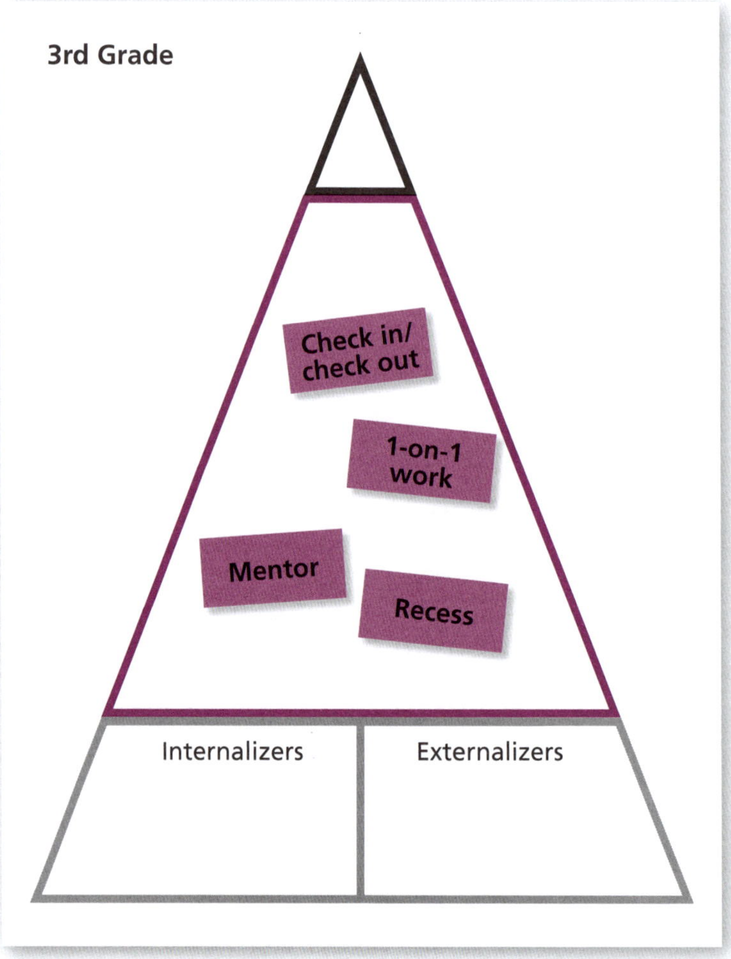

Borchardt, Carter, Miller & Feifarck

When students continue to have skill deficits after Tier 2 interventions, Tier 3 supports are then considered. School staff (e.g., interventionist, school psychologist, behavior specialist, special education teacher, etc.) conduct Tier 3 processes, including complex functional behavior assessments and discussion at a larger problem-solving MTSS Tier 3 team meeting (see chapter 6 for additional information on Tier 3).

With a better understanding of aligned practices, it's time to examine your own school/district.

ACTIVITY: Flowchart

Complete a flowchart on the systems, data and practices in your school (based on Figure 3.2 and similar to Sugar Creek's example in Figure 3.4).

- What data do you examine across each Tier?
- How often do you review data? How is data disaggregated?
- What systems (e.g., policies, procedures, etc.) do you have in place at Tier 1? At Tier 2/3? How often do you examine systems for inequities? How do you ensure systems are culturally sustaining?
- What practices do you have in place? Review the lists of evidence-based practices listed in chapters 4, 5 and 6. Which programs do you have access to within your school counseling program and within MTSS? What other interventions can the school counseling team use to support students across the tiers?
- How often do you examine practices for inequities? How do you ensure practices are culturally sustaining? What partnership opportunities do you see to work alongside of other professionals in your school to coordinate data, systems and practices?

In sum, Steps 3 and 4 include an integrated approach in which the school counselors and MTSS teams work in collaboration to examine data and systems, provide culturally sustaining evidence-based practices/interventions and monitor effectiveness. Clearly within these steps, having aligned interventions and systems allows school counselors to work smarter not harder.

VOICES FROM THE FIELD:

"Usually the school counselor knows most of the kids, if not all the kids. I think if they can help determine what might be a good strategy and help brainstorm the kids that we do intervene with...maybe not being the person who implements the strategies, but definitely overseeing the strategies as they get implemented."

DESCRIPTION: STEPS 5, 6, AND 7: ALIGNING EVALUATION, ADVOCACY AND SYSTEMIC CHANGE

Activities and interventions across tiers should be continuously evaluated. Due to the persistent gaps in student achievement and behavior, school counselors play an important role in evaluating data to address disproportionality and advocate for systemic change. In fact, research has noted a relationship between schools that integrate MTSS with decreased suspensions and increased school success, particularly for marginalized populations

(Swain-Bradway, Gulbrandson, Galston, & McIntosh, 2019). Thus, school counselors can serve as leaders to ensure equitable, culturally sustaining systems are in place in schools using Steps 5, 6 and 7.

Step 5: Evaluate: Within step 5, both school counselors and the MTSS team should disaggregate and analyze data to evaluate the effectiveness of interventions. In the following example, let's take a look at how Sugar Creek Elementary School counselors examine data in concert with the MTSS teams.

Case Example: When integrating school counseling program and MTSS data, data disaggregation should be at the forefront of the intervention evaluation process. Twice a year the Sugar Creek Elementary School MTSS team student services/Tier 2 team (school counselor, school psychologist, school social worker and principal) create two graphs. The first graph shows office discipline referrals disaggregated by race and percentages divided by race. The second graph provides the risk-ratio data, which show that Asian and Black students are at higher risk than all other groups for receiving office discipline referrals. The school counselor, as a member of the team, noted an inequity and examined the systems. The school counselor then created professional development for school staff. The school counselor (1) reviewed the MTSS T-chart (see chapter 4 for additional examples of T-charts); (2) reviewed the school's buddy classroom protocol, which included how to respond to behavior in the classroom; (3) defined and discussed the impact of implicit bias; and (4) offered strategies for staff members to manage vulnerable decision points. The focus included working with staff on implicit bias and fine-tuning system supports rather than focusing the intervention solely on students.

Graph of Office Discipline Referral Disaggregated by Race/Ethnicity

Log Distribution by Race/Ethnicity

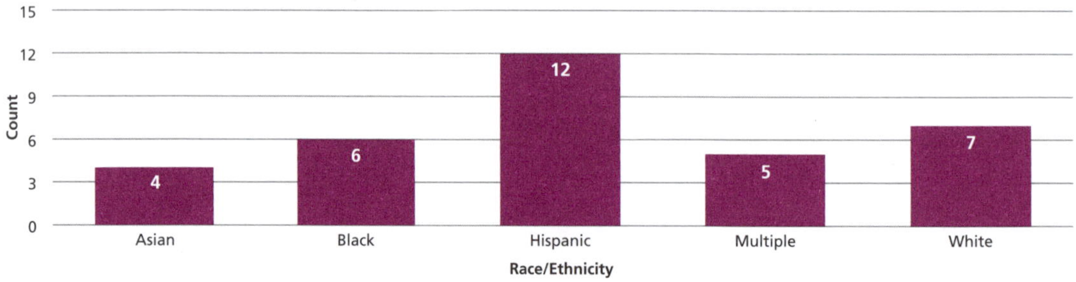

Total Logs Found	Average	Maximum	Minimum
34	6.80	12	4

Race/Ethnicity	Count	Portion
Asian	4	11.8%
Black	6	17.6%
Hispanic	12	35.3%
Multiple	5	14.7%
White	7	20.6%

Equity Risk Ratio

School Name: Sugar Creek	Number of Students Enrolled at the School	Number of Students in Group Who Received a Referral	Total Number of Referral from Group	Group's Percent of Student Body	**Student Composition** *The % of students with referrals who belong to a target group; **WHITE cells suggest disproportionality***	**Referral Ratio** *Referral Rate for that group divided by the Referral Rate for all other students; **1.0 is equal***	**Referral Rate** *Total number of referrals for group divided by the number of enrolled students from that group*	**Risk Ratio** *Group's risk of receiving a referral compared to all other students; **3.0 is equal***	**Difference in Student Composition** *Student Composition minus the Percent of the Student Body; **Positive values suggest disproportionality***
White	283	33	69	52.3%	55.0%	1.12	0.24	1.11	2.7
Hispanic/ Latino	194	10	14	35.9%	16.7%	0.23	0.07	0.36	–19.2
African American/Black	22	7	26	4.1%	11.7%	6.20	1.18	3.12	7.6
Indian/Alaskan Native	0	0	0	0.0%	0.0%	N/A	N/A	N/A	N/A
Asian	14	4	5	2.6%	6.7%	1.57	0.36	2.69	4.1
Hawaiian/ Pacific Islander	0	0	0	0.0%	0.0%	N/A	N/A	N/A	N/A

The school counselor, as a member of the Tier 1 and Tier 2 MTSS teams, noted an inequity in that Black and Asian American students were more likely to receive discipline referrals (Step 5: Evaluate). After conducting a root-cause analysis, she learned staff may be imposing white middle-class values on their definition of "disruption." As an advocate of systemic change (Steps 6 and 7), the school counselor created a Tier 1 systems intervention aimed at the school staff. Specifically, the school counselor created a professional development presentation for school staff, reviewing the MTSS T-chart on discipline procedures and discussing the impact adults have on students. Further, the school counselor, school psychologist and school social worker started monthly consultation times with classroom teams, where they discussed equity, neutralizing discipline, culturally sustaining principles and overall cultural awareness. Thus, the school counselor was fully engaged in Steps, 5, 6 and 7, aligning efforts to evaluate data and advocate for systemic change.

What is a risk ratio?

Risk ratios represent the likelihood of the outcome (e.g., office discipline referrals) for one group in relation to a comparison group. There are many calculators that school counselors and MTSS teams can use to determine this for their schools. See the appendix for resources.

Questions for Review and Discussion

- What can school counselors do to address inequity in schools?
- What practices can school counselors use to close gaps?
- How can you use data to examine the system – not just students – to build culturally sustaining systems and inclusive school environments?

VOICES FROM THE FIELD:

"We look at sub-groups within our populations, such as English-language learners or students who are on free or reduced lunch, and think about how we can better serve those students. ... We do use data a lot."

VOICES FROM THE FIELD:

"[Several] students reported they were affected by racial and cultural bullying. It was a disproportionately high number of Hispanic and African American students. We might have to work on racial, cultural understanding and respect and awareness."

As you read from the previous case example, it takes time and thoughtful reflection, to complete Young and Kaffenberger's (2018) seven steps. As a final review and summary, let's return to the school data profile you completed in chapter 2. This will allow you to better understand potential ways to create systemic change in your own buildings.

Activity: Review the school data summary you completed in chapter 2. Pay particular attention to question number 3: Disaggregate relevant school data by race/ethnicity, gender, grade level, socioeconomic status, disability status. Then, reflect on and answer the following five questions):

- Are your systems and practices culturally sustaining? In other words, do your systems support the success of all students?
- What is it about policies, people and practices that contribute to any inequities?
- What equitable, culturally sustaining practices can address this discipline inequity?
- If applicable (based on your answer to question 3), did the equitable, culturally sustaining strategies decrease discipline disparity?
- Who is at the table when systemic or policy decisions are made in your school?

From: Payno-Simmons (2020)

Given the complexities involved in building culturally sustaining systems, many school teams utilize additional resources, including those listed in the resource section at the end of the chapter (e.g., Loudoun County School District. (n.d.) Equitable Practices; McIntosh, Girvan, Horner, Smolkowski, & Sugai (2018); McIntosh, Barnes, Eliason, & Morris, (2014).

DESCRIPTION: FINAL THOUGHTS ON ALIGNING AND IMPLEMENTING SCHOOL COUNSELING PROGRAMS AND MTSS

Engaging in school counseling program and MTSS alignment takes time and energy. In fact, implementation is a science. The examples we have used throughout this book include school districts and schools that have been engaged in this work for years not months. As such, we provide the following graphic to help you consider the many stages of school counseling program/MTSS alignment and implementation. (WI RTI Center/PBIS Network, n.d.).

Stages of Implementation

Implementation is a science. Research shows that it takes years to see the effects of putting a new evidence-based system in place.

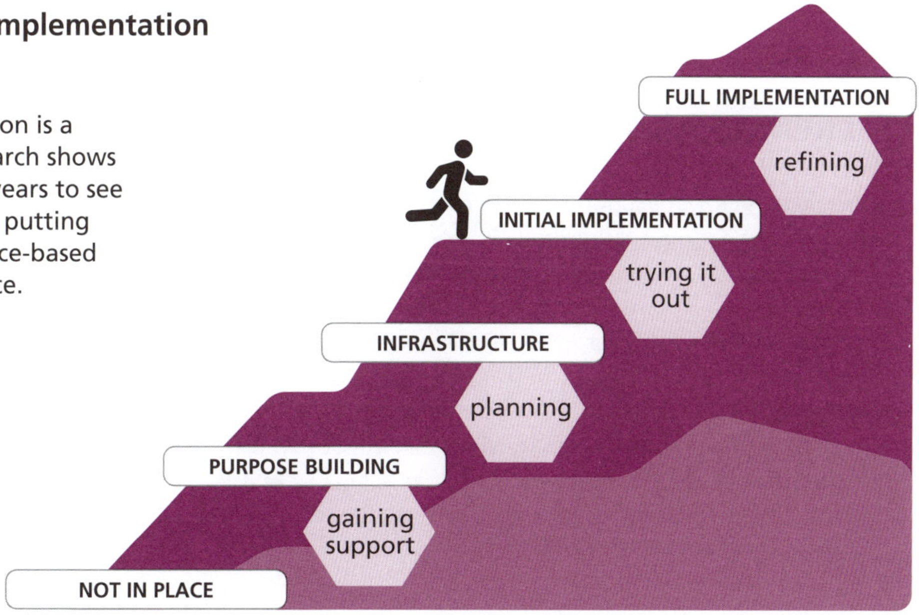

Based on Fixsen, D. L., Naoom, S. F., Blase, K. A., Friedman, R. M. & Wallace, F. (2005)

Questions for Review and Discussion

- Looking at the previous visual, which step best describes your school counseling program implementation? Your MTSS implementation? Your school counseling program and MTSS alignment?
- Who can you collaborate with to build purpose and infrastructure?
- What steps can your team take to ensure the systems you are building are culturally sustaining?
- See Sugai, La Salle, Everett, and Feinberg (2019) and Wisconsin RTI Center/Wisconsin PBIS Network (2018) for additional reading on implementation.]

Fidelity. While too lengthy to cover in this chapter, school counseling program and MTSS systems alignment and practices must be completed with fidelity. See the following websites and templates for an MTSS and school counseling program fidelity assessments:

- PBIS applications: *www.pbisapps.org/Applications/Pages/PBIS-Assessment.aspx*
- PBIS assessments: *www.pbis.org/resource-type/assessments*
- ASCA (2019) school counseling program assessment and ASCA (2019) school counseling program appraisal, *www.schoolcounselor.org*

CONCLUDING THOUGHTS

This chapter highlights the cyclical process of how and why school counselors use data, demonstrating that school counselors can create data, systems and practices within their school counseling/MTSS alignment to create a stronger and more culturally sustaining school counseling program, such as one based on the ASCA National Model, and best serve students. We are hopeful that through this chapter and others in this book, you learned implementation is a process that can take years and you gained ideas and strategies to continue to move your school counseling program forward and have a positive impact on all students as you seek to nurture a safe and inclusive school environment.

REFERENCES AND RESOURCES

ASCA. (2019). *School Counseling Program Assessment.* Retrieved from https://www.schoolcounselor.org/school-counselors/asca-national-model/templates-and-resources

ASCA. (2019). *School Counseling Program Appraisal* Retrieved from https://www.schoolcounselor.org/school-counselors/asca-national-model/templates-and-resources

Betters-Bubon, J., Kortemeier, H., & Smith-Durkin, S. (2019). Culturally responsive MTSS: Advocating for equity for every student. In E. Goodman-Scott, J. Betters-Bubon, & P. Donohue (Eds.), *A School Counselor's Guide to Multi-tiered Systems of Support* (pp. 298-329). New York City, NY: Routledge.

Conley, K., Kittelman, A., Massar, M. & McIntosh, K. (2018). *What are Patterns and Predictors of CICO Participation in U.S. Schools?* OSEP Technical Assistance Center on Positive Behavioral Interventions and Supports.

Fixsen, D.L., Naoom, S.F., Blasé, K.A., Friedman, R.M. & Wallace, F. (2005) Implementation Research: A Synthesis of the Literature. Tampa, FL: University of South Florida, Louis de la Parte Florida Mental Health Institute, The National Implementation Research Network (FMHI Publication #231).

Loudoun County Public Schools. (n.d.). Equitable Practices. Retrieved from: https://sites.google.com/lcps.org/mtss/positive-behavioral-interventions-and-support-pbis/equitable-practices?authuser=0

Maggin, D. M., Zurheide, J., Pickett, K. C., & Baillie, S. J. (2015). A systematic evidence review of the check-in/check-out program for reducing student challenging behaviors. *Journal of Positive Behavior Interventions, 17*(4), 197-208.

McIntosh, K., Barnes, A., Eliason, B., & Morris, K. (2014). *Using discipline data within SWPBIS to identify and address disproportionality: A guide for school teams.* OSEP Technical Assistance Center on Positive Behavioral Interventions and Supports. www.pbis.org.

McIntosh, K., Girvan, E. J., Horner, R. H., Smolkowski, K., & Sugai, G. (2018). *A 5-point intervention approach for enhancing equity in school discipline.* OSEP Technical Assistance Center on Positive Behavioral Interventions and Supports.

Northeast Positive Behavioral Interventions and Supports(NEPBIS). (2018). *Advanced tiers. Tier 2 School Team Training Workbook. Northeast Positive Behavioral Interventions and Supports.* Retrieved from https://nepbis.org/advanced-tiers/

Olson, J. (2019). Tier 2: Providing supports for students with elevated needs. In E. Goodman-Scott, J. Betters-Bubon, & P. Donohue (Eds.), *A School Counselor's Guide to Multi-tiered Systems of Support* (pp. 133-162). New York City, NY: Routledge.

Payno-Simmons, R. (2020). *Five Questions Every Team Should Ask About Racial Disproportionality.* Retrieved from https://www.pbisapps.org/community/Pages/5-Questions-Every-Team-Should-Ask-About-Racial-Disproportionality.aspx

Sugai, G., & Horner, R. (2009). Responsiveness-to-Intervention and School-Wide Positive Behavior Supports: Integration of Multi-Tiered System Approaches. Exceptionality, 17(4), 223-237. doi: 10.1080/09362830903235375

Sugai, G., La Salle, T., Everett, S., & Feinberg, A. (2019). Multi-Tiered Systems of Support: The What, Why and How for School Counselors. In E. Goodman-Scott, J. Betters-Bubon, & P. Donohue (Eds.), *A School Counselor's Guide to Multi-tiered Systems of Support* (pp. 1-28). New York City, NY: Routledge.

Swain-Bradway, J., Gulbrandson, K., Galston, A., & McIntosh, K. (2019). Do Wisconsin Schools Implementing an Integrated Academic and Behavior Support Framework Improve Equity in Academic and School Discipline Outcomes? OSEP Technical Assistance Center on Positive Behavioral Interventions and Supports. www.pbis.org.

Wisconsin RTI Center/Wisconsin PBIS Network. (2019) *Go Higher: High schools implementing an equitable multi-level system of supports with fidelity over time show positive student outcomes.* Evaluation Brief. Retrieved from: https://www.wisconsinrticenter.org/wp-content/uploads/2019/04/High-school-evaluation-brief-Spring-2019-web.pdf

Wisconsin RTI Center/Wisconsin PBIS Network. (2018). Five factors that facilitate sustained implementation of a culturally responsive multi-level system of support in Wisconsin. Evaluation Brief. Retrieved from: https://www.wisconsinrticenter.org/wp-content/uploads/2019/01/1493996457_2017-Evaluation-Brief-Sustainability-Five-Factors.pdf

Wisconsin RTI Center/Wisconsin PBIS Network (n.d.). Assess System. Retrieved from: https://www.wisconsinrticenter.org/school-implementation/assess-system/?fbclid=IwAR13HEWxOYJz50CdPNUOh4vRPDvwF8U0gIGmurdDwYPxA1ODGEEYTrqzZJA

Young, A., & Kaffenberger, C. (2018) *Making Data Work*. Alexandria, VA: American School Counselor Association.

CHAPTER 4

Aligning Tier 1 Supports

In the introduction and Chapter 1, we described the ASCA National Model and MTSS, as well as how they could be aligned. Then in Chapters 2 and 3, we described the integral role of data in this alignment. In this chapter, we will delve deeper by describing key tenets of Tier 1 MTSS supports and aligning Tier 1 supports with the school counselor's role. Although MTSS includes academics, behaviors, social/emotional, etc., the school counselor's role in academics is largely that of a supporter, which you'll see reflected in the content over next few chapters.

DESCRIPTION: TIER 1 SUPPORTS

There are several factors to consider when aligning the ASCA National Model with Tier 1 supports, specifically: (1) using a systems approach, (2) using a culturally sustaining approach (3) addressing prevention, (4) teaching expectations or behaviors, (4) creating schoolwide protocols and (5) using data. For more in-depth information on data, see the previous two chapters.

Systems Perspective

Imagine you're at a pond, and you throw bread into the pond to feed the ducks. The bread landing in the water creates ripples, and those ripples will, to some extent, reach all parts of the pond. The pond is a system; changes, or ripples, in one part of a system affect all parts of the whole. Systems can be families, communities and even schools. They are affected by a range of factors, both internal and and external. For an example, see the following image portraying Bronfenbrenner's ecological systems theory, below.

Bronfenbrenner's Ecological Model of Human Development

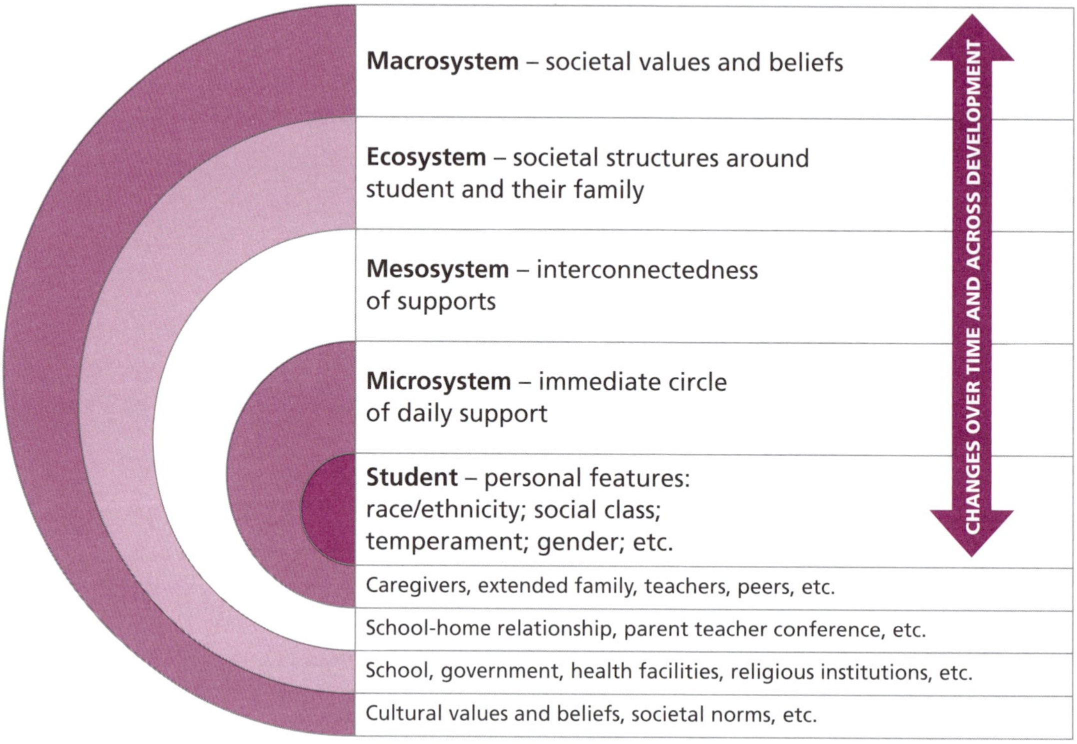

(Bronfenbrenner, 1979). *The ecology of human development.*

ACTIVITY: Personal Systems Factors

Each of us is shaped by a unique intersection of culture, experience, demographics, access and so many other variables. In reflecting on Bronfenbrenner's model, look at the following image, and write your name in the center circle. What are the ecological or systems factors that have and continue to influence your development? In the image, write these factors in the nested circles surrounding your name. Consider:

- Personal factors: such as your generation, race/ethnicity, social class, gender, sexual/affectional orientation, education level, etc.
- Relationships, communities, culture, access to resources: such as family, mentors, peers, neighborhood, hobbies, community relationships, place of work, religious beliefs, community, cultural values, structural racism and privilege, access to health care, etc.

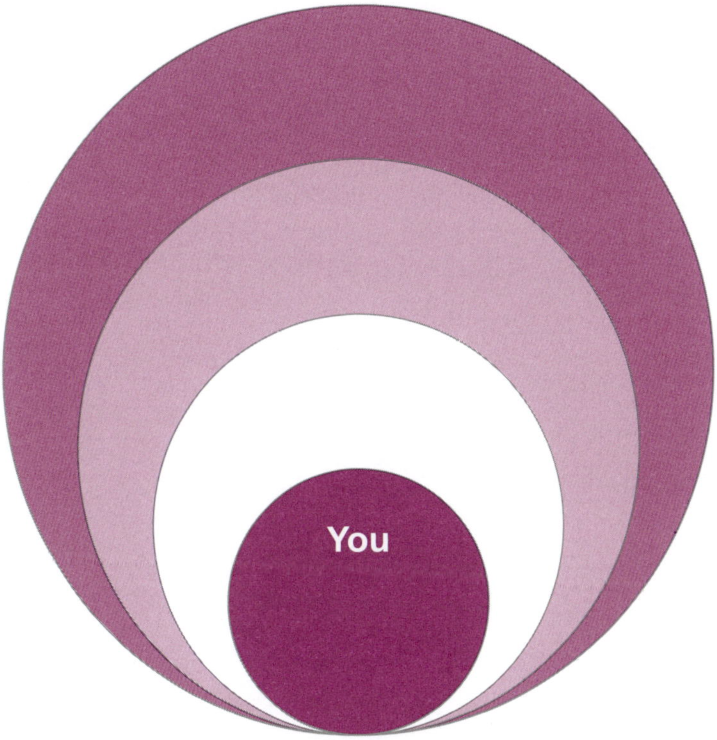

ACTIVITY: **School Systems Factors**

Just as you can view yourself through a systems perspective, MTSS also uses a systems perspective, by viewing the school as a whole and realizing a variety of internal and external factors have an affect on the school:

- Internal factors: school leadership decisions, organizational climate, spoken and unspoken policies, procedures, norms, students' cultural backgrounds, staff biases, relational dynamics between staff, available resources, etc.
- External factors: school board budgetary decisions, state policies, community crises and events, local and national cultural trends and movements, etc.

In the following image, write the name of your school in the middle of the center circle. Each ring, or circle, around your school represents factors influencing your school. The smaller circles closest to the center represent the factors within your school, and each larger circle represents more distant, increasingly external factors affecting your school. Complete this image, listing the factors that affect your school, both internally and externally. What do you notice about your completed picture?

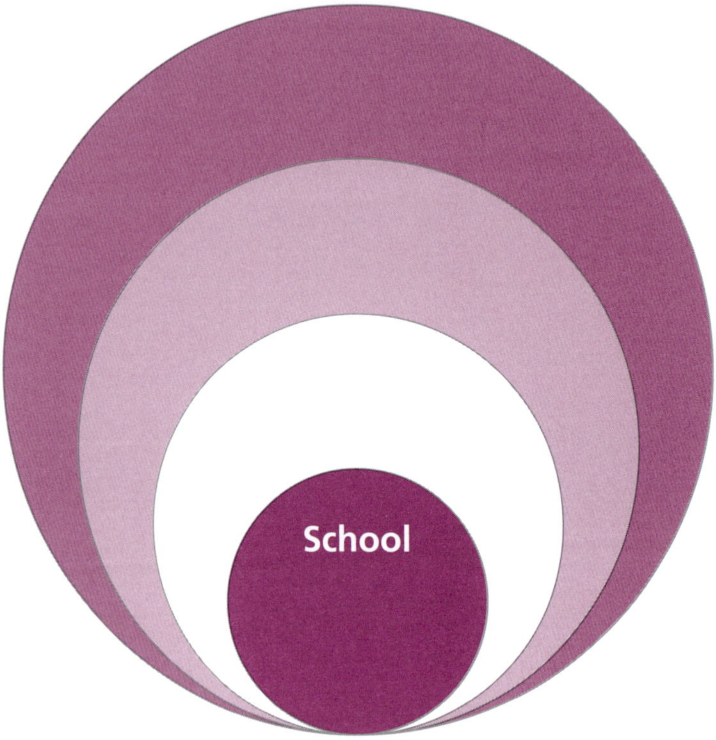

To continue this activity, when looking at the image above of your school and the factors that influence your school, list:

- What are the strengths and positive factors across these different systems, affecting your school's functioning and environment? (e.g., perhaps your school district's superintendent prioritizes decreasing disproportionate discipline referrals for students of color or is especially knowledgeable and supportive of social/emotional learning.)
- What factors pose a challenge or negatively affect your school community? (e.g., perhaps the factory in your town has recently closed, and many of your students' families lost their source of income; many high school students are increasingly absent from school, as they are working to help support their families.) Are there ways you can provide extra advocacy or support in these areas? (e.g., perhaps your local school board chronically denies funding to lower the school counseling ratio. Can you organize stakeholders and school counselors to speak at the next school board meeting, sharing data and stories, to demonstrate the school counselors' impact? Or, perhaps you can advocate for your district to provide more comprehensive translation services and related supports, to assist students and families who are English-language learners.)

As school counselors, we must implement culturally sustaining systems. Specifically, schools must sustain, or continue, the cultures of the school families and community. Thus, schools must partner hand-in-hand with their students, families and communities to ensure procedures and practices include, or sustain, these stakeholders' cultures. Culturally sustaining procedures and practices should be implemented in all aspects of MTSS, not only Tier 1 but across all three tiers, through the use of data, etc.

Both the ASCA National Model and MTSS encourage school counselors to be systems thinkers, to consider that students and schools are influenced by a variety of factors or systems. As such, we are called to make systemic change, to remove systemic barriers that hinder students' access, opportunity, and achievement. In using this systems lens in MTSS and school counseling, school counselors focus on evaluating and then changing unjust, inequitable, oppressive systems.

EXAMPLE FROM THE FIELD:

We must use a social justice lens as we examine the systems in our schools. Do the systems, procedures and resources privilege some students over others? Do they penalize some students over others? For instance, high school principal Kelly Wickham Wurst described systemically biased discipline rules and practices at her school (Hurst, 2016). Her school's dress code prohibited sagging pants, which disproportionately affected Black males. Further, she noticed that school staff enforced this school rule more often with Black males compared with their white classmates. This is an example of systemic racism, as well as teacher bias. As school counselors, we are called to examine and evaluate systems, questioning if the systems are biased toward or privilege certain subgroups of students over others, and then work with school leaders to change the systems to be more culturally just for all students.

Questions for Review and Discussion:

- How can you evaluate your school's systems to determine the existence of inequities, biases and privileging? What would you do if you found such disparities at your school?
- Who would you build alliances with to address disparities?
- What suggestions do you have for staff professional development that would help address such disparities?

PREVENTION AND TEACHING CULTURALLY SUSTAINING EXPECTATIONS

Another premise behind Tier 1 supports is that just as we teach academics, we should also teach schoolwide, developmentally appropriate, culturally sustaining behaviors, such as schoolwide expectations. Thus, Tier 1 supports include explicitly defining and teaching schoolwide expectations to all students, giving them a common message, providing ample opportunities for them to practice these behaviors and receive feedback, such as positive reinforcement or acknowledgements.

VOICES FROM THE FIELD:

"It should be the same. The systematic approach across the school, everybody: same goal, same words, same vocabulary that we're using with the students."

It is crucial that school expectations and protocol are culturally sustaining; they must represent and incorporate the unique culture of all members of the school community. Thus, all student should see aspects of their culture positively represented throughout the school day: language of expectations, types of acknowledgements, etc. To do this, the MTSS team responsible for creating these expectations must include members from throughout the school community: teachers, hourly-paid staff and teaching assistants, family and community members and students. In fact, some schools have had a specific parent/community/student council specifically to review the MTSS expectations, protocol and data to provide continual input on MTSS processes. Relatedly, schoolwide expectations and procedures must be representative of the entire school population, rather than privileging dominant groups (e.g., white, European descent, cisgender, heterosexual, middle-class, able-bodied, college-educated, etc.). We need to be purposeful that the school expectations/behaviors taught are based on the cultures and expectations of the local families and communities, rather than the school staff. After deciding on these expectations and procedures, the school teaches them in a uniform method across all students.

VOICES FROM THE FIELD:

Once the school community decides on culturally sustaining expectations, we teach them to all students. "We can't assume students will walk into the building and automatically know how we expect them to walk into this classroom, interact with other students or walk down the hall, so we teach those expectations."

In school we teach reading, writing, math... shouldn't we also teach behavior?

Did you know? MTSS schoolwide expectations focus on social skills, behaviors and social/emotional content; thus, they go hand-in-hand with ASCA's Mindsets & Behaviors, as well as ASCA's social/emotional domain.

EXAMPLES: Schoolwide Expectations

Schools teach culturally sustaining behavioral expectations to students at the start of the school year, throughout the school environment, and reinforce and re-teach over the duration of the school year. The following are examples of tools to teach expected student behaviors.

VOICES FROM THE FIELD:

"Going through the process of teaching expectations, students really buy into you... they learn to trust you because you're going to actually follow through with the expectations that, as a class, you set in place."

Schoolwide expectations (Milwaukee Public Schools): For this schoolwide behavioral matrix, schools typically list their schoolwide expectations in the far-left column (Be Safe, Be Respectful, Be Responsible), and the school setting/location/transition across the top row (e.g., arrival, reading centers, etc.). Then, teachers and students complete this matrix together, creating individualized expectations pertinent to their class and location, and list those within the table.

MTSS Classroom Matrix

(List locations and transitions along top row)			
Be Safe			
Be Respectful			
Be Responsible			

Elementary school schoolwide expectations (Milwaukee Public Schools): here is an adapted example of schoolwide expectations, listing the location (bathroom) and the expected behaviors in the bathroom, that correspond with the schoolwide expectations (Be Safe, Be Respectful, Be Responsible).

Taylor Elementary School Bathroom Behavior

Be Respectful:
Give privacy to others
Wait for your turn

Be Responsible:
Use a soft voice
Keep hands and feet to yourself
Flush the toilet

Be Safe:
Wash hands with soap and water
Water stays in the sink
Dry hands

Be "Spotted" Using Taylor Elementary School Bathroom Behavior

Elementary school matrix: English and Spanish: A high percentage of students in this community speak Spanish as their first language. Thus, Loudoun County provides its matrixes in English and also Spanish. It is the MTSS team's responsibility to ensure school-wide expectations and protocols are culturally sustaining and truly represent all members of the school community.

Guilford Elementary School PBIS Teaching Matrix

	EXPECTATIONS			
	Respectful	**Responsible**	**Ready to Learn**	**Build Relationships**
Definition	Show courtesy, appreciation, and regard for others	Be accountable for your actions	Be prepared	Treat others the way you want to be treated
Classroom I will	■ Use kind words and actions ■ Be an active listener	■ Keep my hands and feet to myself ■ Use materials appropriately ■ Complete my work	■ Come prepared to learn and do my best work	■ Treat others as I want to be treated
Technology I will	■ Use my account only ■ Use my device only as directed by my teacher	■ Put devices back correctly when finished ■ Always carry devices safely	■ Treat all the devices as if they are my own	■ Use my device to positively collaborate with classmates
Cafeteria I will	■ Raise my hand for help ■ Use quiet voices	■ Eat my lunch ■ Keep food to myself ■ Keep hands and feet to myself	■ Make sure I've cleaned up my messes ■ Line up quietly	■ Offer to help others in need
Hallway I will	■ Walk on the right ■ Have a quiet voice	■ Keep hands and feet to myself ■ Face the front	■ Be ready to move on to my destination	■ Be silent in the hallway so others can continue learning
Bus I will	■ Use kind words ■ Use quiet voice	■ Stay seated ■ Keep my feet out of the aisle ■ Face the front	■ Ride the bus	■ Look out for other people's things
Playground I will	■ Use equipment properly ■ Use good sportsmanship	■ Keep hands and feet to yourself ■ Go down the slides safely ■ Stay in the designated area	■ Go and play the whole time	■ Include all students in games
Bathroom I will	■ Flush the toilet	■ Wash my hands	■ Leave and go back to class	■ Keep our bathroom clean for the next person

Guilford Elementary School PBIS Teaching Matrix

	EXPECTATIVAS			
	Respetuoso	Responsable	Listo para Aprender	Construye Relaciones
Definición	Demuestra cortesía, apreciación y cuidado por otros.	Se hace responsable de sus acciones	Está preparado	Trata a otros como quiere ser tratado
Salón Yo	■ Usaré palabras y acciones agradables ■ Escucharé activamente	■ Tendré mis manos y mis pies quietos ■ Usaré los materiales adecuadamente ■ Completaré mi trabajo	■ Vendré preparado para aprender y haré lo mejor que puedo	■ Trato a otros como quiero ser tratado
Technologia Yo	■ Usaré mi cuenta solamente ■ Usaré mis aparatos solo cuando me lo indica el maestro	■ Pondré el equipo correcto cuando termino ■ Siempre usaré el equipo de una manera segura	■ Trataré todos los aparatos como si fueran míos	■ Uso mis aparatos para participar colectivamente con otros positivamente
Cafetería Yo	■ Levantaré mi mano para pedir ayuda ■ Usaré mi voz baja	■ Comeré mi lunch ■ Mantendré mi comida conmigo ■ Mantendré mis manos y pies quietos	■ Me aseguraré de limpiar todo lo que ensucie ■ Me formaré de manera callada	■ Ofrezco ayuda a otros cuando la necesitan
Corredor Yo	■ Caminaré por la derecha ■ Usaré mi voz baja	■ Mantendré mis manos y pies quietos ■ Tendré mi cara hacia el frente y veo hacia adelante	■ Estaré listo a moverme a donde tengo que ir	■ Estoy callado para que otros continúen aprendiendo
Autobús Yo	■ Usaré palabras amables ■ Usaré mi voz baja	■ Permaneceré sentado ■ Mantendré mis pies fuera del pasilio ■ Veré hacia el frente	■ Iré en el autoús	■ Cuido las cosas de otras personas
Afuera Yo	■ Usaré el equipo appropiadamente ■ Usaré buen espíritu de equipo	■ Tendré mis manos y mis pies quietos ■ Usaré la resbaladilia de una manera segura ■ Permaneceré en elárea designada	■ Iré y jugaré todo el tiempo	■ Incluyo a todas las estudiantes cuando juego
Baño Yo	■ Jalaré el baño	■ Me lavaré las manos	■ Me iré de regreso a clase	■ Dejo el baño limpio para la siguiente persona

VOICES FROM THE FIELD:

One school described bringing in community members to assist with MTSS planning and implementation: "It takes a village. There are so many people that are members of our village: partnership with colleges, high schools, the alumni, the parents, our feeder schools."

Secondary example schoolwide expectations and matrix: To build on the elementary expectations/matrix listed above, see these at the middle school level. (Adapted from Loudoun County Public Schools)

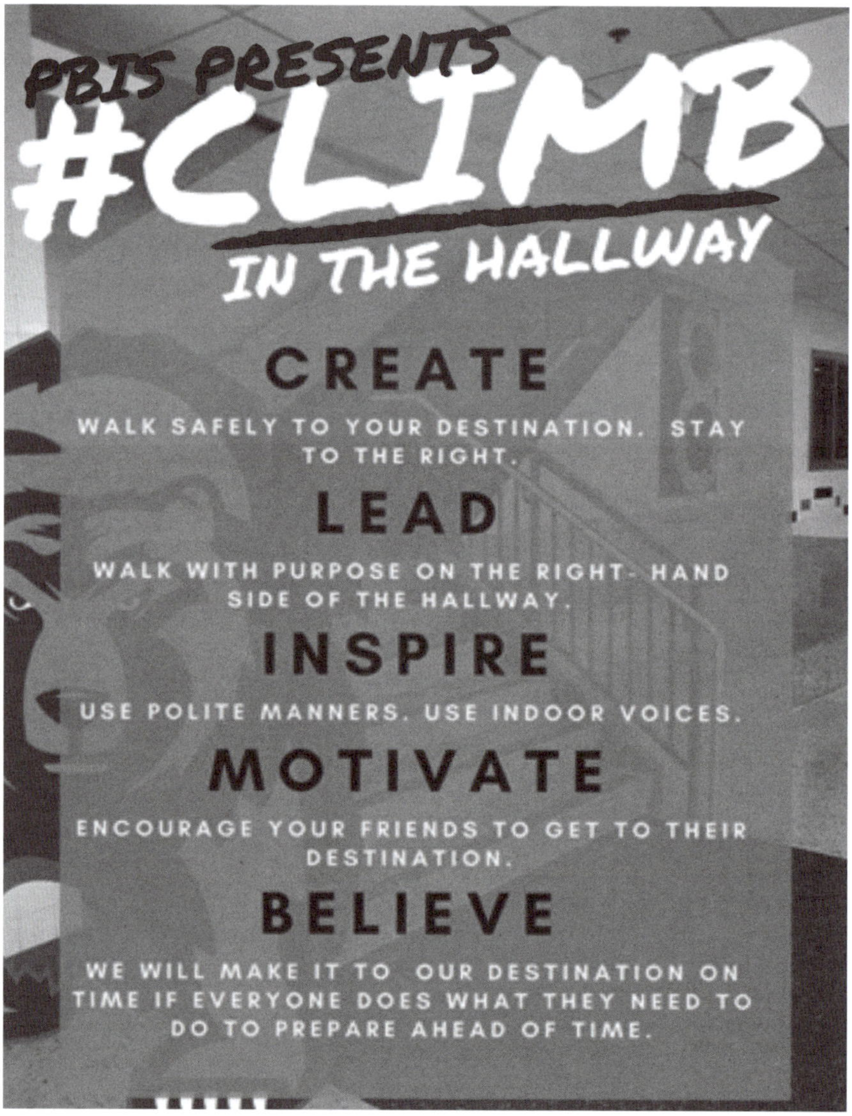

Mustangs Race to Success with the 3 "Rs"

	Respect Ourselves	Respect Others	Respect Property
Hallway and Lockers	■ Keep your surroundings clean and organized at all times ■ Take pride in how your locker looks ■ Get to class on time and with all materials (get it and go)	■ Use school language and volume ■ Keep all hands and objects to yourself ■ Walk on the right side of the hallway	■ Use lockers and hallways during designated times ■ Pick up any trash you see
Cafeteria	■ Stay seated ■ Raise your hand to get up	■ Wait your turn in line ■ Be kind to others in the cafeteria ■ Eat your own lunch	■ Keep trash off the floor ■ Clean up your table before you leave ■ Keep all food items contained
Classroom	■ Come prepared with agenda and materials ■ Complete assignments	■ Show consideration for others	■ Follow instructions when using classroom and school materials ■ "Does it belong to you?"
On the Bus	■ Be at your bus stop on time ■ Stay seated while the bus is moving ■ Go directly home once you get off the bus	■ Be kind to bus driver and other students ■ Follow and respond to adult directions	■ Leave the bus cleaner than you found it
At Home	■ Study and review materials ■ Complete homework assignments and projects	■ Treat others with kindness ■ Follow and respond to adult directions	■ Keep your backpack and binders organized
BYOT	■ Only take out your device with teacher permission	■ Use only your device or a school borrowed device	■ Fully charged battery ■ Keep in locker area when not being used in class

VOICES FROM THE FIELD:

One secondary principal discussed teaching students expectations, "For every grade, during the first two weeks in September, we have built into the master schedule 30 minutes a day for behavioral instruction. Classes do role-playing, social stories, practice routines, learn from our school staff and more. New students who arrive during the year receive the same lessons in an abbreviated format with a classmate as a peer model and a school counselor."

VOICES FROM THE FIELD:

As one secondary school teacher stated, "Teaching MTSS routines and expectations takes about the first 20 minutes of every day for the first two weeks of school, but it's the most valuable time we've ever spent."

While we focus on matrixes for behaviors, these matrixes can include other domains as well. For example, some schools collaborate with families, to create an expectation matrix for homework. How could your school use a matrix to teach and reinforce academic or career expectations?

The highest percentage of educators (including school counselors) in the U.S. are white, educated women. However, are all our students and school communities composed of white, educated women? Absolutely not. As such, we need to ensure MTSS expectations, norms and protocols represent the culture of the school and are created by members of the school community. This means seeking out community members, in and out of the school, to serve on the MTSS team and provide insight to the culture and needs of the school communities. Or, consider creating a separate parent/community/student advisory council to also provide input. Also ensure expectations are applied in a culturally sustaining way. If students are asked to be responsible in the cafeteria, that could look different to a teacher than a student, or from one family to another family. Thus, it is crucial that students and family/community are active in defining respectful behavior and that school staff aren't imposing their cultural and behavioral expectations upon students and families.

Home expectations (Sugar Creek): Not only can the MTSS team create student behavioral matrixes for the school, but they can also help families facilitate a similar conversation at home. A blank matrix can be shared with families, for each family to define how their home behavior expectations are aligned with the schoolwide expectations. This can facilitate a conversation between the school and families about culturally sustaining practices, code-switching and ensuring the school's language/expectations represent the families. See the example below. The school sent home a blank matrix, and the following matrix was created by a family at home.

	Be Respectful	Be Responsible	Be Safe
Morning	■ Use a quiet voice until others are awake ■ Use kind words – say "good morning" ■ Follow directions the first time	■ Get up on time ■ Brush teeth ■ Get dressed ■ Make bed ■ Get materials ready for school	■ Stay indoors/in room ■ Put shoes and clothes away
Meal times	■ Use manners – say "please" and "thank you" ■ Chew with mouth closed ■ Take turns listening and talking ■ Try new foods	■ Wash hands ■ Clean up dishes after eating ■ Keep food on the table	■ Stay in your seat ■ Keep chair legs on the floor ■ Use utensils properly
Homework	■ Work quietly ■ Ask for help (if needed)	■ Fill out assignment book ■ Finish all of your homework ■ Pack up backpack for the next day	■ Stay in designated homework spot ■ Clean up materials when finished ■ Hang up backpack
Free time/ Play	■ Include others ■ Share and take turns	■ Take care of belonging (toys, games, etc.) ■ Turn off electronics when finished ■ Clean up when you are finished playing	■ Use toys as intended ■ Keep hands and body to self ■ Tell an adult where you are playing
Bedtime	■ Use a quiet voice at nighttime ■ Use kind words – say "good night"	■ Put on pajamas ■ Wash up and brush teeth ■ Use bathroom ■ Go to bed on time	■ Stay indoors/in room ■ Put shoes and clothes away ■ Calm body in bed

EXAMPLES: Acknowledgements

In MTSS, it is common for school staff to positively reinforce or acknowledge students as a way to provide affirmative feedback for following the school expectations. Schools engaging in MTSS typically have schoolwide, grade/team and classroom acknowledgements. For instance, at the elementary level, students may receive a ticket; students may redeem a given number of tickets for a prize.

> Do acknowledgements always need to be things that are given to students? The answer is no. Acknowledgements can be words, events or a host of other ideas, rather than concrete tangibles. In fact, over time, the goal is to fade out students' reliance on concrete, external reinforcement and to focus on greater intrinsic, internal methods

> Are acknowledgement or reinforcement systems only for young students? Absolutely not. Positive reinforcement can be used with any age, including school staff. Check out the Wisconsin RTI's guide for using positive feedback in high schools, listed in the resource section at the end of this chapter.

Elementary school acknowledgement menu (Adapted from Loudoun County Public Schools):

Liberty Fourth Grade PBIS Menus

BLUE Eagle Menu	WHITE Eagle Menu
10 Show & Tell Spotlight	10 Extra recess
20 Trade seats for a day or sit in teacher's chair	20 Dance party
30 Homework Pass	30 Safari montage
40 Treasure Chest	40 PJ Party
50 Eat lunch with another 4th grade class or visit another classroom in the building	50 An awesome surprise (lunch in the classroom, class kickball game, etc.)
Trade 5 Blues for 1 White	*5 mins of Music for every 5*

Middle school acknowledgements (Adapted from Loudoun County Public Schools): "The Bus Stop Bandits are a Stone Hill Middle School initiative in which staff volunteers choose a highly referred bus stop location based on monthly data to visit and check-in on student behaviors. The Bandits wear specially made T-shirts, blast music and cheer while the students arrive at their bus stop. If the students exhibit positive behavior on the bus that day as determined by the bus driver, all students receive an incentive the following day. We do not inform students which route or stop will be visited in order to encourage all students to exhibit positive behavior."

High school acknowledgements (ABC Unified School District): "If 80% or more students who attend class during a particular block meet expectation (e.g., pre-determined school-wide/class expectations), the class is entered into a weekly raffle for a classwide incentive."

Staff acknowledgements (Milwaukee Public Schools): Positive acknowledgements aren't just for students. School staff may appreciate them too. "Staff members will receive a Green PBIS Card from fellow staff members for being caught promoting and implementing Lancaster's PBIS Initiatives (Be Safe, Be Respectful, Be Responsible) with fidelity. Staff members can redeem their Green PBIS Cards once they have earned 10 cards and pick from the Equity/Treasure Box)."

CREATING CULTURALLY SUSTAINING SCHOOLWIDE PROTOCOLS

As mentioned earlier, rather than looking at students' behavior and academics in isolation, we consider factors both within and outside of the school that could be contributing to students' outcomes. Then, we strive to assist students by making changes to the system, such as changing the school procedures and practices. Thus, to build upon the systems approach, Tier 1 preventions (e.g., schoolwide protocols) are put in place throughout the school, such as the classroom, schoolwide, and with family/communities. And as described above, these schoolwide protocols must be culturally sustaining.

From a systems perspective: MTSS emphasizes changing the school's procedures and practices, as well as the staff behavior, rather than focusing on changing the student behavior.

The importance of a systems perspective: "When a flower doesn't bloom, you fix the environment in which it grows, not the flower." – Alexander den Heijer

This culturally sustaining, preventive, systems perspective emphasized in MTSS also aligns with the ASCA National Model themes: school counselors are leaders and advocates who collaborate with stakeholders across the school to enact systemic change by removing equity and access barriers to student success.

EXAMPLES: Adult Expectations

In addition to student expectations, behavioral expectations and matrixes can also be created and used for the adults in the school community during their school-related meetings and routines.

Adult behavioral expectations: MTSS behavioral expectations can be used to inform norms used during school-related adult meetings (e.g., staff meetings, PTA meetings, committee meetings, family workshops, meetings with local community members, etc.) These expectations can be based on the schoolwide expectations and modified by the participants in each meeting or created in advance by the MTSS team, whichever is most appropriate and respectful to participants.

Community Meeting Norms

Be Responsible	▪ Complete assigned tasks
Be Respectful	▪ Turn off cell phone volume ▪ Listen to others
Be Engaged	▪ Share your knowledge, information, and ideas ▪ Share questions with the group

MacDowell Montessori Staff Expectations for Non-Classroom Settings 2012-2013

STAFF EXPECTATIONS	Be Responsible	Be Respectful	Be Safe	Be Productive
	■ Enforce MacDowell student expectations at all times ■ Use MacDowell PBIS language	■ Model the behavior you want from students	■ Use active supervision **Move** **Scan** **Interact**	■ Know the T-Chart ■ Follow protocol to manage minor violations quickly and quietly and refer major violations
	■ Interact with and correct all students in the building (not just your own)	■ Use a positive tone and language when interacting with students	■ Keep students in your line of sight ■ Pause periodically for students to catch up	■ Participate in all-school PBIS boosters ■ Conduct your own boosters when needed
	■ Use pre-corrects before all transitions	■ Verbally praise and acknowledge positive student behavior ■ Goal: 4 to 1 ratio of positive to negative	■ Keep personal electronic devices turned off and not visible	■ Help new students learn all school and classroom expectations within one week
	■ Be visible and active during transitions	■ Correct students calmly and privately when possible	■ Be on duty on time and ready to give your full attention to the students	■ Set up the environment to help students be successful

Examples: As stated before, with MTSS the focus is on changing the system. As such, the MTSS team creates protocols and procedures for school staff, which can assist with their classroom-level routines and procedures, and increase the consistency of these practices throughout the school.

VOICES FROM THE FIELD:

Some critics say MTSS is more effective at the elementary level. However, common procedures and practices are particularly important at the secondary level due to the large size of the school. "Because the school is large, we need to have structures in place, across the board, that everyone buys into."

Building a lesson (Capistrano Unified): Teachers and school counselors can use this framework to design their lessons as they teach schoolwide expectations.

Building A Lesson Plan

Location:

Be Safe	Be Respectful	Be Responsible

TELL (Introduce)

SHOW (Teach and Inform)	
Looks Like	Sounds Like

PRACTICE/MODEL/ACKNOWLEDGE

EXAMPLES: Building A Lesson Plan

Location: Bathroom

Be Safe	Be Respectful	Be Responsible
■ Wash your hands ■ Keep water in the sink	■ Allow people to have their privacy ■ Close the stall door ■ Flush the toilet ■ Voice Level 1	■ Enter quietly ■ Report all problems and spills to an adult ■ 2 pumps of soap ■ 3 pulls for paper towels

TELL (Introduce)
Objective: By the end of the lesson students will be able to follow schoolwide PBIS Bathroom Procedures. Today we are going to learn about always being safe, respectful, and responsible at LMS. ■ Being safe always means being free from harm. ■ Being respectful always means being polite and cooperative. ■ Being responsible means being dependable and trustworthy. Check for student understanding.

SHOW (Teach and Inform)	
Looks Like	Sounds Like
■ Students respecting the space of others. ■ Students washing hands and throwing away paper. ■ Students exiting the bathroom quickly.	■ Students using the indoor voice level. ■ 3 pulls for paper towels. ■ 2 pumps of soap.

PRACTICE/MODEL/ACKNOWLEDGE
Teachers provide practice of the Bathroom Procedures in the classroom. ■ Teachers and students should model: appropriate voice level, washing hands and putting paper towels in the trash. ■ Teachers should model: inappropriate voice level, leaving paper towels on the floor and not washing hands after using the bathroom. Students practice Bathroom Procedures with teacher giving immediate feedback and praise.

Teacher/staff classroom intervention plan (Milwaukee Public Schools): This document serves as a guide to provide teachers with recommended steps to teach and respond to classroom behaviors.

Classroom Intervention Plan Template

TEACHING BEHAVIOR	**Classroom Expectations & Rules** (rules are specific to classroom and fit under the expectations) 1. Be Safe 2. Be Respectful 3. Be Responsible *Are posted and positively stated
	Teaching Behavior (how and when will you teach behavior, how will you re-teach/ remind students)
	Classroom Procedures (what is your daily routine when entering class, when asking for help or bathroom, when sharpening pencil, turning in homework, getting missing work, etc)

ACKNOWLEDGEMENT SYSTEM	**Acknowledgement System** (how will you acknowledge, and what behaviors will you acknowledge?) (in addition to schoolwide system, how will you acknowledge desired behaviors within your classroom setting?) Examples: verbally, calls home, letter home, raffles, etc.

RESPONDING TO PROBLEM BEHAVIOR	**Responding to Problem Behavior:** (what is your system for dealing with students who don't follow the rules and procedures?) What is the sequence of your actions? What can students expect to occur?

ACTION PLAN	
	Physical Environment and Procedures:
	Communication to parents/ students:
	Instructional Practices:
	Resources/Assistance Needed

Teacher Name: ______________________________

Classroom Number: ____________

T-chart: Student behavior management/referral process: The MTSS team creates flow-charts outlining the process for school staff to manage student behaviors. Specifically, these charts define student behaviors that are classroom-managed vs. office-managed, as well as the roles and responsibilities of the involved staff member.

Some teachers may send students to the office for discipline concerns more frequently than others. For instance, imagine two students display the same aggressive behaviors in two different classrooms. Teacher #1 sends Student #1 to the office with an office discipline referral, while Teacher #2 keeps Student #2 in the classroom and provides discipline. When the MTSS team looks at office discipline referrals across the school, it appears Teacher #1 has a higher number of students with aggressive behaviors. Is this accurate? Does Teacher #1 actually have more students with aggressive behaviors? Or does Teacher #1 refer students more readily? Are students referred to the office more often because of the teacher's own biases or lack of cultural knowledge? This scenario is ripe for inequities in how students are treated. How do we combat this? For starters, with a T-chart. T-charts specifically define which student behaviors warrant an office referral vs.which should be managed within the classroom. This process helps level the playing field for more consistent behaviors across teachers, which can lead to more equitable treatment of all students.

Questions for Review and Discussion:

- What is a collegial way for school counselors to discuss trends in how teachers discipline and report students?
- What are the benefits and challenges of implementing T-charts in your school?
- How could T-charts be received by your school staff? What types of professional development would help teachers understand and engage with the T-charts in culturally sustaining ways?

Elementary school T-chart:

Byron Kilbourn Elementary Student Discipline Process

We believe optimal student achievement, both academically and behaviorally, can be attained by utilizing a proactive systems approach for creating and maintaining a safe and effective learning environment

Chaparral Elementary School Behavior Management

Classroom Teacher
minor behavior

1st Step
Give a verbal warning and re-state expectation/rule

2nd Step
Try 1–2 interventions

3rd Step
Apply additional intervention(s)

4th Step
Send a Parent/Family Notification Form home and when returned keep copy in classroom file

5th Step
Refer to administrator

Provide copy of Parent/ Family Notification Form if Step 4 was implemented

SAMPLE INTERVENTIONS

- ☐ 5:1 verbal positive feedback
- ☐ Redirection
- ☐ Proximity
- ☐ Verbal & Non-verbal Prompts
- ☐ Provide choice
- ☐ If ______, Then ______
- ☐ Seating Change
- ☐ Apology
- ☐ Working recess
- ☐ Loss of Privilege
- ☐ Other ______________
  ____

RESPECT, RESPONSIBILITY AND READY TO LEARN
Sample Behavior Offenses

Minor
- Defiance
- Disrespect
- Disruption
- Inappropriate Language
- Physical Contact

Major
- Defiance/ Insubordination
- Repetitive Disrespect
- Major Disruption
- Profanity/ Abusive Language
- Physical Aggression
- Out-of-Bounds

Office
Major behavior

Administrator is contacted

Administrator investigates

Incident resolved. Student sent back to class

Administration determines consequence

Discipline Referral Form (DRF)

Copy of DRF given to teacher to sign

Copy retained at school

Copy sent to parent for signature

(Capistrano Unified)

High school T-chart:

Milwaukee Public Schools Student Behavior Management Process

Observe problem behavior

↓

Problem solve with students

↓

Determine is behavior office managed?

NO → Use Intervention Strategies

↓

Level 1 – Redirection Model/ discuss correct student behavior

↓

Level 2 – Options Provide an option – assign detention, sit down & do your work, etc.

↓

Level 3 - Action Teacher discipline, phone call home – PEP (proximity, eye control, privateness)

↓

Document the strategies you have used PRIOR to writing a referral. If these don't work, go to level 4.

↓

Level 4- Referral Write the referral and send student to administration.

YES → Write referral to office

↓

Administrator determines consequence

↓

Administrator follows through on consequence

↓

Administrator provides teacher feedback

Classroom Managed	vs. **Office Managed**
■ Lack of supplies	■ Fights physical/ verbal
■ Sleeping in class	■ Weapons
■ Refusal to work	■ Drugs
■ Profanity (expletive)	■ Sexual innuendo
■ Ribbing	■ Selling food
■ Off task	■ Extortion
■ Dress code	■ Verbal/physical intimidation
■ Out of seat	■ Profanity at adult
■ Not following teacher directions	■ Smoking
■ Throwing things	■ Sexual harassment
■ Late to class	■ Vandalism
■ Eating in class	■ Defiance
■ Ipods	■ Stealing
■ Texting	■ Gang related activity
■ Horseplay	■ Instigating fights
■ Pass abuse	■ Secure home contact
■ Doesn't serve detention	■ Cheating
■ Cell phone	■ Walks out of class
	■ Chronic minor infractions
	■ Threats
	■ Threat intended profanity

Minor Incident Referrals (same form as regular incident referrals)

- Issue slip when student does not respond to pre-correction, re-direction or verbal warning.
- Once written, notify parent with phone call or letter.
- Take concrete action to correct behavior (i.e. assign detention, complete behavior reflection).
- Whenever possible, have the corrective action correspond to the behavior being corrected.

Cerritos High School, ABC Unified District

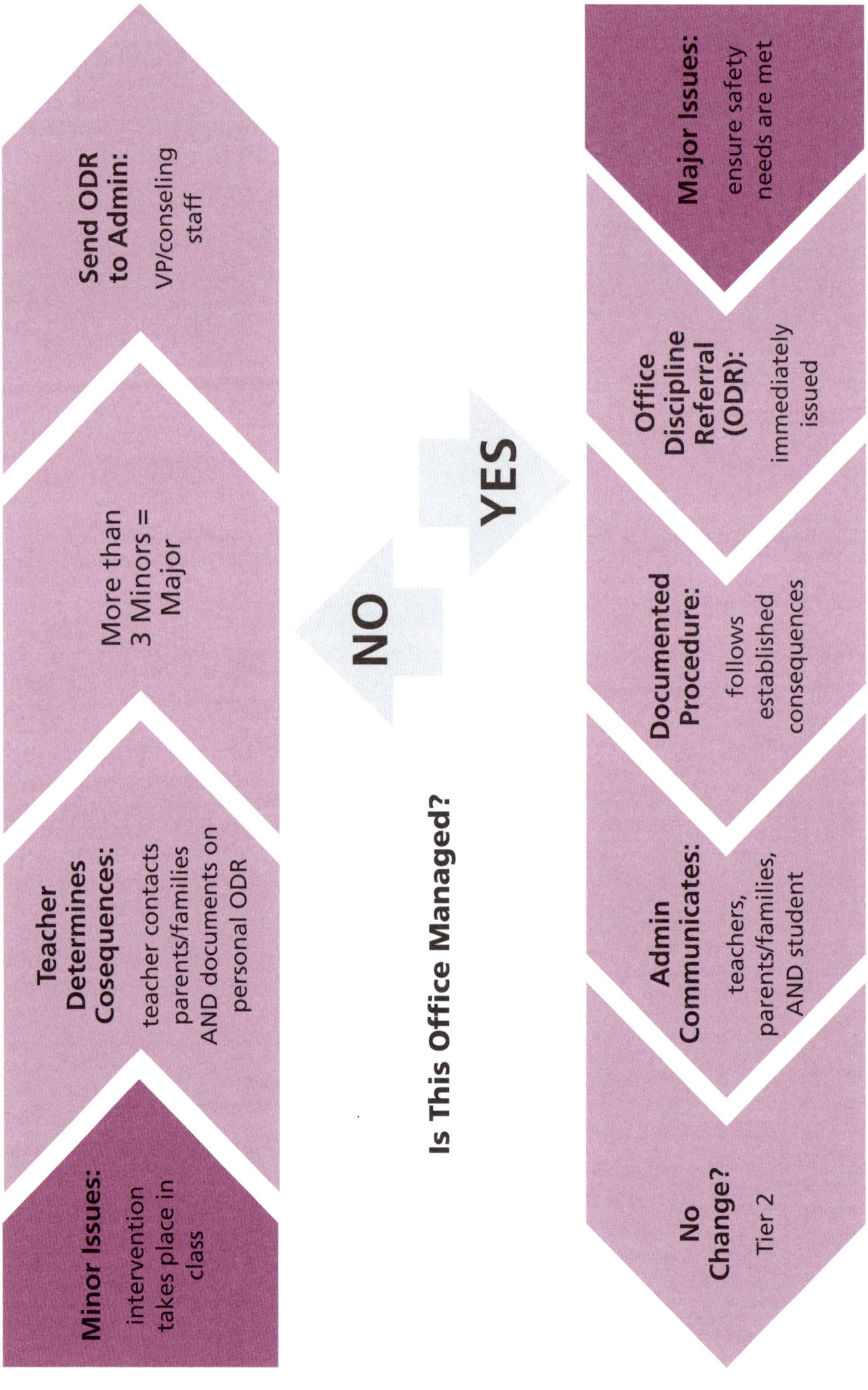

Remember, it's important to have an MTSS team that includes the school's community and cultures and perhaps a separate parent/community/student council to provide input as well. It's crucial these teams help design and implement the referral process and all similar documents that guide staff procedures and practices, aspiring for practices to be culturally sustaining, and address staff and student biases. As we discussed, "defiant" and "respectful" behavior can vary by context, by teacher, by family and by community. This must be considered when creating and following T-charts.

See the Appendix for more examples of MTSS tools and resources commonly used in Tier 1 supports. For more information on the systems approach, see Bronfenbrenner (1979), Sink (2019), and McMahon and colleagues (2014). For more information on MTSS, including Tier 1 supports, see Brown-Chidsey and Bickford (2016), McIntosh and Goodman (2016), Sugai and colleagues (2019), and Mason and Lopez-Perry (2019). A new resource by Leverson and colleagues (2019) provides examples of culturally sustaining PBIS/MTSS, as does the book by Paris and Alim (2017): "Culturally Sustaining Pedagogies."

DESCRIPTION: SCHOOL COUNSELORS' ROLE IN TIER 1

In aligning the ASCA National Model and MTSS, school counselors provide both direct and indirect services, also known as an intervener and supporter (Ockerman et al., 2012).

Direct Services/Intervener:

School counselors serve as interveners by providing direct services to students. The direct services, rooted in the school counseling program's mission and vision and the ASCA Mindsets & Behaviors, focus on academic, career and social/emotional development. Direct services are based on data and the annual student outcome goal. Let's take a look at how these activities can align with MTSS, particularly school counseling classroom instruction, large group/schoolwide activities and initiatives, and student appraisal and advisement.

School counseling classroom instruction: As school counselors provide classroom lessons to all students, they can incorporate the MTSS-generated schoolwide expectations into this instruction. For example, during lessons, school counselors can reinforce the schoolwide behavioral expectations at the start of each lesson and also weave these expectations into the lesson itself, such as presenting content through the lens of how it relates to the expectations. Further, during lessons, school counselors can acknowledge students' positive behaviors through implementing the schoolwide and/or classwide incentive system, whether distributing school tickets or other means determined by the school or teacher. Lesson content is based on the ASCA Mindsets & Behaviors, the annual student outcome goals and data gathered from the school counseling program and the MTSS team.

True alignment between school counseling lessons and MTSS reduces redundancies: School counseling lessons, based on ASCA Mindsets & Behaviors, reinforce MTSS schoolwide expectations, and these schoolwide expectations simultaneously address the ASCA Mindsets & Behaviors.

VOICES FROM THE FIELD:

One teacher communicated how school counselors' lessons were interwoven with MTSS supports, "When our MTSS data shows us we need some kind of Tier 1 supports, then the school counselors will design lessons and figure out the best classes to go into to deliver that instruction."

VOICES FROM THE FIELD:

"Our school counseling classroom lessons piggyback on these schoolwide MTSS positive expectations."

Large group/schoolwide activities and initiatives: School counselors can directly serve every student through presenting during schoolwide activities, such as assemblies, presentations and events. For instance, school counselors can partner with MTSS team members to deliver engaging schoolwide content to also teach the schoolwide expectations, as well as practice school procedures (e.g., walking in the hallway, practicing desired behaviors in the school cafeteria, etc.). Relatedly, working in tandem with the MTSS team, school counselors can present to students on topics aligned with both the school counseling program and MTSS Tier 1 prevention, such as social media safety initiatives, strategies for academic success, mental health and mindfulness.

Student appraisal and advisement: Another aspect of providing direct services is the school counselor meeting with every student for appraisal and advisement. As such, school counselors can meet with all students on their caseload to develop an academic/graduation/career plan, thus promoting student engagement in academic and career goals, with the aim of reducing the number of students requiring Tier 2 small-group intervention. Another idea are minute meetings, in which the school counselors uses a platform such as Google Forms to ask every student on their caseload three to five questions (e.g., I have an adult at school I can talk to, etc.), as a way to introduce themselves and conduct a needs assessment regarding appraisal and advisement.

ACTIVITY: Integrated Expectations

List your school MTSS expectations. How can you integrate your school expectations into your Tier 1 school counseling activities? Specifically, your classroom instruction/lessons, large group/schoolwide activities, and student appraisal and advisement?

VOICES FROM THE FIELD:

As one school counselor explained, "MTSS schoolwide expectations are just so embedded in what we do on a daily basis."

VOICES FROM THE FIELD:

Conveying the importance of prevention and teaching the schoolwide expectations early in the school year,"We're getting in front of the negative student behaviors rather than just reacting to it."

Examples:

Elementary lesson introduction (Adapted from Loudoun County Public Schools): At the start of the lesson, school counselors can review the schoolwide expectations with students. They can prompt students by asking: "What three things does a Pinebrook Puma [school mascot] do at school to create a safe and happy place to learn?" Students respond with: "Ready, Respectful, Responsible."

Elementary lesson introduction (Adapted from Loudoun County Public Schools): At the start of the lesson, the school counselor can ask: "How do we know someone is being a respectful?" "What does it look like, sound like, feel like to listen?" Have students draw responses on the board or point to the body part that is responsible for that action (e.g., heart, ears, mouth, etc.)

Complete schoolwide expectations and behavioral matrix specific to school counselors (Milwaukee Public Schools): During a school counseling lesson at the start of the school year, students can complete a blank schoolwide expectations document pertaining to school counseling.

For instance, as in this example, students can review expectations for various settings throughout the school (see the first three images), then describe how they will behave during school counseling lessons (completing the fourth, blank document):

Taylor Elementary School Playground Behavior

Be Respectful:
Share the equipment
Take turns
Help others

Be Responsible:
Listen for the bell or whistle
Put equipment away
Line up quickly

Be Safe:
Dress for the weather
Play by the rules
Ask for adult help when needed

Be "Spotted" Using Taylor Elementary School Playground Behavior

Taylor Elementary School Bathroom Behavior

Be Respectful:
Give privacy to others
Wait for your turn

Be Responsible:
Use a soft voice
Keep hands and feet to yourself
Flush the toilet

Be Safe:
Wash hands with soap and water
Water stays in the sink
Dry hands

Be "Spotted" Using Taylor Elementary School Bathroom Behavior

Taylor Elementary School Library Behavior

Be Respectful:
Listen to the teacher
Use a soft voice
Wait for your turn

Be Responsible:
Return books on time
Take care of the books
Put materials away

Be Safe:
Walk in the library
Push in your chair
Line up quietly

Be "Spotted" Using Taylor Elementary School Library Behavior

Taylor Elementary School Behavior: School Counseling Lessons

Be Respectful:

Be Responsible:

Be Safe:

Be "Spotted" Using Taylor Elementary School Behavior: School Counseling Lesson

Also, students can complete a behavioral matrix for their school counselor, describing how the school counselor can meet the schoolwide expectations in various settings (e.g., during classroom instruction, during large-group activities, during advising/appraisal).

MTSS School Counseling Matrix

	School Counselor Lesson	School Counselor Assembly	School Counselor Counseling/Advising
Be Safe			
Be Respectful			
Be Responsible			

Student exit ticket (Utah school counselors): School counselors can align their exit ticket (e.g., post-test) with the schoolwide expectations. For instance: "What did you learn from this lesson that will help you Respect Self? Respect Others? And Respect Property?"

Student role play (Utah school counselors): Have students experientially demonstrate their understanding of the schoolwide expectations, such as: (a) role play or create a play acting out their school expectations or (b) engage in a debate, comparing and contrasting the expectations, such as benefits and challenges, suggestions, etc.

Acknowledge students: School counselors can utilize the existing acknowledgement structure in the school during their work directly and indirectly serving students. Specifically, school counselors can provide specific, positive verbal feedback (e.g., thank you for arriving to class on time, Rashad). Further, students can earn privileges based on the class/grade/school menu or directives (e.g., recognizing the top five classes/teams with model cafeteria behavior).

VOICES FROM THE FIELD:

One teacher communicated how school counselors' lessons were interwoven with MTSS supports, "When our MTSS data shows us we need some kind of Tier 1 supports, then, the school counselors will design lessons and figure out the best classes to go into to deliver that instruction."

VOICES FROM THE FIELD:

A school counselor at a middle school described how they distributed the schoolwide incentive: "Whether it's in the classroom, in the hallway, whether it's working with students individually or in a small group with the school counselor, we provide what we call School Bucks, our schoolwide incentive program to reward students when they're doing things that they should be doing or even things they're doing that go above and beyond."

Indirect Services/Supporter:

In an effort to serve students as a supporter, school counselors provide a range of indirect services to school staff through their involvement on committees such as the MTSS team, as well as by providing collaboration, consultation and education to school staff, parents/family members and community members, thus enhancing stakeholders' work with students. Specifically, in this section we'll outline schoolwide leadership and advocacy, consulting and collaborating with school staff, and providing staff and family training/workshops.

Schoolwide leadership and advocacy: School counselors serve students by being actively involved in schoolwide leadership teams. As members of the MTSS team, they can consult on schoolwide Tier 1 activities, offering their expertise on youth development, mental health and wellness, prevention, etc. Also, school counselors can ensure the MTSS team includes diverse stakeholders and represents the school community, thereby working toward culturally sustaining supports.

In Tier 1, data is used to evaluate the implementation of school counseling programs and MTSS and identify student and school needs. Thus, school counselors can help the MTSS leadership team make data-informed decisions, as well as develop schoolwide expectations, protocols, practices and events for students, staff and community members. Further, during leadership meetings, school counselors can provide background information on students and families (as ethically appropriate) and advocate for systems level changes.

VOICES FROM THE FIELD:

When implementing MTSS, one school counselor highlighted the importance of culturally sustaining equity, "There is no one-size-fits-all. It's all based on your community and addressing the needs of your community. It is systemic change, making sure all students have the resources."

VOICES FROM THE FIELD:

Through their school counseling program, "The school counselors support the process of [MTSS] in a lot of different ways, building a supportive atmosphere and climate."

Consult and collaborate with school staff: In the role of supporter, school counselors often consult and collaborate with school staff on a range of topics, such as classroom management, behavioral concerns, developmental considerations, students' academics, etc. For instance, school counselors assist teachers in using the MTSS protocol and procedures, such as teaching, practicing and reinforcing schoolwide behavioral expectations and classroom routines. Further, in recent years, advisory meetings have become increasingly popular in middle and high school, in which students meet with a small group of peers, led by a staff member, to discuss academic, career and social/emotional topics. School counselors can create curriculum, resources and content for school staff to use when leading these advisory sessions with students.

VOICES FROM THE FIELD:

One teacher described that school counselors consulted and collaborated with them pertaining to using the schoolwide MTSS incentive system, "School counselors encourage teachers to distribute cougar cash and give us suggestions on how we can use cougar cash with students."

VOICES FROM THE FIELD:

Another teacher highlighted appreciating the school counselors' consultation and collaboration on MTSS procedures, "The school counselors are a really great sounding board for figuring out classroom management."

VOICES FROM THE FIELD:

A school counselor communicated how the preventive schoolwide approach helped in consulting and collaborating with teachers, "As a school, we talk about being ready and prepared. Not only be prepared for the next school year but being prepared for academic success and job success. I love that I've been able to pull that in and make that a schoolwide conversation. It's given me a good in to start talking with the teachers."

Staff and family training/workshops: School counselors provide trainings to school staff and students' family members that are aligned with school counselors' services to students (e.g., classroom instruction, schoolwide initiatives, advisory sessions, advisement/appraisal, etc.), as well as the school counseling program goals and ASCA Mindsets & Behaviors. For instance, school counselors can provide educational trainings or workshops on topics such as youth coping with anxiety, college and career planning, the rights of nondocumented students and families, organizational and study skills, substance use, etc. In addition to trainings, school counselors can also provide school staff and family with resources and referrals.

EXAMPLE: **Parent Education:**

Mental Health Awareness Series (Adapted from Loudoun County Public Schools):

Mental Health & Wellness Parent Seminar Series 2019–2020
6:30–8:30 p.m.

9/19	Identifying, Supporting, and Managing Childhood Anxiety Potomac Behavioral Solutions
10/24	Angst Film Screening and Panel Discussion for Parents and Teens Student Assistance Services and Panel
11/14	Bullying Behavior and Cyberbullying School Counseling Services and County Sheriff's Office
1/23	Managing Bumps in the Road: Building Resilient Relationships with Your Teen Student Support Services
2/6	Learn CPR! Student Health Services and INOVA Medical Group
2/27	Family Power: Engaging and Collaborating with Your Child Student Support Services
3/19	A Time to Connect in a Busy World Student Assistance Services
4/16	Three Things to Help Students Deal with Stress and Anxiety Neil McNerney, LPC
5/14	Preventing Perfectionism: What Parents Can Do With Young Children Diagnostic and Prevention Services

VOICES FROM THE FIELD:

A principal relayed the many ways of communicating with family members as part of MTSS, "With parents, I have sent home MTSS messages this year including: updates about our goals, data, expectations and acknowledgements; a report on behavior that we presented to our school board; information about our Tier 2 supports; a schoolwide survey on behavior; a request for parent reps to sit on our MTSS committee; our home behavioral matrix, which helps parents connect home and school behavioral expectations and language, and more."

In sum, through the Deliver component of the ASCA National Model, school counselors act as interveners and supporters in aligning their work with MTSS.

Activity and Questions for Review and Discussion

Read the following six case studies, and answer these questions for each case study:

- How is this case study tied into school counseling and MTSS?
- How did school counselors act as interveners and supporters, providing direct and indirect services in these Tier 1 activities?
- What systemic supports do you notice (e.g., practices across multiple parts of the system, such as the student, class, schoolwide, staff, family or community-level)?
- What aspects of these case studies are preventive?
- Was data used in this case study, and if so, how?
- Were these supports culturally sustaining? Did they promote social justice? Do you have suggestions for infusing culturally sustaining principles in these practices?
- Was an evidence-based program used?

CASE STUDY 1: ELEMENTARY SCHOOL BULLY PREVENTION

Elementary schools can take a multipronged approach to bully prevention using the evidence-based curriculum Bully Prevention in Positive Behavior Support (BP-PBS; Ross, Horner, & Stiller, 2008), which promotes bully prevention within the MTSS framework.

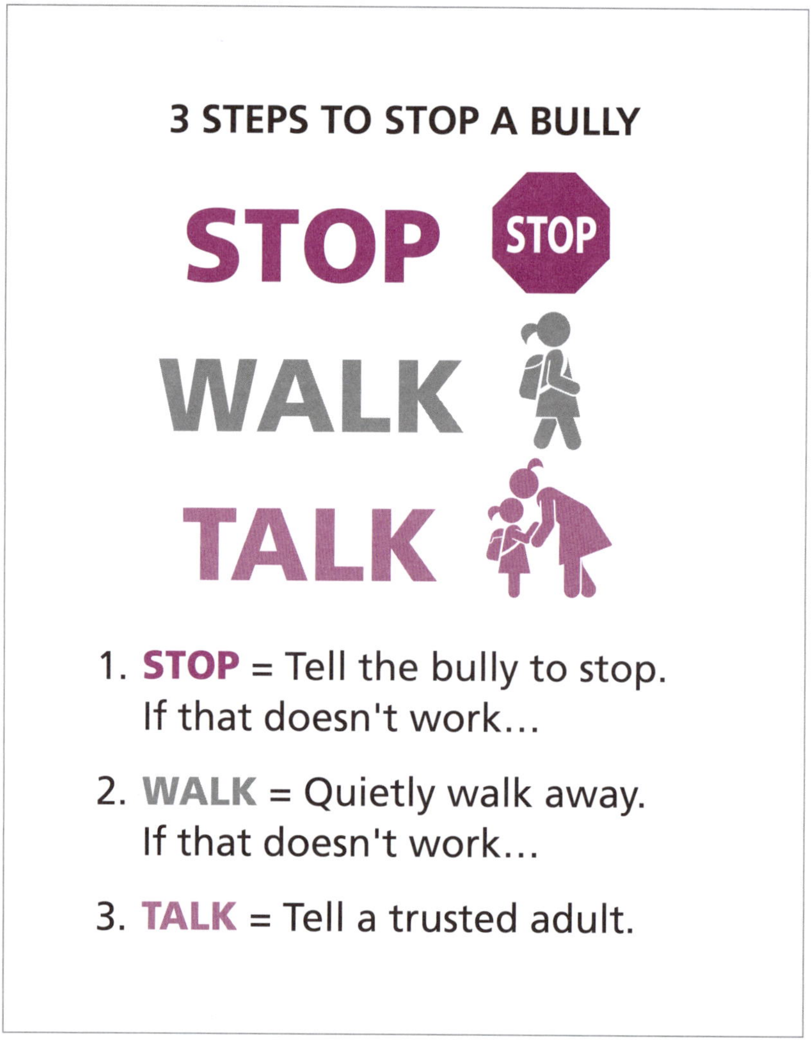

To start with, school counselors teach a series of classroom lessons to students, using the BP-PBS curriculum. They provide the classroom teacher with follow-up content to use and reinforce with students, between school counseling lessons. Next, the MTSS team, including the school counselor, plans and facilitates a schoolwide, upbeat assembly, reinforcing key points of the BP-PBS framework to students, to build off the classroom lessons. Last, school counselors conduct a parent workshop, titled Coffee with the Counselor, in which they described the BP-PBS lessons and related content, provided bullying data from the school, staff members' roles in bully prevention and intervention, and suggested strategies for family and student follow-up at home. (modified from Loudoun County Public Schools)

School data presented at the parent coffee, listing the location and frequency of previous bullying at the school:

2017-2018: Student Incident Locations

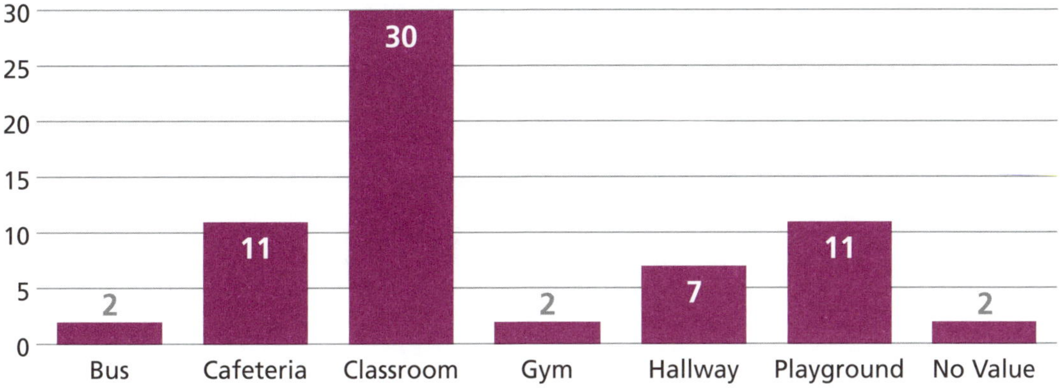

Content presented at the parent coffee, showing school staff roles pertaining to bully prevention and follow-up

School Roles

School counselor will:	Teacher will:	Administration will:
■ Provide Bullying Prevention Education in K-5 ■ Collect data to ensure students understand concepts taught ■ Provide Restorative Circles ■ Provide support for victim in bullying situation ■ Notify administration ■ Conference with parents and teachers	■ Reinforce Stop, Walk, Talk ■ Promote communication through circles and class climate ■ Keep accurate records of incidents and discipline ■ Report bullying to Admin. ■ Communicate with parents, counselors, or admin when a situation is occurring.	■ Speak with the student who caused harm ■ Use restorative questions to understand the situation ■ Speak with students involved ■ Consider discipline ■ Speak with parents ■ Communicate "next steps or actions"

Bully Prevention MTSS Pyramid: see this pyramid, for bully prevention supports at the district level, as implemented by a range of related stakeholders, one of whom is the school counselor.

Loudoun County Public Schools Multitiered System of Supports (MTSS)

Bullying Behavior Prevention and Education

Bullying Behavior Prevention and Education includes: verbal, emotional/relational, social, cyber, and physical

Social-Emotional Interventions

Increase Intensity, Frequency and/or Duration of Tier 2

- Intensive Long-Term Individual Counseling
- Threat Assessment/Safety Plan
- Restorative Conferences
- Follow-up and Referral for Suicide Screening Results

Tier 3 Systems Planning Team and Tier 3 Problem Solving Team (PSSST, CST, UMHT)

Social-Emotional Interventions

Increase Intensity, Frequency and/or Duration of Tier 1

- Targeted Evidenced-Based Strategies/Intervention
- Check In/Check Out
- Short-Term Individual Counseling
- Mentoring
- Group Counseling
- Restorative Circles
- Support Groups

Tier 2 Systems Planning Team and Tier 2 Problem Solving Team (CLT, IT, SAT, UMHT)

Social-Emotional Strategies

- PBIS Bullying Prevention (Stop-Walk-Talk & Expect Respect)
- PBIS Bullying Prevention (Stop-Walk-Talk & Expect respect) Staff Training
- Bullying Prevention & Education Curriculum Action Plan
- Classroom Counseling/Advisory Lessons
- Bulletin Boards/PSA's/Newsletters/Website
- Parent/Guardian/Community Bullying Prevention & Education Presentations
- Restorative Language
- Differentiation (Reteach/Model/Reassess)
- Sources of Strength
- PEER
- Signs of Suicide & Signs of Suicide-Training Trusted Adults
- Dating Matters Lessons (FLE)

Tier 1 Systems Planning Team (PBIS/SEL, Bullying Prevention Committee, UMHT)

Revised July 2019

CASE STUDY 2: ELEMENTARY SCHOOL SOCIAL/EMOTIONAL LEARNING

This initiative is led by a district-level social/emotional learning (SEL) specialist, who is housed under district-level MTSS efforts. The specialist created an SEL initiative involving several members of the school community, including the school counselor. What do you notice about the school counselor's role in this comprehensive and proactive Tier 1 SEL effort? (modified from Loudoun County Public Schools)

Social/Emotional Learning

Coordinated by Dr. Lindsay Orme, Social-Emotional Learning Specialist

Vision for Social/Emotional Learning

All elementary schools will implement an evidenced-based social/emotional learning curriculum to promote student skill development in the areas of social awareness, self-awareness, self-regulation, relationship skills and responsible decision making, based on CASEL (Collaborative for Academic, Social, and Emotional Learning).

Schoolwide SEL Integrated into the MTSS framework

This SEL initiative is aligned with: MTSS, Restorative Practices, Trauma-Informed Practices, Academic Standards, ASCA Standards

Steps to SEL Implementation

- The district established Second Step as the Tier 1/Universal Social Emotional Learning Curriculum
- Second Step's grade-specific materials include games, visuals, songs and activities to engage students
- Utilizing a systemic approach with Second Step, the school district infuses social/emotional learning into every part of students' daily lives: in their classrooms, throughout the school day, and in their homes and communities
- This initiative is being implemented through a cohort model:
  - Year 1: 33 elementary schools begin implementation
  - Year 2: 45 elementary schools begin implementation
  - Year 3: All elementary schools begin implementation
- This initiative includes:
  - Trainings for administrators, lead teachers, school counselors, SPED support staff, school psychologists, and school social workers
  - Education and awareness for families and the community

Teachers' Roles

- Deliver Second Step curriculum
- Reinforce throughout the day
- Integrate with academic content
- Anticipate, Reinforce, & Reflect
- Create an equitable, supportive and safe environment
- Model strong social-emotional competencies
- Send content home to families
- Assess knowledge acquisition (pre-/post-tests)

School Counselors' Roles

- Consult and collaborate with teachers, to support them in their explicit instruction of the SEL competencies (e.g., Second Step)
- Align school counseling classroom lessons with classroom teachers' Second Step lessons to reinforce and build upon the teachers' lessons
- Support schoolwide SEL initiatives through both direct implementation and planning efforts, as part of the MTSS/PBIS team
- Based on data identifying students with elevated needs, school counselors will provide follow-up, supportive small-group counseling, using the Second Step curriculum (Tier 2 practice)

CASE STUDY 3: MIDDLE SCHOOL UNIFIED MENTAL HEALTH TEAMS

Tier 1 Unified Mental Health Team: Middle School

The Loudoun County Public Schools Unified Mental Health Team (UMHT) is a team at each secondary school composted of school counselors, the school psychologist, the school social worker, student assistance specialist, school nurse and administrators. The UMHT mission is to promote schoolwide mental health initiatives within MTSS and provide a spectrum of prevention and intervention supports and services addressing students' social, emotional, and behavioral needs, and to remove barriers to learning. UMHT members receive district-level training, and complete the School Mental Health Implementation Inventory (SMH-II), as a way to measure the extent to which UMHT is implementing the features of a school-based integrated model of mental health.

The Loudoun County Public Schools Harper Park Middle School UMHT conducted a needs assessment at the start of the school year, asking the following questions: *What can the adults at Harper Park do to make school a more positive place for students? What can students do to help everyone feel included at Harper Park? What could be done to help students feel more connected with adults at HPMS?* and *What do YOU need to be happy at school?* Based on student feedback, the UMHT created at least one lesson a month focused on mental health wellness, such as: stress reduction, study skills, healthy sleeping, resiliency skills, and positive coping strategies. They started a Monday Morning Check-In during homeroom to foster more relationships in the building. Also, the UMHT created The Oasis, which houses a school psychologist, school social worker, and lead school counselor, and is used for individual and group counseling, restorative practices, as well as a resource for staff and students. In The Oasis, students can find flexible seating, stress balls, anxiety reducing manipulatives, therapeutic coloring, kinetic sand, calming music and videos, and can have a conversation with a mental health professional. All students have a chromebook with a "request to see a mental health provider" icon on the student's homepage: giving them immediate access.

The UMHT also creates monthly newsletters for parents and staff that inform them of the content of advisory lessons and offers suggestions for families to try at home that correspond to the UMHT lessons. They also maintain an Instagram, Twitter, and website devoted to the UMHT and use these platforms to share mental health and wellness tips. In addition, the team arranges for parent workshops on mental health and wellness, as well as an Annual Staff Wellness Week.

Beth Weatherford, Loudoun County Public Schools School Psychologist

For more information on unified mental health teams see the article Unified Mental Health Teams by Tracy Jackson, available at *www.schoolcounselor.org*.

CASE STUDY 4: HIGH SCHOOL TIER 1 UNIFIED MENTAL HEALTH TEAMS BOOK TALK

In an effort to meet school counseling standards and academic standards simultaneously, school counselors can engage in a practice called standards blending. Specifically, school counselors and teachers can collaborate to co-deliver content to students that meet both sets of school counseling and academic standards. This is considered a Tier 1 support. For instance, Park View High School was awarded with a grant to host a series of book club discussions around race and racism. Members of the unified mental health team partnered with teachers to hold the book club in a 10th-grade English class and used practices such as restorative circles to increase trust between students during the conversations. This example of MTSS Tier 1 standards blending incorporates academics, mental health/wellness, current events, as well as building students' social skills and critical thinking. (based on Loudoun County Public Schools)

CASE STUDY 5: EMPOWERING ALL STUDENTS

Empowering All Students: Student Assembly, Parent Presentation, and Advisory Lesson

By Jaclyn Smith, Director of School Counseling, Dominion High School, Loudoun County Public Schools

Sam Lucania, Motivational Speaker, shared his powerful story and message with all 9th - 12th grade students and our faculty at Dominion High School on January 9, 2019. Turning his "mess into a message," Sam shared how he turned to substance use and addiction during adolescence to escape and numb the pain of depression, anxiety and bullying. Never feeling comfortable in his own skin, constantly fearing judgment from his peers, and continually striving for peer acceptance, Sam shared his journey through addiction and recovery and a message of hope, help, and strength. Students connected to his authenticity, his brokenness, and his palpable desire to help others learn through his own mistakes. He left students with poignant lessons that they're still talking about in the hallways of Dominion High School to this day. No one succeeds in life alone. What others think of you is not your business. Find a positive mentor. Every decision you make has consequences. Fill your life with healthy activities, positive friends, and mentors, rather than drugs and alcohol. Work on being physically, mentally and spiritually fit. If you make mistakes, experience failure, or face challenges, there is hope and there is help so you emerge stronger.

Later that evening, Sam shared his message with parents at our Parent-Teacher Organization. In addition to sharing his story, Sam included information about how he believes parents can support their children and the names of commonly abused prescription drugs and how to properly store them to prevent abuse. Parents in attendance were highly complimentary of his presentation, and some even purchased several copies of his books as a donation for our students.

The next day, every high school student participated in an advisory lesson facilitated by a faculty member and/or a peer leader. The lesson involved a circle discussion in which students reflected on the parts of Sam's story that resonated with them, the difficulty some students have in asking for help, the importance of asking for help, and the people and resources within the Dominion High School community that students feel they can turn to when faced with various challenges. Sam Lucania's assembly and the follow-up parent presentation and advisory lesson were an overwhelming successful Tier 1 initiative.

CASE STUDY 6: DECREASING HIGH SCHOOL OFFICE DISCIPLINE REFERRALS

A local high school was in the beginning phases of MTSS implementation. When analyzing data, the MTSS team observed the high number of office discipline referrals. In disaggregating the data, the MTSS team determined that most referrals were related students' incorrect use of hall passes and verbal altercations with staff when discussing their use of hall passes. Due to the data, the MTSS team implemented new practices for the subsequent school year. Specifically, they color-coded the main hallways of the school and corresponding hall passes. Thus, a student with a class in the blue hall would get a blue pass to use the bathroom in the blue hall. This change cleared up discrepancies and related disagreements regarding where students should be using their hall pass. This one change resulted in a significant change in school office discipline referrals, dropping them from nearly 900 in year one to just over 300 in year two, approximately a 66% decrease. Scholars estimate that each referral takes approximately 15 minutes of student and administrator time. Thus, it is estimated that this decrease in referrals led to 9,000 extra minutes or 150 hours gained back across administrators and students. Overall, the school's MTSS team, including the school counselor, used schoolwide data to change a schoolwide practice, which resulted in improved student outcomes. This is a great example of school staff changing the system to improve student outcomes.

VOICES FROM THE FIELD:

Although MTSS implementation does take time to implement, many school staff consider it a worthwhile investment due to the benefits, especially the positive affect on student outcomes, "It's worth the time, and it actually saves you time in the long-run. It's a marathon, not a sprint."

Evidence-based Practices: Tier 1

To wrap up the chapter, we expand on one final point. We recommend school counselors use evidence-based practices in their role as an intervener in delivering Tier 1 direct services and as supporter consulting and collaborating with school staff who implement evidence-based practices. The following are a sample of evidence-based practices commonly used in Tier 1; for a more exhaustive review, see Mariani and Kuba (2019).

Second Step*: A classroom-based social skills program for students in preschool through junior high (ages 4–14 years). Designed to reduce impulsive, high-risk and aggressive behaviors and increase children's social competence and other protective factors. Intended to teach children to identify and understand their own and others' emotions, choose positive goals and successfully manage reactions when emotionally aroused.

Strong Kids*: A set of curricula that teach social/emotional skills, promote resilience, strengthen assets and increase coping skills of children and adolescents. For the K–12 age range: Strong Start (grades K–2), Strong Kids (grades 3–8, including versions for both elementary and middle school students) and Strong Teens (grades 9–12). Program goals are to increase knowledge of social/emotional concepts and coping skills while decreasing problem symptoms.

Responding in Peaceful and Positive Ways: Developed to provide conflict-resolution strategies and skills to sixth-, seventh- and eighth-grade students. Goals are to reduce aggressive behavior and violence in school-aged youth and to intervene with young children to help them avoid potential violence in adolescence.

Too Good Program: Promotes character values, social/emotional skills and healthy beliefs of elementary and middle school students. All lessons are scripted and engage students through role-playing and cooperative learning games, small-group activities and classroom discussions. Two related programs are addressed in the intervention reports on Too Good for Drugs and Violence (high school) and Too Good for Drugs (K–8).

Student Success Skills*: A structured school counseling curriculum and training scheme that equips practitioners with relevant and useful activities designed to support achievement and related school behaviors in students grades 4 through 12. Students set specific goals and monitor aspects of daily living that affect achievement (i.e. rest, social support, exercise and nutrition).

*can be used as a Tier 2 interventions as well

REFERENCES AND RESOURCES

Bronfenbrenner, U. (1979). *The ecology of human development.* Harvard university press.

Hatch, T., Duarte, D., & De Gregorio, L. K. (2018). *Hatching results for elementary school counseling: Implementing core curriculum and other tier one activities.* Corwin Press.

Hatch, T., Triplett, W., Duarte, D., & Gomez, V. (2019). *Hatching results for secondary school counseling: Implementing core curriculum, individual student planning, and other tier one activities.* Corwin Press.

Hurst, K. W. (2016, December 7). Biased discipline at my school: A public high school administrator recounts the moment she recognized that her teachers disciplined black and white students differently. Retrieved from: https://www.edutopia.org/article/biased-discipline-at-my-school-kelly-wickham-hurst?utm

Kendi, I. X. (2016). *Stamped from the Beginning.* Nation Books.

Mason, E., & Lopez-Perry, C. (2019). Tier 1: School counseling core curriculum and classroom management for every student. In E. Goodman-Scott, J. Betters-Bubon, & P. Donohue (Eds.), *A School Counselor's Guide to Multi-tiered Systems of Support* (1st ed. 133-162). New York City, NY: Routledge.

McMahon, H. G., Mason, E. C. M., Daluga-Guenther, N., & Ruiz, A. (2014). An ecological model of professional school counseling. *Journal of Counseling & Development, 92*, 459-471. doi:10.1002/j.1556-6676.2014.00172.x

Leverson, M., Smith, K., McIntosh, K., Rose, J., Pinkelman, S. (2019). *PBIS Cultural Responsiveness Field Guide: Resources for Trainers and Coaches.* Retrieved from: https://assets-global.website-files.com/5d3725188825e071f1670246/5d70468ef10ca28bb416e7b0_pbis%20cultural%20responsiveness%20field%20guide.pdf

Ockerman, M. S., Mason, E. C. M., & Hollenbeck, A. F. (2012). Integrating RTI with school counseling programs: Being a proactive professional school counselor. *Journal of School Counseling, 10*(15). Retrieved from tp://jsc.montana.edu/articles/v10n15.pdf

Ross, Horner, & Stiller (2008). *Bully-prevention in Positive Behavior Support.* Retrieved from: https://assets-global.website-files.com/5d3725188825e071f1670246/5d6ff1ec72843e4ad1d44b55_bullyprevention_es.pdf

Paris, D., & Alim, H. S. (Eds.). (2017). *Culturally sustaining pedagogies: Teaching and learning for justice in a changing world.* Teachers College Press.

Sink, C. (2019). Tier 1: Creating strong universal systems of support and facilitating systemic change. In E. Goodman-Scott, J. Betters-Bubon, & P. Donohue (Eds.), *A School Counselor's Guide to Multi-tiered Systems of Support* (1st ed. 62-98). New York City, NY: Routledge.

Sugai, G., La Salle, T., Everett, S., & Feinberg, A. B. (2019). Multi-tiered Systems of Support: The what, why, and how for school counselors. In E. Goodman-Scott, J. Betters-Bubon, & P. Donohue (Eds.), *A School Counselor's Guide to Multi-tiered Systems of Support* (1st ed. 1-28). New York City, NY: Routledge.

Wisconsin RTI's guide: Using specific, positive feedback in high schools. Retrieved from: https://www.wisconsinrticenter.org/wp-content/uploads/2020/03/specific-positive-feedback-hs.pdf

CHAPTER 5

Aligning Tier 2 Supports

Chapter 4 focused on Tier 1, particularly aligning school counseling programs with Tier 1 supports, and provided a variety of examples to help you strengthen the school counseling work you are already doing. In this chapter, we will focus on evidence-based, culturally sustaining Tier 2 supports guided by a MTSS team, aligning school counseling programs with these Tier 2 supports and sharing numerous examples of this alignment.

DESCRIPTION: TIER 2 SUPPORTS

Tier 2 supports are put in place when data indicates students may have elevated needs and require additional support beyond what is provided at Tier 1. When data indicates elevated needs, it is critical to examine Tier 1 systems and staff practices using root-cause analysis as described in Chapter 2. This examination can occur during a dedicated Tier 2 team meeting or be integrated into the Tier 2 data-based decision-making process.

For example, after gathering data from multiple sources, the Tier 2 team can reflect on the following questions when examining Tier 1 systems and staff practices:

- Asking why (e.g., Why is this concern happening?)
- Asking what (e.g., What are potential causes? What trends do you notice?)

After reflecting on these questions, the Tier 2 team can determine the level of intervention needed (e.g., system-, staff- or student-level intervention).

After addressing any system- or staff-level issues resulting from the root-cause analysis, the Tier 2 team can focus on student-level interventions. For Tier 2 supports to be effective, foundational systems and practices need to be in place, including (a) a system for equitably identifying students in need of Tier 2 supports, (b) readily available evidence-based and culturally sustaining small-group supports and (c) a system for monitoring students' progress and making data-based decisions to continue, modify or fade Tier 2 supports.

Identifying Students for Tier 2 Supports

To highlight the importance of systematically and equitably identifying students in need of Tier 2 supports, consider the following two scenarios:

Scenario 1: Students are typically referred for Tier 2 supports in two ways. In the first case, students who are disruptive in class are sent to the office. As a result, the administrator may refer the student to the school counselor for an individual or small-group Tier 2 support. Additionally, students are also referred by school staff, who email, call or stop the school counselor's office after school.

Scenario 2: The Tier 2 team continually collects and analyzes a variety of data (e.g., office referrals, requests for assistance, universal screening). When data indicates students have elevated needs, Tier 1 systems and staff practices are examined using root-cause analysis. After warranted changes have been made, to ensure that Tier 1 systems and staff practices are implemented with fidelity and in a culturally sustaining way, the Tier 2 team leads the process of identifying students' needs and an evidence-based and culturally sustaining support that is most likely to meet those needs.

Questions for Review and Discussion:

Which scenario would be most successful in efficiently, equitably and effectively identifying students who have elevated needs and determining what supports students need? Which school would you rather work for, scenario 1 or 2?

In scenario 1, the process for identifying students in need of Tier 2 supports is reactive: only identifying students who are "disruptive in class" and are regularly recognized by school staff. The first scenario is likely to result in two situations:

1. Students needing Tier 2 support may be overlooked (e.g., student with internalizing behaviors, students with emotional needs); thus these students may not receive needed supports.

2. Staff who are the most vocal, overwhelmed or comfortable making referrals will likely do most of the referring; therefore, a large number of students could be referred by a small number of staff. This reactive process also increases the likelihood that referrals are based on staffs' subjective perceptions and implicit biases, which could result in inequitable student identification and supports.

In scenario 2, the process for identifying students needing Tier 2 supports is proactive and systematic, using multiple sources of data to increase the effectiveness and comprehensiveness of the process. The second scenario is more likely to result in:

1. More students in the school being considered for Tier 2 supports (e.g., those with externalizing and internalizing behaviors).

2. Greater likelihood that school staff buys into the process of tiered supports because they have a predictable and systematic way to request assistance with challenging behaviors, and they know that the MTSS team, including the school counselor, is ready to assist in providing supports.

Identifying students in need of Tier 2 supports using a systematic, equitable and proactive process is an important first step to ensuring we are considering the needs of all our students. To make this process culturally sustaining, we need to examine and reflect on the data we collect to identify students. Much of the data used to identify students for Tier 2 supports is subjective (e.g., office referrals, requests for assistance) and based on school staffs' perception. This perception is influenced by previous experience, culture, implicit biases and, oftentimes, the complex emotions involved in working with students. To be intentional about the data we collect and use to identify students, we can build the strategies below into our Tier 2 process:

- **Disaggregate data** by race/ethnicity, disability and gender, and use disaggregated data to identify patterns of disproportionality in students, as well as patterns related to systems and practices that need to be changed to increase equity (e.g., are certain staff referring certain students? Are students referred because of a policy that may be a cultural mismatch for families?).
- **Collect and use multiple data sources** such as academic and discipline data, and student and family perspective and voice, to decrease the extent to which decisions are made based solely on one perspective (e.g., a referring staff member).
- **Dedicate resources** to developing staffs' knowledge and awareness of their own culture and the culture of students and families to inform interpretation of student behavior.
- **Engage students and families** in the development and implementation of the process for identifying students in need of Tier 2 supports (e.g., the parent/community/student council).

To organize multiple sources of data used to identify students in need of Tier 2 supports, Capistrano Unified developed a quick and easy existing school data inventory to organize their data and data-based decision-making guidelines. Next, let's take a look at the process for using this inventory; these efforts should be led by the MTSS team (including the school counselor as a member).

ACTIVITY: School Data

To organize school data and data-based decision-making guidelines for Tier 2 supports, MTSS teams can complete the following template using the following prompts:

1. What data do you currently use to identify students in need of Tier 2 supports? List the data items in the first column, or use the examples listed for you.
2. For each data point, what are data-based decision-making criteria indicating a student is proficient, at-risk or high-risk?
3. In the frequency column, list the time of year or frequency with which the MTSS team will collect and analyze the data.
4. After completing the table, reflect on the data the MTSS team currently uses. Is the data disaggregated? Do you collect and use multiple sources of data that include student and family perspective and voice? Have resources been allocated to developing staff cultural knowledge and awareness? Have students and families been engaged in the process used to identify students in need of Tier 2 supports? As a school counselor, how can you assist with this process?

5. After evaluating the current MTSS team's data collection and making goals for improvement, how will the MTSS team communicate this to staff and families?
6. How does the team make allowances for students who are transient in the community? How are students who enter after the first day of school welcomed and assessed? These may be students experiencing family transition, job losses, etc.

(modified from Capistrano Unified)

Existing School Data Inventory

Measure	Proficient Score	At-Risk	High Risk	Frequency
1. Office Discipline Referrals				☐ Quarter ☐ Trimester ☐ Semester ☐ End of the Year
2. Classroom Minors				☐ Quarter ☐ Trimester ☐ Semester ☐ End of the Year
3. Absences				☐ Quarter ☐ Trimester ☐ Semester ☐ End of the Year
4. Tardy				☐ Quarter ☐ Trimester ☐ Semester ☐ End of the Year
5. In-School Suspension				☐ Quarter ☐ Trimester ☐ Semester ☐ End of the Year
6. Out-of-School Suspension				☐ Quarter ☐ Trimester ☐ Semester ☐ End of the Year
7. Course Grades/GPA				☐ Quarter ☐ Trimester ☐ Semester ☐ End of the Year
8. Reading Inventory				☐ Quarter ☐ Trimester ☐ Semester ☐ End of the Year
9. Writing Assessment				☐ Quarter ☐ Trimester ☐ Semester ☐ End of the Year

It's important to note, there is no one way to collect and use data. As MTSS is a framework, there is flexibility to collect and use the data, based on each school's unique needs. At the same time, keep in mind that data-based decision-making guidelines for some types of data (e.g., office discipline referrals, academic scores) have been established by research. For example, the commonly used office discipline referral cut points of 0-1 (i.e., average), 2-5 (i.e., at-risk) and 6 or more (i.e., significant) have been validated by research (McIntosh et al., 2009; McIntosh et al., 2010).

Examples:
Capistrano Unified's completed existing school data inventory and Sugar Creek's Tier 2 inventory below illustrate the use of multiple sources of data and data-based decision-making guidelines indicating when a student should be considered for Tier 2 supports.

EXAMPLE: Existing School Data Inventory

Measure	Proficient Score	At-Risk	High Risk	Frequency
1. Office Discipline Referrals	0-1	2 or more	5 or more	Trimester
2. Classroom Minors	2-4	5 or more	15 or more	Trimester
3. Absences	< 10%/trimester	>10%-<20%/ trimester	>20%/trimester	Trimester
4. Tardy	< 4/trimester	4+ trimester	10/trimester	Trimester
5. In-School Suspension	0-1	2	4 or more	End of the year
6. Out-of-School Suspension	0	1	2	End of the year
7. Course Grades/GPA	2.5 or higher	D or F in any course	Ds or Fs in multiple courses	Semester
8. Reading Inventory	800+	799 or lower	599 or lower	Trimester
9. Writing Assessment	3 or 4	2	NS; 1	Trimester

Tier 2 Inventory Sugar Creek

Type of Intervention	Data Rule	How This Meets Student Need
Check-In/ Check-Out	▪ 2 or more ODRs in a month OR ten or more minors ▪ Progress monitoring tool for other Tier 2 interventions ▪ Function of behavior is to obtain attention OR lagging skills	▪ Increased student feedback ▪ Increased adult attention ▪ Increased communication with parents/guardian
Mentoring	▪ Documented internalizing behaviors OR ▪ 2 or more ODRs in a month OR 10 or more minors AND ▪ Function of behavior is to obtain attention	▪ Increased adult attention
Social Academic Instructional Group	▪ 2 or more ODRs in a month OR ten or more minors AND ▪ Function of behavior is lagging skills	▪ Targeted, more intensive, teaching of skill ▪ Increased feedback ▪ Increased communication with parents/guardian

Targeted and Small-Group Supports

Once the MTSS team has developed a systematic, equitable and proactive process to identify students in need Tier 2 supports, the next step is implementing evidence-based and culturally sustaining supports for students. Because the purpose of Tier 2 supports is to meet students' elevated needs, these supports typically involve smaller groups of students. Therefore, Tier 2 supports should align with students' needs (i.e., skill acquisition, skill practice, adult attention, peer attention, etc.) and be culturally sustaining in nature (e.g., shown to be effective with the intended student population, students and families reflected in the supports).

Too often, students who need support beyond Tier 1 are put in a small group or met with individually without a plan for how the school staff can address student standards, develop goals, use evidence-based strategies or curriculum, or monitor progress with data. Accessing, reviewing and implementing evidence-based and culturally sustaining Tier 2 supports may seem like a daunting task. However, we owe it to our students to provide supports that have been shown to have a positive impact on students through research and that can be implemented by educators with typical resources. Fortunately, there are a growing number of evidence-based Tier 2 supports. Further, MTSS teams can utilize any Tier 1 evidence-based curricula to re-teach skills for students needing Tier 2 support. With that said, intentional efforts need to be made to provide these evidence-based Tier 2 supports in a culturally sustaining way. The following practices should be integral to Tier 2 support implementation. For more in-depth descriptions of these practices, see Leverson et al. (2019), Chaparro et al. (2015), McIntosh et al., (2018) and Paris & Alim (2017).

- Ensure students, families, community are understood, validated, reflected.
- Align expectations with culturally sustaining Tier 1 expectations (Leverson et al., 2019).
- Provide engaging small-group instruction, i.e., perpetuates/fosters student culture (Paris & Alim, 2017), multiple opportunities to respond, performance feedback (Chaparro et al., 2015).
- Set goals that communicate high expectations (i.e., goal behaviors, grades, scores on feedback forms, etc.)
- Collaborate with teachers (e.g., strategies for neutralizing implicit bias when facing challenging student behaviors; McIntosh et al., 2018).
- Collaborate with families in multiple languages and modes.

If you or a loved one had an illness and required treatment, what would you want to see in the treatment process? How would you want the medical staff to communicate and collaborate with you before, during and after the treatment? Would you want medical doctors to prescribe a treatment because they liked the treatment? Or because the treatment underwent rigorous clinical trials and was proven to successfully treat the illness? These are similar questions we should ask ourselves when we work with students and families during the Tier 2 process. Similarly, we want to choose educational supports based on evidence and data and that sustain students' culture.

Evidence-based Practices: Tier 2

Following is a sample of evidence-based practices commonly used in Tier 2. These evidence-based practices can be used as a resource, as you reflect on what Tier 2 supports you may need to meet your students' needs. For a more exhaustive review, see Olsen (2019) and Mariani and Perhay Kuba (2019).

Skills for Social and Academic Success: Designed to support students in small groups who experience social anxiety within a school system. Utilizes real-life social situations and input from parents, teachers and peers.

Coping Cat: A cognitive behavioral treatment for children ages 7–14. Designed for children and adolescents dealing with anxiety who may have a diagnosis of generalized anxiety disorder, social phobia or separation anxiety disorder. Includes coping skills training, gradual exposure to anxiety-inducing scenarios and homework assignments focused on helping students recognize and analyze anxious feelings while developing strategies to cope with anxiety-provoking situations.

The Incredible Years Social Skills and Problem-Solving Curriculum: Designed for children (ages 0–12) with challenging behaviors and focuses on building social/emotional skills. Lessons cover recognizing and understanding feelings, getting along with friends, anger management, problem solving and behavior at school. Parent training programs focus on positive discipline, promoting learning and development, and involvement in children's life at school.

Why Try: Curriculum that engages students with Tiers 2 and 3 needs in a series of 10 visual analogies that teach important life skills (e.g., decisions have consequences, dealing with peer pressure, obeying laws and rules, plugging into support systems). Can be taught in an hour-long small group session or in a 10-minute homeroom environment.

Check-In/Check-Out – Practice: Designed to help students improve classroom behaviors through motivation. The student works on three to four target behaviors that have become barriers to learning (i.e. asking for help, completing classwork, etc.). Students are given feedback on those specific behaviors throughout the day and assigned points (1, 2 or 3). Daily progress reports are typically sent home for review and signature.

ACTIVITY: Tier 2 Inventory

As the MTSS team develops or fine tunes the Tier 2 supports, schedule time to take inventory of the existing Tier 2 supports using the prompts below:

1. What Tier 2 supports does the school currently have in place?
2. Are the Tier 2 supports evidence-based and culturally sustaining? How do you know?
3. Based on the current Tier 2 supports, what more is needed?
4. Based on the answers to these first three questions, create an action plan for next steps.

Once the MTSS team completes the activity above, the team can use the resources provided in this chapter to identify evidence-based and culturally sustaining Tier 2 supports to add to what they are currently doing. Finally, the team can organize and document Tier 2 supports so the supports can be quickly referenced and easily shared. Stamford School's Tier 2 intervention index, Kern High School District's targeted intervention skill quick sort, targeted intervention function quick sort and Capistrano Unified's Tier 2 targeted intervention reference guide highlight different approaches teams can use to organize their Tier 2 supports.

Tier 2 Intervention Index

Literacy				
Intervention	Description	Entrance Criteria	Exit Criteria	Interventionist
Example: *Academic Enrichment Class*	*Addresses gaps in literacy skills using Read 180*	*Reading Inventory grade level 2+ years below proficiency*	*Proficiency on Reading Inventory*	*Classroom Teacher, Other Literacy Support Specialist*

Math				
Intervention	Description	Entrance Criteria	Exit Criteria	Interventionist
Example: *Academic Enrichment Class*	*Addresses gaps in literacy skills using Math 180*	*Math Inventory grade level 2+ years below proficiency*	*Proficiency on Math Inventory*	*Classroom Teacher, Interventionist*

Social-Emotional /Behavior				
Intervention	Description	Entrance Criteria	Exit Criteria	Interventionist
Example: *Check-In Check-Out*	*Used to reduce chronic, low-level behaviors*	*2-5 office discipline referrals by end of October*	*Daily goal of 75% of possible points met for more than 80% of days in 8-week period*	*Classroom Teacher, Check-In Check-Out Coach*

Targeted Intervention Skill Quick Sort

SKILL	Check-In/ Check-Out	Social Skills Group	Grief Group	Mentoring	Forward Thinking	Restorative Conference/ Mediation	ART	Why Try	CAT Project	Brief Intervention
Attentional Control	✓				✓			✓		✓
Planning skills								✓		
Inhibitory Control	✓				✓			✓		✓
Cognitive Flexibility					✓			✓		
Emotional Knowledge and Expression	✓	✓	✓	✓	✓	✓		✓	✓	
Emotional and Behavioral Regulation	✓	✓	✓		✓	✓	✓	✓	✓	
Empathy/ Perspective Taking		✓	✓	✓	✓	✓	✓	✓	✓	
Understanding Social Cues		✓			✓					
Conflict Resolution/ Social-Problem Solving					✓	✓	✓			
Prosocial/ Cooperative Behavior	✓	✓		✓	✓	✓	✓	✓		
Character		✓		✓	✓	✓		✓		✓
Mindset		✓						✓	✓	✓
Sense of Belonging	✓		✓	✓		✓		✓	✓	

Targeted Intervention Function Quick Sort

	Check-In/ Check-Out	Social Skills Group	Grief Group	Mentoring	Forward Thinking	Restorative Conference/ Mediation	ART	Why Try	CAT Project	Brief Intervention
Increases opportunities for positive adult attention	✓	✓		✓	✓			✓		
Increases opportunities for positive peer attention		✓			✓	✓				
Promotes a positive, encouraging adult relationship	✓		✓	✓	✓			✓		
Teaches replacement behaviors and/or skills	✓	✓	✓				✓		✓	
Teaches problem solving		✓	✓	✓	✓	✓	✓	✓	✓	
Increases precorrection, prompts and structure		✓			✓		✓	✓	✓	
Monitors risk factors				✓	✓		✓	✓		
Provides access to choice of alternatives/ activities		✓	✓		✓	✓	✓			
Facilitates self-monitoring	✓	✓	✓		✓	✓			✓	
Increases opportunity for stronger incentives/ positive reinforcement	✓			✓		✓		✓		
Supports student at risk for substance abuse				✓	✓					✓

Chaparral Elementary Tier II Targeted Intervention Reference Guide

Evidence Based Practice	Social Skills Group	Behavior/Self-Regulation Group	Skills for Learning Group	Reading Intervention Club	Homework Club	CICO	Individual Counseling
Access to Adult Attention	Yes	Yes	Yes	Yes	Yes	Yes	Yes
Access to Peer Attention	Yes	Yes	Yes	Yes	Yes		
Access to Choice of Alternatives/Activities	Yes	Yes	Yes	Yes	Yes	Yes	Yes
Option for Avoiding Aversive Activities	Yes	Yes	Yes			Yes	Yes
Option for Avoiding Aversive Social Peer/ Adult Attention						Yes	Yes
Structural Prompts for What To Do Throughout the Day	Yes	Yes	Yes			Yes	Yes
At Least 5 Times During the Day When Positive Feedback is Set Up						Yes	
A School-Home Communication System						Yes	
Opportunity for Adaptation into a Self-Management System	Yes	Yes	Yes	Yes	Yes	Yes	Yes

Monitoring Student Progress

Developing a system for identifying students in need of Tier 2 supports and providing efficient, equitable, evidence-based and culturally sustaining Tier 2 supports are essential to the Tier 2 process. However, if we stop there, we have no way of knowing if our Tier 2 supports have an impact on students. To be sure, we need an ongoing system for monitoring students' progress and making data-based decisions. Typically, MTSS teams oversee Tier 2 data procedures, which can be collected on a daily or weekly basis and reviewed at least every two weeks.

Examples:

Milwaukee Public Schools uses the following daily progress reports to monitor students' progress in Tier 2 supports. For example, students participating in check-in/check-out identify goal behaviors collaboratively with the check-in/check-out coordinator. These goal behaviors are written on the daily progress report. Students start their day by checking in with the coordinator to review goal behaviors and set a positive tone. Throughout the day, students use the daily progress report to check in with their teachers to receive feedback on their goal behaviors, and feedback is captured on the daily progress report in the form of points. At the end of the day, students meet with the check-in/check-out coordinator to review the daily progress report, discuss feedback and record the points for the day. To monitor student progress, the MTSS team reviews daily progress report point totals during weekly or biweekly meetings to determine if the intervention is effective. Daily progress reports can also be used in a similar way for other Tier 2 small-group interventions such as school-counselor-led small groups.

Daily Progress Report: Curtin Leadership Academy

Name: ______________________________ Date: ______________

3 = WOW!
2 = OK
1 = Tough Time

Goals	7:45-Recess	Recess-Lunch	Lunch-Recess	Recess-2:35
Be Safe	1 2 3	1 2 3	1 2 3	1 2 3
Be Respectful	1 2 3	1 2 3	1 2 3	1 2 3
Be Responsible	1 2 3	1 2 3	1 2 3	1 2 3
Be a Positive Leader	1 2 3	1 2 3	1 2 3	1 2 3
Total Points				
Teacher Initials				

Total Points = __________ Points Possible = __________

Teacher Comments: Way to be: ______________________________

Name: ______________________________ Date: ______________

_____ I met my goal today! _____ I had a tough day.

One thing I did really well today was ______________________________.

Something I will work on tomorrow is ______________________________.

Parent/Guardian Signature: ______________________________

Comments:

Burbank Bear Tracking System – Check-In Check-Out
Bears Earning Awesome Results!

Student name: ______________________________ Date: __________

Staff mentor: ______________________________ **Goal for Today: 80%**

Rules "The 3 B's"	Optional–put time or subject area here → **Expectations**	**Block 1**	**Block 2**	**Block 3**	**Block 4**	**Block 5**
BE RESPONSIBLE	Had materials	1 2 3	1 2 3	1 2 3	1 2 3	1 2 3
	Was in the right place at the right time	1 2 3	1 2 3	1 2 3	1 2 3	1 2 3
	Completed work (including homework)	1 2 3	1 2 3	1 2 3	1 2 3	1 2 3
BE RESPECTFUL	Stayed in seat	1 2 3	1 2 3	1 2 3	1 2 3	1 2 3
	Spoke respectfully Spoke at appropriate times	1 2 3	1 2 3	1 2 3	1 2 3	1 2 3
BE SAFE	Kept hands, feet and objects to self	1 2 3	1 2 3	1 2 3	1 2 3	1 2 3
	Teacher Initials →					

KEY 1 = No 2 = Somewhat 3 = Yes!!

Points earned: _____ out of _____

Percentage earned: _____% Student Signature: ______________________

Met Goal: _____Yes _____No Parent Signature: ______________________

CICO Daily Progress Report

Name ______________________ 3 = Great Points received ______________

Date ______________________ 2 = Almost Points possible ______________

Goal ______________________ 1 = Try Again Daily Goal met? Yes No

Goals:	Period 1	Period 2	Period 3	Period 4	Period 5	Period 6	Period 7
1. Be Safe (Keep hands, feet and objects to self.)							
2. Be Respectful (Use kind words and actions.)							
3. Be Responsible (Be on task/follow directions.)							
4. Homework							
Teacher Initials							

Comments: ____

Parent Signature: ______________________

SAIG Daily Progress Report

Name ______________________ 3 = Great Points received ______________

Date ______________________ 2 = Almost Points possible ______________

Goal ______________________ 1 = Try Again Daily Goal met? Yes No

Goals:	Period 1	Period 2	Period 3	Period 4	Period 5	Period 6	Period 7
1. **Be Safe** (Keep hands, feet and objects to self.)							
2. **Be Respectful** ■ Use "I" messages with feeling words ■ Use problem solving skills (define problem, look at all solutions, pick one and use it) ■ Use appropriate words and tone for situation (friendly vs. assertive)							
3. **Be Responsible** ■ Set a friendship goal for the day/week ■ Use positive self-talk ■ Ask to join a friend/group ■ Ask for help							
4. **Homework**							
Teacher Initials							

Comments: ____

Parent Signature: ______________________

Milwaukee Public Schools' Student Goal Monitoring

Student Name: ____

Week:1 **Personal Goal:**	Circle Personal Score: **1** (struggled to obtain this goal) **2** (made some progress towards obtaining this goal, but more progress needed) **3** (was successful in obtaining this goal)	One area I was successful with this goal:	One area I need to improve with this goal:
Week:2 **Personal Goal:**	Circle Personal Score: **1** (struggled to obtain this goal) **2** (made some progress towards obtaining this goal, but more progress needed) **3** (was successful in obtaining this goal)	One area I was successful with this goal:	One area I need to improve with this goal:
Week:3 **Personal Goal:**	Circle Personal Score: **1** (struggled to obtain this goal) **2** (made some progress towards obtaining this goal, but more progress needed) **3** (was successful in obtaining this goal)	One area I was successful with this goal:	One area I need to improve with this goal:
Week:4 **Personal Goal:**	Circle Personal Score: **1** (struggled to obtain this goal) **2** (made some progress towards obtaining this goal, but more progress needed) **3** (was successful in obtaining this goal)	One area I was successful with this goal:	One area I need to improve with this goal:
Week:5 **Personal Goal:**	Circle Personal Score: **1** (struggled to obtain this goal) **2** (made some progress towards obtaining this goal, but more progress needed) **3** (was successful in obtaining this goal)	One area I was successful with this goal:	One area I need to improve with this goal:

Week:6 **Personal Goal:**	Circle Personal Score: **1** (struggled to obtain this goal) **2** (made some progress towards obtaining this goal, but more progress needed) **3** (was successful in obtaining this goal)	One area I was successful with this goal:	One area I need to improve with this goal:
Week:7 **Personal Goal:**	Circle Personal Score: **1** (struggled to obtain this goal) **2** (made some progress towards obtaining this goal, but more progress needed) **3** (was successful in obtaining this goal)	One area I was successful with this goal:	One area I need to improve with this goal:
Week:8 **Personal Goal:**	Circle Personal Score: **1** (struggled to obtain this goal) **2** (made some progress towards obtaining this goal, but more progress needed) **3** (was successful in obtaining this goal)	One area I was successful with this goal:	One area I need to improve with this goal:
Week:9 **Personal Goal:**	Circle Personal Score: **1** (struggled to obtain this goal) **2** (made some progress towards obtaining this goal, but more progress needed) **3** (was successful in obtaining this goal)	One area I was successful with this goal:	One area I need to improve with this goal:

Students do not continue with Tier 2 supports forever. How do we know when a student has "graduated" or no longer needs Tier 2 supports? Many MTSS teams have formal and informal strategies for determining if a Tier 2 support is effective and when students should discontinue participation. For instance, a formal process organized into a decision-making process might involve the steps in the table below, when considering these two scenarios. Less formally, perhaps all that is needed to discontinue Tier 2 supports is the MTSS team engaging in a systematic process (i.e., organized, efficient, regular communication) discussing, clarifying and documenting the process used for each Tier 2 support.

Scenario 1: Student Responds to Supports	Scenario 2: Student Does Not Respond to Supports
Supports implemented for four weeks	Supports implemented for four weeks
Data is collected	Data is collected
Student is responding to support	Student is not responding to support
Supports are implemented for another four weeks	MTSS team assesses if supports are good fit for student (e.g. cultural fit, needs accurately identified) Team identifies systems and staff practices that are barriers to student success and need improvement (e.g., fidelity of implementation) Student and family perspective and voice are heard and incorporated
Data is collected	After adjustments, supports implemented another four weeks
Supports are faded	Data is collected
	Student is not responding to support
	Advance for referrals to Tier 3 individualized, intensive supports

Questions for Review and Discussion:

The MTSS team can use the prompts below to discuss developing a system for monitoring student progress:

1. Do we monitor student progress for all Tier 2 supports?
    - If not, which Tier 2 supports do we need to monitor or monitor more effectively?
    - How often do we monitor student progress?

2. Do we use data to make decisions about continuing, modifying or fading Tier 2 supports?
    - If so, what data is used for each Tier 2 support?
    - Is there other data we need (e.g., student and family perspective and voice)? If so, how do we get the data?
    - Do we have data-based decision-making guidelines rules for our Tier 2 supports?

3. Do we document our process for monitoring students' progress and making data-based decisions about Tier 2 supports? Has the process been shared with all staff? Has the process been informed by students and families?

What if students are not successful with a range of Tier 2 supports over time? How should the MTSS team decide if Tier 3 supports are needed? Chapter Six: Tier 3, addresses this topic.

Bringing it all Together: As the MTSS team develops and fine-tunes the Tier 2 support systems and practices discussed so far, it's important to document the process. This increases organization, predictability and sustainability for the MTSS team and allows the process to be easily shared with staff and stakeholders. The following examples from Kern High School District and Culver City illustrate their Tier 2 supports process. In the Kern process, reviewing multiple sources of data, providing evidence-based Tier 2 interventions and using data to make decisions are emphasized, while the Culver City process highlights the importance of ensuring Tier 1 supports are examined for effectiveness and illustrates Tier 2 supports in the context of the other tiers.

KHSD PBIS Flowchart for Tier II Support

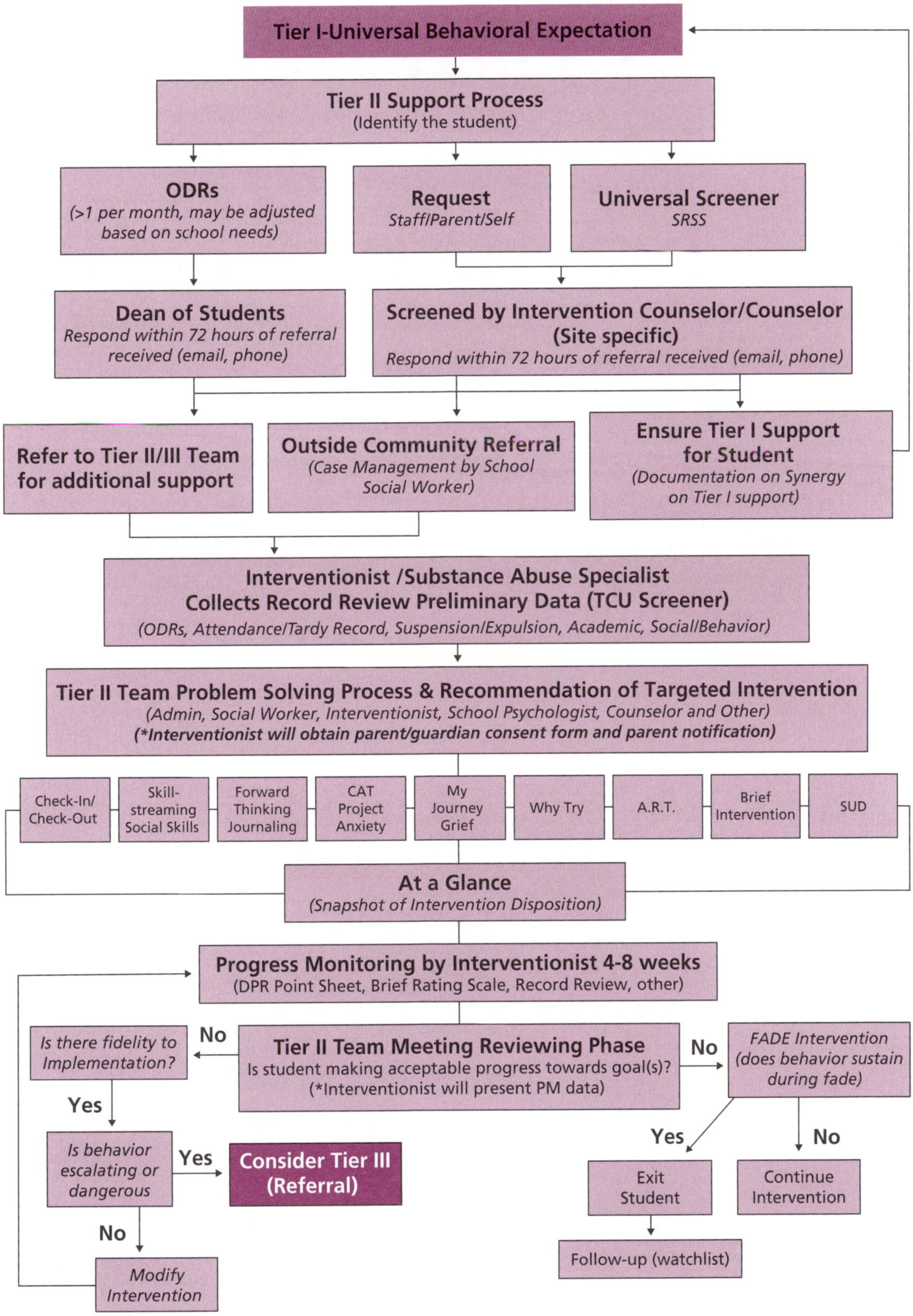

CCUSD Flowchart for Tiered Support and Intervention

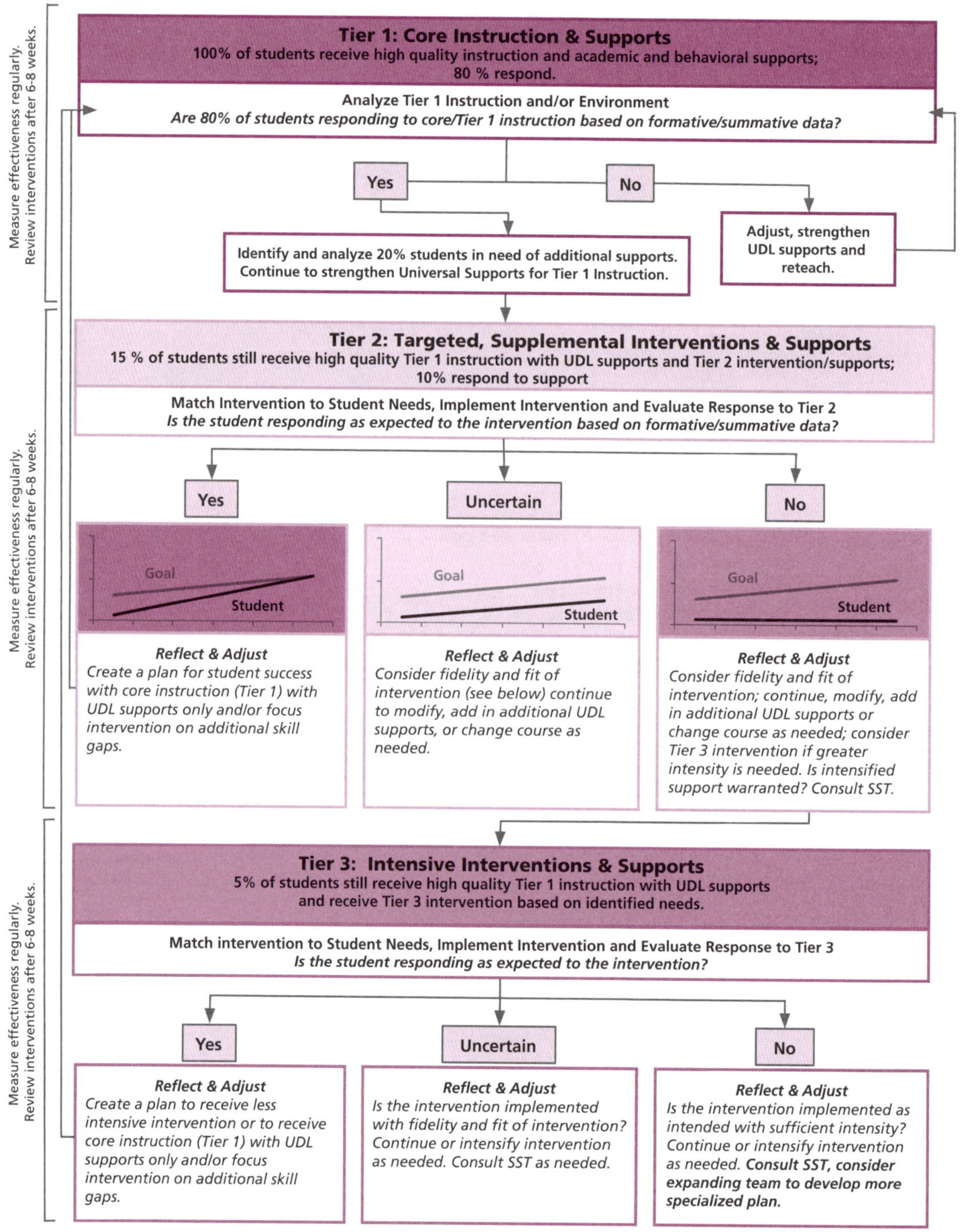

Fidelity: *Has the intervention been implement as intended?* Consider delivery, quality, student engagement, and attendance.
Fit: *Is the intervention matched appropriately to students need?*

ACTIVITY: Tier 2 Documentation

To document your school's Tier 2 supports process, your MTSS team can develop a visual representation that includes the following steps:

- a system for identifying students in need of Tier 2 supports
- readily available evidence-based and culturally sustaining targeted and small-group supports
- a system for monitoring students' progress and making data-based decisions.

This document serves as a map or flowchart to guide the team along the Tier 2 process. For instance, the first part should include a section that lists a variety of data that will be collected and how that data will be analyzed with a focus on equity. The second section should list available evidence-based and culturally sustaining Tier 2 supports. Think of this section as a menu of supports the team can use to decide what supports to provide students. The last section should include information to help the team make data-based decisions about systems, staff practices and the effectiveness of the intervention, including:

- What systems and staff practices are barriers to student success?
- Are supports implemented with fidelity?
- How long will the support be provided?
- When will data be collected?
- What are the data-based decision-making guidelines that will help the team determine to continue, modify or fade a support?
- How can your MTSS team document and communicate the process with all staff, students, families and stakeholders to increase awareness, input and buy-in?

Now that we've provided background information on Tier 2 supports, describing how the MTSS team facilitates these processes, let's talk about alignment. How can school counselors align their work, implementing the ASCA National Model, with these Tier 2 supports, to increase their efficiency and effectiveness?

DESCRIPTION: SCHOOL COUNSELORS' ROLE IN TIER 2

The Deliver component of the ASCA National Model is action-oriented and focuses on the supports school counselors provide for students, which are particularly important in the context of Tier 2 of the MTSS framework. When students need additional support beyond what all students receive (Tier 1), school counselors operate within the Deliver component to provide Tier 2 supports to some students as an intervener and supporter. Specifically, at Tier 2, school counselors provide:

- Individual and group supports: instruction, counseling, advising (intervener)
- Consultation and collaboration with teachers, staff, parents and community providers (supporter)

VOICES FROM THE FIELD:

As an administrator for Kern High School district said, "The school counselors must play an active role in the MTSS implementation process. Since they play such an integral role in the supports provided to students, their input and perspective have helped shape the detailed processes we use in how students are referred, discussed and matched with interventions that best fit student need."

Direct Services/Intervener:

As an intervener, school counselors provide evidence-based and culturally sustaining Tier 2 supports including (a) individual and small-group instruction, (b) counseling and (c) advisement.

- **Instruction:** School counselors use individual and small-group instruction to deliver content and teach need-based skills, as well as to provide opportunities for practice, feedback and to help students improve.
- **Counseling:** As an intervener, school counselors have a unique skillset to provide time-bound individual and small-group counseling to support students when they experience situations that impede their success (e.g., transitions, stress, crisis, academic, career, social/emotional problems, etc.). Individual and small-group counseling are based on counseling theory and techniques relevant and effective in school settings and intended for students who have elevated needs best met through short-term counseling. Compared with instruction, counseling is more process-focused rather than content-focused.
- **Advisement:** School counselors use individual and small-group advisement to help students explore opportunities, make decisions and set goals for their future. The advisement process can be used as a Tier 2 support by collecting academic and career/college assessment data and engaging students in goal setting.

Further, these school counseling Tier 2 individual and small-group supports are aligned with Tier 1 schoolwide expectations, as well as the ASCA Mindsets & Behaviors and the academic, career and social/emotional domains. For instance, school counselors can use the MTSS schoolwide expectations to generate group norms for individual and small-group instruction and counseling. To make the expectations culturally sustaining for individual students and groups of students, school counselors can facilitate conversations with students and families about what their expectations are at home and integrate home expectations with school expectations. Further, school counselors, students and families can explore how expectations at school and home may differ and how to navigate those differences.

Next, MTSS-generated outcome data could be used to identify students with elevated needs who could be potential candidates for these individual and small-group supports. Thus, the MTSS data can inform school counselors' student outcome goals, their action plans and their direct supports. In another role as an intervener, school counselors can create and then participate in check-in/check-out with students, discussing their daily, time-bound Tier 2 behavior plans. Last, these school-counselor-led Tier 2 supports are integrated into schools' MTSS framework alongside other Tier 2 supports provided by a wealth of other school staff and often in collaboration with the MTSS team.

Through these individual and small-group supports, school counselors can deliver several of the Tier 2 interventions, including the evidence-based practices mentioned previously in this chapter, as highlighted in the examples below.

Examples:

Social Academic Instructional Groups (Milwaukee Public Schools): A social academic instructional group (SAIG) is a type of small group used to meet the needs of students requiring Tier 2 supports. As such, the SAIG curriculum can be used as a resource for school counselors delivering small-group instruction to support students with building academic and social/emotional skills. In this example, Milwaukee Public Schools developed a SAIG, drawing from evidence-based curriculum, such as Second Step. The Milwaukee Public Schools' SAIG curriculum has three-units (e.g., academic, emotion management and attendance) with nine lesson plans per unit, and is taught in a small-group setting to support students' skill development. Key features of SAIGs, in general, typically include:

- Teaches students academic, emotion management, and attendance and responsible behavior skills
- Developed in collaboration with multiple stakeholders across the district, including school counselors
- Draws from evidence-based practices
- Encompasses elementary, middle and high school levels
- Organized into nine small-group lesson plans per unit
- Exemplifies how small-group instruction can be aligned with Tier 2 of the MTSS framework

Additional information about the SAIG curriculum can also be found on the resource list at the end of the chapter.

Check-In/Check-Out (CICO): CICO is a widely implemented and researched group-oriented Tier 2 support for students who are not responding to Tier 1 supports. Key features include:

- Increased positive adult contact
- Frequent feedback on goal behavior that is aligned with schoolwide expectations
- Positive reinforcement for meeting goals
- Embedded social skills instruction
- Individual progress monitored by a daily progress report
- Group progress reviewed at least bi-weekly

Although CICO is efficient and relatively simple to maintain once it is in place, it requires some initial setup, staff training and planning. To learn more about CICO, see the resource list at the end of the chapter.

Aligning Tier 2 Supports with Tier 1 Schoolwide Expectations (Culver City): When school counselors deliver small-group instruction and counseling as well as advisement, they use an adapted schoolwide behavior matrix to develop small-group behavior expectations. Developing small-group behavior expectations with students collaboratively sets the tone for the group, increases student buy-in and reinforces schoolwide expectations.

Culver City Middle School Panther Behavior Expectations

	Small Group Entrance and Exit	Small Group Instruction	Small Group Skills Practice
Prepared & organized	■ Be aware of the time ■ Go directly to your destination ■ Bring materials	■ Be prepared to share update on goal behavior ■ Be prepared to share your ideas ■ Be ready to learn	■ Be prepared to participate in skills practice ■ Stay organized by knowing your skills practice role
Respectful	■ Follow office procedures to get to school counselor's office	■ Use an appropriate voice and language ■ Be respectful of others	■ Cooperate with group members ■ Respect other people's personal belongings and space
Integrity	■ Come to all scheduled group meetings ■ Come to group with a positive attitude	■ Be honest with group members	■ Be a good model for the skills we are learning
Diligent & punctual	■ Arrive on time ■ Complete group "homework" before coming to group	■ Use group time effectively	■ Stay focused during skills practice ■ Follow start and stop prompts from school counselor
Engaged	■ Arrive ready to participate in group activities ■ Know what your group "homework" is before leaving group	■ Ask questions ■ Pay attention to your teachers and classmates	■ Actively participate ■ Respond appropriately

Indirect Services/Supporter:

The role of supporter is particularly critical in the context of Tier 2 supports. Delivering and progress monitoring Tier 2 supports often involves the MTSS team, students' teachers and family, and other school staff who interact with the student on a daily basis to teach and reinforce goal behaviors. Because of the number of people involved in MTSS, and Tier 2 supports specifically, school counselors can use their consultation and collaboration skills to provide background information, referrals and expertise (e.g., counseling, knowledge of youth development, data, mental health, etc.) and ensure systems and practices are equitable and effective for students receiving the supports.

- **Consultation:** School counselors use consultation to provide information and offer recommendations to school staff who are working directly with students receiving Tier 2 supports. In other words, using consultation, school counselors work with others on behalf of students. In this case, school counselors may offer consultation regarding how school staff can implement a Tier 2 support with fidelity, collect data or problem solve challenging situations. School counselors may also consult with classroom teachers pertaining to reinforcing school-counselor-led small-group goals or giving students feedback on their group daily progress report goals. In addition to school staff, consultation with families should involve school counselors seeking out culturally sustaining strategies that families use to support their student at home. These strategies can be incorporated into Tier 2 supports.

- **Collaboration:** School counselors collaborate by working with school staff, teachers, administrators, families and community partners to effectively deliver Tier 2 supports to students. This includes teaming and partnering, participating in school and district committees and engaging families in discussion and workshops. For example, school counselors should be an integral part of the MTSS Tier 2 team because of their use of data-informed decisions, knowledge and skills in delivering individual and group supports and overall leadership role in the school. Thus, they can assist the MTSS team in identifying students for services, monitoring students' progress, determining future steps and ensuring the Tier 2 process is implemented with equity.

School counselors can also participate in district-level MTSS committees to contribute their knowledge and skills to improve MTSS implementation, such as ensuring schools across the district have a defined Tier 2 process and students have access to evidence-based, culturally sustaining Tier 2 supports. Finally, as a supporter, school counselors can collaborate with families to engage in discussion about the Tier 2 process and supports and provide information and workshops in partnership with families. This collaboration is an opportunity to incorporate students' and families' culture into the Tier 2 process and Tier 2 supports. For example, school counselors can learn effective strategies and cultural norms used by parents at home that can be incorporated into small-group goals and activities. When parent collaboration is done consistently, a line of communication is opened up, and the Tier 2 process is demystified for parents with students who participate in Tier 2 supports or may do so in the future.

Through consultation and collaboration, school counselors work with stakeholders to ensure students have equitable access to Tier 2 supports and Tier 2 supports are developed and delivered with fidelity, as highlighted in the following examples.

Consultation with classroom teachers: Milwaukee Public School school counselors use the Tier 2 Teacher Checklist below to consult with teachers, as the teacher works with their students participating in CICO.

PBIS Tier 2 Teacher Checklist

- ☐ Greet student positively in the morning, take DPR card, and prompt student
  - Things you may say: "It's great to see you today! Let's have a great day! I bet you can meet you goal today!"
- ☐ At the time periods listed on the DPR, rate student on the goals based on the following scale: 3 pts = great day, 2 pt = so-so day, 1 pts = tough day AND initial your rating. See guideline below for how to assign points...
  - Note: You may have to ask lunch/recess monitors regarding students' behavior during that time
  - Total points will be calculated by student with "mentor" and the DPR card will be taken home for parent signature. When it is convenient for you, there is additional space to write notes for the parent(s) to review.
- ☐ Guidelines for giving points...
  - Give a 3 if the student meets the expectation
  - Give a 2 if the student had brief incidents of inappropriate behavior and had been warned twice (individually) and then repeated an incident of the behavior (i.e. after asking to be safe twice, student engages in unsafe behavior, then rate as 2)
  - Give a 1 if the student has repeated instances (3 or more) of not following directions, being off-task repeatedly, or doing something more serious, such as fighting
    - Note: A score of "1" should be given sparingly, as this indicates serious concerns. If a student repeatedly receives "1," an additional intervention may be necessary for that student. Data from the DPR will be graphed and shared with you to determine whether this is needed. Please contact Ms. Pelsue if you have any concerns!!
- ☐ When circling ratings with student, give ***specific, positive feedback*** (should take less than <1 min)
  - "Given your behavior, you earned ... " "I'm so proud of you - you..."
  - "Look's like you had a rough time... I know you can do it tomorrow"
- ☐ At the end of the day, prompt student to check-out by sending them to their "mentor"
  - Again, ***stay positive*** – "I look forward to seeing you tomorrow!" "Remember to work on ... tomorrow!"
- ☐ If a student's mentor is absent, the classroom teacher will do the check in/check out with the student. Extra daily behavior report sheets will be provided to classroom teachers.

** IT IS VITAL THE DPR CARD BE COMPLETED EVERY DAY THE STUDENT IS PRESENT**

Check In-Check Out Trouble-Shooting Guide

1. **The student (or mentor) forgets to "check in" or "check out"**

   This is common, especially for younger students or during hectic times of a day. If the student forgets to check in or the student's mentor is absent, the classroom teacher may "check in-check out" the student. However, it is important that the student checks in with their mentor whenever possible. If the problem becomes consistent (2-3 days per week), contact Ms. Pelsue and we will come up with a plan.

2. **The student loses the DPR**

   Pick a place in the classroom to keep the DPR. You may also tape the DPR to the student's desk. Do not allow the student to carry the DPR to lunch or recess unless it is necessary. Start a new DPR (in your package) when a DPR is lost.

3. **The student "loses" the DPR if they are having a bad day**

   If during the day the student says that the DPR is lost after having a bad rating, begin to use a new DPR. If you remember the ratings that you previously gave, record on the new DPR. Keep the DPR with you for the rest of the day, but still briefly meet with the student to provide the ratings and feedback.

4. **The student arrives late to school**

   Begin a DPR (from your packet) and start when the student arrived. Note on the DPR if the student was absent for a specific rating period (i.e reading) by writing an "A" in that space for the rating period (i.e write an "A" under reading). When the student arrives, explain that you will start the DPR, and that they may turn in the DPR home report (from the previous day) during check out with their mentor.

5. **The student becomes angry and throws the DPR or rips it up**

   Discontinue the DPR for the day. Explain that having the DPR is a special privilege, and they must not destroy it. The student should still check out at the end of the day if possible. If this continues to be a problem, please let Ms. Pelsue know.

Collaboration through teaming and partnering: Loudoun County Public Schools' decision tree for school counselors below illustrates (a) how school counselors can collaborate with problem solving teams to plan, develop and make decisions about Tier 2 supports and (b) how collaboration can be used to align school counseling programs with MTSS.

Proactive and Responsive Decision Tree for School Counselors

Proactive: Using effective data (discipline, attendance, academic, perception) if a student is identified as needing additional support, the school counselor chooses to:
Responsive: Student is identified by staff, parents, administration, self or other students as needing additional support. After speaking with the referral source, student and reviewing appropriate data, the school counselor chooses to:

Provide **short-term individual** counseling support for students during times of:
- A transition
- Heightened stress
- Critical change
- Other situations impeding success

Identify problem, causes, potential consequences and benefits, alternative outcomes so student can make decisions and take appropriate action.

School counselor makes parents aware of the goals of the three sessions and explains the difference between appropriate short-term counseling and inappropriate longterm therapy.

Counselor designs sessions to promote academic, career, and or social/emotional development using counseling theories and techniques effective in the school setting. Progress is communicated with parents.

Provide **short-term group** counseling support for students during times of:
- A transition
- Heightened stress
- Critical change
- Other situations impeding success

Identify problem, causes, potential consequences and benefits, alternative outcomes so students can make decisions and take appropriate action.

School counselor makes parents/families aware of the need and goals of the group. School counselor gains parent permission using Loudoun County Public Schools group permission slip.

School counselor designs group to promote academic, career and or social/emotional development using counseling theories and techniques effective in the school setting (evidence-based when possible). School counselor monitors and communicates student progress.

Provide **check-in** support for students during times of:
- A transition
- Heightened stress
- Critical change
- Other situations impeding success

Identify problem, causes, potential consequences and benefits, alternative outcomes so they can make decisions and appropriate action.

Counselor makes parents/families aware of the of the students visits (after 3-same concern) and explains the roles and limitations of a school counselor.

Counselor can continue to check in with the student as a responsive service, with goal to provide brief strategies to help student reintegrate into normal schedule.

If student continues to need support after the above strategies/Interventions:

- Consult with team MTSS (Tier 2 Kid Talk)
- Make referral to appropriate school or community resource
- Consult school social worker or school psychologist
- Continue to check in with student as needed as a responsive service
- Keep parents and teachers aware of progress and concerns
- Review academic and discipline data to identify possible need for additional support (CST)
- Attempt a different intervention or strategy above
- Record necessary data and share with problem solving team

(Loudoun County Public Schools)

CASE STUDY EXAMPLE: SMALL-GROUP ADVISEMENT

After the MTSS team (including the school counselor) reviewed the schoolwide data and examined (e.g. using root-cause analysis) and made necessary changes to the school's system and staff practices, they created annual student outcome goals focusing on increasing ninth-grade students' career and college readiness.

Specifically, they aimed to increase (a) students' completion of academic and career plans, (b) students' achieving their ninth-grade plan goals, (c) students' connection between high school experiences and their plan's postsecondary goals and (d) on-time graduation. The MTSS team called these career- and college-readiness indicators. The MTSS team met with all the school counselors in the school to collaborate on ways the school counselors could address the career- and college-readiness indicators of developing the academic and career plans, exploring the connection between high school experiences and students' postsecondary goals and developing skills to plan for and monitor on-time graduation.

As a result of this meeting, the school counselors decided to use these indicators to develop and deliver classroom instruction (i.e., Tier 1) for all ninth-graders. To assess the lesson impact, the school counselors used a pre-/post-test survey to measure the content knowledge students gained and another pre-/post-test survey to measure students' career- and college-readiness self-efficacy. Based on the pre-/post-test survey data, the school counselors identified a small group of students who gained significantly less content knowledge than other students and had particularly low self-efficacy toward their career and college readiness. The school counselors developed a small advisement group (i.e., Tier 2) to support students in completing their academic and career plans in a more personalized and targeted way, discuss connections between high school experiences and postsecondary goals in a small-group setting and identify barriers to on-time graduation.

To enhance the group's effectiveness, school counselors consulted with families and community leaders from the students' neighborhoods who reflected the race/ethnicity, social class and gender of the students in the group. These family and community leaders, from a variety of career fields, met with students in the group to discuss how their high school experience connects to their postsecondary goals. The school counselors used the same pre-/post-test surveys to assess the impact of the small-group meetings.

Questions for Review and Discussion:

Consider the Tier 1 supports (e.g., classroom instruction lessons) offered in your district or school.

1. Similar to the school counselors in the example above, how can you align Tier 2 supports with Tier 1 supports you already have in place?
2. What direct and indirect supports do the school counselors in the example above conduct?
3. What data do you and the MTSS team need to collect and analyze to determine students in need of these Tier 2 supports?
4. Who is available to provide Tier 2 intervention? (School counselors, teachers, school social workers, school psychologists, etc.). What if the number of students in need of Tier 2 supports exceeds current staffing? Are there non-direct-service tasks that can be eliminated to make way for more intervention group time? How can we ensure those staff entrusted to provide Tier 2 interventions have adequate training?

5. How will Tier 2 supports supplement rather than simply repeat your Tier 1 supports?
6. Based on your responses to the questions above, document a brief action plan with steps to collect data, determine the Tier 2 supports needed to align with Tier 1 supports and develop the content and scope and sequence of the Tier 2 supports.

REFERENCES AND RESOURCES

Betters-Bubon, J., Kortemeier, H., & Smith-Durkin, S. (2019). Culturally sustaining MTSS: Advocating for equity for every student. In E. Goodman-Scott, J. Betters-Bubon, & P. Donohue (Eds.), *A school counselor's guide to Multi-tiered Systems of Support.* Routledge.

Chaparro, E. A., Nese, R. N. T., & McIntosh, L. (2015). *Examples of engaging instruction to increase equity in education.* OSEP Technical Assistance Center on Positive Behavioral Interventions and Supports. www.pbis.org.

Hatch, T., Kruger, A., Pablo, N., & Triplett, W. (2019). *Hatching Tier Two and Three Interventions in Your Elementary School Counseling Program.* Corwin.

Leverson, M., Smith, K., McIntosh, K., Rose, J., & Pinkelman, S. (2019). *PBIS cultural responsiveness field guide: Resources for trainers and coaches.* OSEP Technical Assistance Center on Positive Behavioral Interventions and Supports. www.pbis.org.

Mariani, M., & Perhay Kuba, S. (2019). Evidence-based practices across MTSS. In E. Goodman-Scott, J. Betters-Bubon, & P. Donohue (Eds.), *A school counselor's guide to multi-tiered systems of support.* New York, NY: Routledge.

McIntosh, K., Barnes, A., Eliason, B., & Morris, K. (2014). *Using discipline data within SWPBIS to identify and address disproportionality: A guide for school teams.* OSEP Technical Assistance Center on Positive Behavioral Interventions and Supports. www.pbis.org.

McIntosh, K., Campbell, A. L., Russell-Carter, D., & Zumbo, B. D. (2009). Concurrent validity of office discipline referrals and cut points used in schoolwide positive behavior support. *Behavior Disorders, 34*(2), 100-113.

McIntosh, K., Frank, J. L., & Spaulding, S. A. (2010). Establishing research-based trajectories of office discipline referrals for individual students. *School Psychology Review, 39*(3), 380-394.

McIntosh, K., Girvan, E. J., Horner, R. H., Smolkowski, K., & Sugai, G. (2018). *A 5-point intervention approach for enhancing equity in school discipline.* OSEP Technical Assistance Center on Positive Behavioral Interventions and Supports. www.pbis.org.

Milwaukee Public Schools. (2020, March 11th). *Social academic instruction groups.* Milwaukee Public Schools. https://mps.milwaukee.k12.wi.us/en/Families/Family-Services/Intervention---PBIS/SAIG-Curriculum.htm.

Northeast PBIS. (2020, March 11th). *Advanced tiers. Tier 2 School Team Training Workbook.* Northeast Positive Behavioral Interventions and Supports. https://nepbis.org/advanced-tiers/.

Ockerman, M. S., Mason, E. C. M., & Hollenbeck, A. F. (2012). Integrating RTI with school counseling programs: Being a proactive professional school counselor. *Journal of School Counseling, 10*(15). Retrieved from tp://jsc.montana.edu/articles/v10n15.pdf

Olsen, J. (2019). Tier 2: Providing increased supports for students with elevated needs. In E. Goodman-Scott, J. Betters-Bubon, & P. Donohue (Eds.), *A school counselor's guide to multi-tiered systems of support*. New York, NY: Routledge.
Paris, D., & Alim, H. S. (Eds.). (2017). *Culturally sustaining pedagogies: Teaching and learning for justice in a changing world*. Teachers College Press.

CHAPTER 6

Aligning Tier 3 Supports

Chapter 4 described the core features of Tier 1 supports and how to align school counseling programs with MTSS, at this universal level for all students. Chapter 5 focused on this alignment across Tier 2 supports for some students with elevated needs. This chapter addresses Tier 3 supports for few students with the most intensive needs and aligning school counseling programs with Tier 3 supports. Alignment examples are also provided.

DESCRIPTION: TIER 3 SUPPORTS

Students needing more than Tier 1 and Tier 2 supports to be successful in school may be considered for additional services at the Tier 3 level, characterized by increased intensity and frequency. Foundational components of Tier 3 supports include (a) a team-based process, (b) development and implementation of individualized supports, including evidence-based and culturally sustaining practices and (c) frequent monitoring of student progress using data (Scott, Alter, Roseberg, & Borgmeier, 2010; Scott, Anderson, & Spaulding, 2008).

Team-Based Process

Given the scope of expertise needed to effectively support the complex and intensive needs of students receiving Tier 3 supports, the composition of the Tier 3 MTSS team is particularly important. MTSS teams should include:

- Tier 2 and 3 supports coordinator
- Staff with applied behavioral expertise (e.g., school psychologist, school social worker, interventionist)
- Administrator
- Staff with knowledge of students, local family and community cultures and systems and practices across all grade levels and programs
- Staff representing diverse cultural perspectives

Example:
See this example of a Tier 3 team, including the needed roles and who can fulfill these roles.

Tier 3 Team Roles		
Team Composition:	**Roles Needed:**	**Who Can Fill These Roles?**
■ Tier 2 systems coordinator ■ Applied behavioral expertise ■ Administrative authority ■ Knowledge of students ■ Knowledge of operation of school across grade levels and programs	■ Team leader/Coach ■ Intervention coordinator ■ Minute Taker ■ Data Analyst ■ Action Plan Recorder ■ Time Keeper	■ General Education Teachers ■ Special Education Teachers ■ Paraprofessionals ■ Special Content Teachers (Music, PE, Librarian) ■ Administrators ■ Mental Health Agency Partners ■ Social Workers ■ School Psychologists ■ School Counselors ■ Community Liaisons ■ Etc.

The MTSS team coordinates a process that includes (a) data collection, (b) developing and implementing evidence-based and culturally sustaining Tier 3 supports, (c) monitoring student progress and (d) collecting and analyzing data to make decisions. Similar to the process for Tier 2, the MTSS team should consider the school's systems, staff practices and related impact when organizing and providing Tier 3 supports. Thus, Tier 3 supports must be viewed in the context of the school, as well as the family/community.

A central aspect of Tier 3 data collection is functional behavioral assessment. MTSS teams use these assessments and checklists to better understand the environmental factors that influence and maintain students' behavior so they can specifically address the function of students' problem behavior (Loman & Horner, 2014; McIntosh et al., 2008).

Individualized Supports

Individualized and intensive supports (i.e., more depth, frequency and duration than Tier 1 and 2) are needed for students who have chronic and complex needs that haven't yet been met by the other tiers of support. That's where Tier 3 supports come in. The process of developing individualized Tier 3 supports includes:

- **Collaborating** with the MTSS team, the student's classroom teachers, family and others who support the student on a daily basis
- **Collecting and analyzing of schoolwide data** (e.g., academic, office discipline referrals, attendance, student and family perspective and voice) and data related to previously attempted Tier 2 supports
- **Conducting a functional behavioral assessment** to identify a summary of the problem behavior (i.e., setting events, trigger, behavior, consequence) and student needs
- **Developing a behavior intervention plan** with individualized strategies to address the needs identified through data collection and functional behavioral assessments

Example:
The school psychologist conducted a functional behavioral assessment to help the Tier 3 teams develop a clearer understanding of a student's behavior and develop a behavior intervention plan based on student needs. See the Appendix for an example of (a) the behavior summary that is generated as a result of using the readily available Functional Assessment Checklist: Teachers and Staff (FACTS) and (b) an example behavior intervention plan based on the FACTS behavior summary. For a thorough description of the functional behavioral assessment process, see Ziomek-Daigle, Cavin, Diaz, Henderson and Huguelet (2019). In addition, the strategies for conducting a culturally sustaining functional behavioral assessment outlined by Moreno, Wong-Lo, Short and Bullock (2014) should be an integral part of the functional behavioral assessment process. Finally, for information on planning Tier 3 interventions and function-based interventions for Tier 3, see the National Center on Intensive Intervention (2014).

Features of a Culturally Sustaining Functional Behavioral Assessment (Moreno et al., 2014)

- Use a team approach to reduce individual biases
- Collect and analyze multiple data sources that include anecdotal and archival data
- Refrain from the overgeneralization of cultural stereotypes
- Conduct thorough assessment of the family culture
- Create safe atmosphere for family to share information regarding family history and practices

Implementation of evidence-based and culturally sustaining Tier 3 supports is coordinated by the MTSS team and involves school staff, the student's family and community-based professionals who support the student directly and indirectly. Tier 3 supports may be focused on academics (e.g., increasing in-class work completion), behavior (e.g., appropriate ways to ask for help) or a combination of both. Student goals related to academics and behavior are specified in a behavior intervention plan. This plan outlines who delivers supports (e.g., classroom teacher, school counselor, teaching assistant, parent), how replacement skills are taught and reinforced and how progress will be measured. Similar to Tier 2 supports, intentional efforts need to be made to provide evidence-based Tier 3 supports in a culturally sustaining way. The following practices should be integral to Tier 3 support implementation. For more in-depth descriptions of these practices, see Leverson et al. (2019), McIntosh et al., (2018) and Paris & Alim (2017).

- Ensure students, families, community are understood, validated, reflected.
- Collaborate and communicate, in multiple languages and modes, with families about the nature of the concerns and the supports to be implemented.
- Set goals that communicate high expectations (i.e., goal behaviors, scores on feedback forms, grades, etc.)
- Collaborate with teachers (e.g., strategies for neutralizing implicit bias when facing challenging student behaviors; McIntosh et al., 2018)

Evidence-based Practices: Tier 3

The following is a sample of evidence-based practices that can be implemented as a Tier 3 support. For a more exhaustive review, see Ziomek-Daigle, Cavin, Diaz, Henderson and Huguelet (2019) and Mariani and Perhay Kuba (2019).

First Step Next: An early-intervention program for young children who exhibit challenging behaviors such as defiance, conflicts with peers and disruptive behaviors in the classroom.

Solution-Focused Brief Therapy – Practice: A goal-directed collaborative approach to psychotherapeutic change that is conducted through direct observation of a students' responses to a series of precisely constructed questions. Focuses on addressing what students want to achieve while exploring the history and source of problem(s).

Motivational Interviewing – Practice: A directive, student-centered counseling style for eliciting behavior change by helping students explore and resolve ambivalence. School counselors use motivational interviewing to attempt to influence students to consider making changes, rather than engaging in nondirective therapeutic exploration.

Cognitive Behavioral Therapy – Practice: A psycho-social intervention that aims to improve mental health by challenging and changing unhelpful cognitive distortions and behaviors while improving emotional regulation and the development of personal coping strategies.

Wraparound Supports – Practice: A collaborative, student- and family-centered process for developing an individualized plan to support students in achieving academic and future goals. Team includes student, family, school personnel, community agencies and additional support systems; works through phases of the process that include engagement and team preparation, initial plan development, plan implementation and transition.

Monitoring Student Progress

Progress monitoring in Tier 3 is similar to the process described in Tier 2; however, there are some additional key features to consider:

- First, data reflecting students' response to Tier 3 supports must be collected and analyzed more frequently. Typically, data for Tier 3 supports is collected on a daily basis and reviewed weekly. Monitoring progress frequently allows the MTSS team to make quick adjustments to systems and staff practices that may be barriers to student success and the implementation of supports. It also prevents academic decline or problem behavior from escalating or continuing for too long.
- Second, because of the number of people potentially involved in implementing Tier 3 supports (e.g., classroom teacher, school counselor, teaching assistant, family, etc.), measuring fidelity of implementation is critical. It's important, for example, to track the extent to which all adults are providing the support they are responsible for implementing as outlined in the behavior intervention plan and as agreed upon by staff, the student and the student's family. For more formalized assessments, see the Tier 3 component of the tiered fidelity inventory (TFI; Algozzine et al., 2019) and the wraparound integrity tool from Milwaukee Public Schools in the Appendix.

Examples:
Monitoring students' progress frequently is key to determining the effectiveness of Tier 3 supports. For examples of Tier 3 data tracking tools, see the resource list at the end of this chapter.

DESCRIPTION: SCHOOL COUNSELORS' ROLE IN TIER 3

The Deliver component of the ASCA National Model defines the way school counselors provide services for students, including Tier 3 supports. As we know, students receiving Tier 3 supports continue to receive Tier 1 and Tier 2 supports. Recall that in Tier 2, school counselors play a particularly critical role in providing direct services (e.g., individual and small-group instruction, counseling and advisement) as interveners within the Deliver component of the ASCA National Model, as well as supporters through consultation and collaboration.

In Tier 3, typically school counselors only provide indirect services as supporters through consultation, collaboration and facilitation of referrals. Students in need of Tier 3 supports typically have complex and chronic concerns; thus, direct supports (e.g., long-term counseling) is typically not within the scope of school counselors' roles (e.g., time-bound, short-term individual and group instruction, counseling and advisement). Thus, school counselors' primary role in Tier 3 is typically as members of the MTSS team (e.g., providing consultation, collaboration and referrals); this multidisciplinary team together oversees Tier 3 implementation, utilizing the expertise and roles of each unique member.

Indirect Services/Supporter:

As supporters, school counselors participate in consultation, collaboration and facilitate referrals as part of the Tier 3 process. This includes providing and seeking consultation to support students, collaborating with key stakeholders on the MTSS team and in the community and providing referrals and resources for students receiving Tier 3 supports and their families. In a way, school counselors are the bridge between the MTSS team, school staff and families.

Consultation: School counselors provide and seek consultation to support students receiving Tier 3 supports. As a member of the MTSS team, school counselors are involved in providing information and directly modeling strategies to classroom teachers and other staff who are implementing Tier 3 supports. For instance, a school counselor could provide consultation to a classroom teacher by modeling how to pre-teach a replacement behavior (e.g., students using a signal to take a break instead of getting out of their seat to avoid work). The Tier 3 process is data-intensive; therefore, school counselors may also assist teachers and school staff with data collection related to Tier 3 support implementation, such as describing how to record the number of times a student uses a replacement behavior instead of a problem behavior during academic instruction time. As part of consultation, school counselors can also seek out information and recommendations from the student's family and experts in the community and at the district and state level to improve their own school counseling practice.

Collaboration: As collaborators, school counselors work with multiple individuals to ensure students receive evidence-based and culturally sustaining Tier 3 supports. Collaboration in Tier 3 includes teaming and partnering with the MTSS team and the student's family. For instance, school counselors often have rapport with and knowledge about students and their families that other school staff may not have. As a result, school counselors may be aware of the complex needs of students including academic, social/emotional and familial challenges affecting students' success. This information can be appropriately shared as the MTSS team seeks to better understand students' academic concerns or problem behaviors and develop individualized Tier 3 supports.

Next, school counselors develop and maintain community partnerships and provide students and their families with referrals. Specifically, these partnerships involve mental health agencies, mentoring programs, work-based experiences, tutoring, social services and afterschool programs. Finally, school counselors provide up-to-date and culturally sustaining referrals for supports outside the scope of the school building, including mental health counseling, academic resources or career-related opportunities to supplement the Tier 3 supports provided in school.

VOICES FROM THE FIELD:

Here is an example of one special education teacher who requests consulting with the school counselor: "More than half of my students have a social/emotional goal. And almost all of their indicators of students' academic achievement and functional performance are sprinkled with statements of how the student is unable to complete work independently, to participate in collaborative learning or to resolve conflict with peers. I see statements of students shutting down or only working with trusted adults. I did not feel equipped to meet such important needs. So, I turned to the experts in our building – our school counseling department. I needed to know how to equip my students to be ready to learn each day. If a student is not emotionally ready to learn, I know the best math or reading lesson in the world would be worthless. I wanted to have strategic tools to help my students spend less time in a state of emotional emergency."

See the exercise in Chapter 1 outlining steps for school counselors to generate a list of referrals and resources. Then look at the activity below.

ACTIVITY: Resource Mapping

In Chapter 1: Alignment, we suggested collaborating with internal and external resources and developing a resource list to make referrals outside of the school or to make recommendations to the MTSS team. In the context of culturally sustaining Tier 3 supports, diversity-informed resource mapping can be used in a similar way. Diversity-informed resource mapping is the intentional mapping of personal, local and institutional resources in a community that are relevant to a particular student's needs (Achola, 2019). Diversity-informed resources may include mental health agencies, community organizations or advocacy groups specifically intended for students from traditionally underserved populations (e.g., racial/ethnic minority, student with disability). School counselors can contribute to supporting students receiving Tier 3 supports by providing resources and referrals through diversity-informed resource mapping. To develop a context-specific diversity-informed resource map, follow the prompts below:

1. In the first column, write the type of resource (e.g., mental health, academic resources, mentorship, etc.).
2. In the second column, write the name of the resource.
3. In the third column, write a brief description of the resource.
4. In the fourth column, write the type of student the resource is intended for (e.g., LGBTQ, Latinx, etc.).
5. In the final column, write the contact information for the resource (website, email, etc.).

Diversity-Informed Resource Map (Achola, 2019)

AAUW				
Description	**Primary category**	**Supports (examples)**	**Contacts**	**Sample transition activities**
Nonprofit organization that advances equity for women/girls through advocacy, education, and research	■ Female students ■ At-risk youths	■ Campus safety ■ sexual assault ■ legal advocacy	Website: www.aauw.org Phone: 202.785.7700 Email: connect@ aauw.org	With the support of her parents, Rebecca will register for the campus safety workshop organized by AAUW.
SF LGBT Center				
Description	**Primary category**	**Supports (examples)**	**Contacts**	**Sample transition activities**
Nonprofit organization serving the LGBTQ population of San Francisco and nearby California communities	■ LGBTQ	■ Employment programs ■ Immigration ■ Counseling ■ Mentoring ■ Cultural programs	Website: www.sfcenter.org Phone: 415.865.5555 Email: AlbertoL@ SFCenter.org	Jamila will volunteer at the SF LGBT center to learn more about more about community dialogues between law enforcement and the LGBTQ community.
Financial literacy and education commission				
Description	**Primary category**	**Supports (examples)**	**Contacts**	**Sample transition activities**
Government agency that offers support relevant to financial literacy	■ Broad range of groups	■ Financial literacy	Website: www.mymoney.gov Email: OFE@ treasury.gov	Rebecca will take the online money quiz to assess her knowledge of the five financial principles.

Note. PSE = postsecondary education; AAUW = American Association of University Women; SF= San Francisco; LGBTQ = lesbian, gay, bisexual, transgender, questioning.

Students who are not successful after the thorough implementation of Tier 3 interventions may be referred for special education testing or mental health assessments. Important to note, prior to the advent of MTSS, a disproportionate number of students of color were referred to special education. Implementing a process of tiered interventions is another way to ensure that only students who are not successful with general education MTSS interventions are accurately identified as students with special needs and thus referred for special education evaluation.

REFERENCES AND RESOURCES

Achola, E. O., (2019). Practicing what we preach: Reclaiming the promise of multicultural transition programming. *Career Development and Transition for Exceptional Individuals, 42*(3), 188-193.

Algozzine, B., Barrett, S., Eber, L., George, H., Horner, R., Lewis, T., ... & Sugai, G (2019). *Tier 3: Intensive SWPBIS Features. School-wide PBIS Tiered Fidelity Inventory. OSEP Technical Assistance Center on Positive Behavioral Interventions and Supports.* www.pbis.org.

Goodman-Scott, E., Betters-Bubon, J., & Donohue, P. (2016). Aligning comprehensive school counseling programs and positive behavioral interventions and supports to maximize school counselors' efforts. *Professional School Counseling, 19*(1), 57-67.

Leverson, M., Smith, K., McIntosh, K., Rose, J., & Pinkelman, S. (2019). *PBIS cultural responsiveness field guide: Resources for trainers and coaches.* OSEP Technical Assistance Center on Positive Behavioral Interventions and Supports. www.pbis.org.

Loman, S. L., & Horner, R. H. (2014). Examining the efficacy of a basic functional behavioral assessment training package for school personnel. *Journal of Positive Behavior Interventions, 16*(1), 18-30.

March, R. E., Horner, R. H., Lewis-Palmer, T., Brown, D., Crone, D., Todd, A. W., & Carr, E. G. (2000). *Functional assessment checklist: Teachers and staff (FACTS).* Eugene, OR: Educational and Community Supports.

Mariani, M., & Perhay Kuba, S. (2019). Evidence-based practices across MTSS. In E. Goodman-Scott, J. Betters-Bubon, & P. Donohue (Eds.), *A school counselor's guide to multi-tiered systems of support.* New York, NY: Routledge.

McIntosh, K., Borgmeier, C., Anderson, C. M., Horner, R. H., Rodriguez, B. J., & Tobin, T. J. (2008). Technical adequacy of the functional assessment checklist: teachers and staff (FACTS) FBA Interview measure. *Journal of Positive Behavior Interventions, 10*(1), 33-45.

McIntosh, K., Girvan, E. J., Horner, R. H., Smolkowski, K., & Sugai, G. (2018). *A 5-point intervention approach for enhancing equity in school discipline.* OSEP Technical Assistance Center on Positive Behavioral Interventions and Supports. www.pbis.org.

Midwest PBIS. (2020, March 11th). *Evaluation resources.* Data tracking tools. Midwest Positive Behavioral Interventions and Supports. Retrieved from http://www.midwestpbis.org/

Midwest PBIS. (2020, March 11th). *Wraparound.* Midwest Positive Behavioral Interventions and Supports. Retrieved from http://www.midwestpbis.org/materials/wraparound

Milwaukee Public Schools. (2020, March 11th). Educational Wraparound. Milwaukee Public Schools. Retrieved from https://mps.milwaukee.k12.wi.us/en/Families/Family-Services/Intervention---PBIS/Educational-Wraparound.htm

Moreno, G., Wong-Lo, M., Short, M., & Bullock, L. M. (2014). Implementing a culturally attuned functional behavioural assessment to understand and address challenging behaviours demonstrated by students from diverse backgrounds, *Emotional and Behavioural Difficulties, 19*(4), 343-355.

National Center on Intensive Interventions. (2014). *Planning intensive tier 3 function-based interventions.* American Institutes for Research. Retrieved from https://intensiveintervention.org/sites/default/files/Handout1_BehaviorCEC2014.pdf

National Wraparound Initiative. (2020, March 11th). I*mplementation overview.* National Wraparound Initiative. Retrieved from https://nwi.pdx.edu/system-organizational-development-overview/

Paris, Django, & Alim, H. Samy. (2017). *Culturally sustaining pedagogies.* Teachers College Press.

Scott, T. M., Alter, P. J., Rosenberg, M., & Borgmeier, C. (2010). Decision-making in secondary and tertiary interventions of school-wide systems of positive behavior support. *Education & Treatment of Children, 33*(4), 513-535.

Scott, T. M., Anderson, C. M., & Spaulding, S. A. (2008). Strategies for developing and carrying out functional assessment and behavior intervention planning. *Preventing School Failure, 52*(3), 39-50.

Ziomek-Daigle, J., Cavin, J., Diaz, J., Henderson, B., & Huguelet, A. (2019). Tier 3: Specialized services for students with intensive needs. In E. Goodman-Scott, J. Betters-Bubon, & P. Donohue (Eds.), *A school counselor's guide to multi-tiered systems of support.* New York, NY: Routledge.

CHAPTER 7

Conclusion

In the introduction, we invited readers to consider their role as a leader versus a doer (Young, 2019). School counseling leaders expand their circle of influence, identify systemic barriers in their schools, promote culturally sustaining, safe and inclusive learning environments and act as purposeful leaders and change agents. Aligning school counseling programs based on the ASCA National Model with MTSS helps us meet these goals. Rather than being one more thing to do, we believe MTSS, when implemented with culturally sustaining principles, fidelity, buy-in from and collaboration with other school leaders, can help school counselors be more efficient, effective and further weave ourselves into the fabric of their schools. Also, aligning school counseling programs with MTSS is a strategy for advocacy and education, to assist our stakeholders (e.g., building and district administrators) understand our roles implementing school counseling programs, within MTSS, a framework widely understood and implemented in education.

ACTIVITY: Self-Assessment

As we wrap up this practical guide to school counseling/MTSS alignment, we invite you to reflect and create goals for your next steps: Where are you now? Where would you like to be? Re-take the self-assessment in Chapter 1.

As a result of reading this book and completing this self-assessment again:

- What is one goal you have for yourself regarding aligning your school counseling program and MTSS? What is one step you can implement this week? What are steps you can implement over the next year? Over the next several years?

- What is at least one way you can help your fellow stakeholders address racial or other disparities in your school? What data do you need to examine to ensure you are making progress in this area?

At the beginning of this book, we asked you to describe your "why?" Why are you in school counseling? As you read this book, chock-full of triangles, protocols and tips for efficiency, we hope you were able to hold steadfast to your "why" and remember why we are striving to create the best schools possible, serving every student.

Although this book is a journey into aligning the ASCA National Model and MTSS, the light at the end of that tunnel, or our "why," remains – making a difference for all our students.

Additional MTSS Resources for School Counselors

In addition to the resources listed at the end of every chapter, following are additional helpful books and websites.

BOOKS

"School Counselor's Guide to Multi-Tiered Systems of Support" (Goodman-Scott, Betters-Bubon & Donohue 2019): This is the first book to provide school counseling practitioners, students and faculty with in-depth information and resources regarding the alignment and implementation of school counseling programs and MTSS across all K–12 settings and all tiers. This book is an essential resource for pre-service and practicing school counselors, as well as their leaders, supervisors and faculty looking to better understand and utilize the overlap between school counseling programs and MTSS, to strengthen school counseling programs to better serve students, schools and communities.

"Evidence-Based School Counseling Student Success Approach" (Brigman, Villares & Webb, 2017): The book presents a unique method for training graduate students to become effective school counselors, is presented in a "tell, show, do, coach" approach to instruction and reflective of ASCA, CACREP and CAEP standards. This method is based on three interrelated components: (a) the ASCA National Model, especially its Mindsets & Behaviors for Student Success and its related student competencies, (b) the extensive research base associated with social/emotional learning, noncognitive factors and college/career readiness and (c) evidence-based programs tied to this research base and suited to school counselor implementation.

"Facilitating Evidence-Based, Data-Driven School Counseling: A Manual for Practice" (Zyromski & Mariani, 2016): This user-friendly manual helps school counselors make the essential shift to evidence-based practices and interventions in a data-informed school counseling program based on the ASCA National Model. The book contains helpful visuals, guides and checklists for every step of the process; examples of successful program evolution; guidance on developing and submitting a successful Recognized ASCA Model Program (RAMP) application; and supporting documents in an online resource center.

"New England PBIS High School Advanced Tiers: Getting Started Workbook" (Swain-Bradway & Horner, 2010): This Tier 2 systems readiness guide supports the implementation of Tier 2 and Tier 3 behavioral interventions and systems for high school students. It was developed to accompany team training and is updated regularly. These training materials have been developed to assist educators in their efforts to improve school climate and schoolwide positive behavior support for all students.

ONLINE RESOURCES

School Counselors For MTSS: This website accompanies "The School Counselor's Guide to Multi-Tiered Systems of Support" and provides regularly updated access to MTSS information, resources, research and consultation. www.schoolcounselors4mtss.com/

National Technical Assistance Center on Positive Behavioral Interventions and Supports (PBIS) website: funded by the U.S. Department of Education, Office of Special Education Programs and Office of Elementary and Secondary Education. *www.pbis.org*

Midwest PBIS Network: In partnership with the OSEP-funded Center on PBIS, this network supports PBIS implementation in state, local and community agencies throughout the Midwest. Excellent information on MTSS implementation and mental health integration. *www.midwestpbis.org/home*

Northeast Positive Behavioral Interventions and Supports: NEPBIS provides information for PBIS implementers on all tiers and hosts an annual conference each May in Connecticut. It's upported by the National Technical Assistance Center on Positive Behavioral Interventions and Supports, which is housed at the University of Connecticut. *www.nepbis.org*

Wisconsin RTI Center: This website, composed of both the Wisconsin RTI center and PBIS networks, contains a host of information on an equitable MLSS (multilevel systems of support), including excellent resources; videos; and content on behavior, math and reading. *www.wisconsinrticenter.org/*

PBIS World: This website contains links to hundreds of interventions, supports, resources and data collection tools, all of which are organized into the Tier 1 through Tier 3 framework. It is designed to help guide users through the PBIS implementation process, starting with behavior identification and offering suggestions for interventions and data collection tools. *www.pbisworld.com/*

Appendix

Introduction

From Doer to Leader

By Anita Young, Ph.D.

Are school counselors doers or leaders? Schools across the nation serve students from all walks of life. Whether in urban, suburban or rural settings, many students enter school buildings with solid levels of academic readiness, buckets full of energy and a positive outlook on life. On the other hand, some students start the school day with lower levels of academic readiness, low energy and riddled with social/emotional deficiencies limiting their ability to concentrate or live fulfilled lives as a child or adolescent.

Regardless of how students enter the building, school counselors can use their leadership capacity to remove barriers and promote sustainable outcomes for students. Rather than lead, school counselors in K–12 settings often simply do what is needed to respond to the day-to-day obstacles limiting students' academic achievement and prohibiting social/emotional wellness. It is easier and more comfortable to respond by doing something rather than doing nothing. And, doing is a safe zone that does not necessarily require leading.

However, by simply doing are you creating a sustainable impact? Are you a doer or leader? Let's think about implications of being a doer. Being a doer need not imply negative connotations. As a matter of fact, doers are like first responders, trained to make a situation better. The attention given improves the situation but not necessarily the outcome. Being a doer isn't enough for school counselors. Student needs demand school counselors move beyond reacting to leading.

Two basic principles transform a school counselor from a doer to a leader. The first step is acknowledging you have all the capacity and power to lead. Identifying your own leadership characteristics and style, coupled with the presence of effective leadership practices, is essential to build sustainable school counseling programs.

The second step is to expand your leadership capacity by seeking opportunities to develop and increase current leadership skills. Familiarize yourself with leadership theories and principles applicable for your school setting. Simple habits such as reading journal articles, participating in district professional development trainings or attending professional conferences that emphasize the value of leaders in educational settings broadens your leadership capacity and ability to identify personal leadership characteristics and styles.

As a profession, we have operationalized the term school counselor leader as a responsive change agent who is able to integrate instructional and school counseling best practices to initiate, develop and implement equitable services to all students. School counselor leaders move beyond doing because they have confidence to influence and effect change from a social justice advocacy stance. School counselor leaders propel above doing because they also know how to collaborate with others to resolve problems.

Let's explore opportunities for school counselors to lead, rather than do, by examining a continuum of school counselor leadership dimensions and how they can be manifested in practice within the ASCA National Model.

ASCA National Model Components

The themes of leadership, collaboration, advocacy and systemic change are integrated within the ASCA National Model components of Define, Manage, Deliver and Assess. Similarly, advocacy, collaboration and systemic change all require using leadership skills at varying degrees.

In the Define component, the ASCA Mindsets & Behaviors for Student Success, the ASCA School Counselor Professional Standards & Competencies and the ASCA Ethical Standards for School Counselors are guiding documents for school counselors. The empirical research and evidence-based practices embedded in the standards serve as foundational resources for school counselor leaders.

The Manage component presents organizational tools and assessments to design and assess school counseling programs based on students' priorities and needs. Managing is an aspect of leadership. While all leaders are managers, not all managers are leaders. The Manage component presents opportunities for school counselors to lead by engaging stakeholders in conversations about student learning that manifest within the mission and vision statements as living documents to serve the needs of all students.

The Deliver component describes how school counselors should deliver programs to students through direct and indirect student services. A paramount responsibility of a school counselor leader working within the context of the Deliver component is to ensure a minimum of 80% of school counselors' time is spent providing direct and indirect services. The school counselor leader integrates all elements to make informed decisions about students' instructional needs.

The Assess component allows school counselors to continually assess the design and delivery of the school counseling program and to demonstrate how students are different as a result of the school counseling program. Thus, school counselor leaders use outcome data to report to multiple stakeholders.

Let's further examine school counselors' capacity to move beyond doing through the dimensions of school counselor leadership. Five dimensions for school counselor leaders identified in a psychometric study measure school counselor and school counselor supervisors' leadership practices: interpersonal influence, professional efficacy, resourceful problem solving, systemic collaboration and social justice advocacy.

The narratives provided are cursory aspects of the dimensions and intended to invoke reflective school counselor leadership characteristics and future innovative practices. Contact the author for a copy of the survey used to identify the five dimensions.

Interpersonal influence: Leadership is defined in myriad ways. Regardless of the source, influence and vision are common terms used to capture the characteristics of a leader. Influence is exerted through verbal and nonverbal communication and how others perceive the school counselor's role.

When school counselors volunteer or are selected to serve on schoolwide, district and community councils, they are in a position of power and influence. Their presence allows a pathway to communicate the value of school counseling interventions aligned with the instructional mission and vision. For example, they can communicate to stakeholders how the ASCA Mindsets & Behaviors for Student Success can be used as an innovative resource to close achievement gaps and promote college readiness. Serving on a schoolwide or district committees is "doing," initiating policy changes as a member of the committee is leading.

To further explore your level of influence as a school counselor leader, ask yourself the following questions and provide evidence.

- How can you expand your circle of influence?
- How do you encourage colleagues to share their new ideas?
- Are you knowledgeable about communication styles? If so, how do you use communication to impact student outcomes?
- Do you effectively navigate through the politics of the school? District?
- Do you have a clear vision for the school counseling program?

Professional efficacy: Leading takes courage. The belief in your ability to lead creates efficacy and confidence that helps school counselors challenge mediocrity. Not only does efficacy breed confidence, it also fertilizes advocacy for self and others. Efficacy is what keeps school counselors returning each day to face the perils presented by students. To design and execute all of the components of the ASCA National Model requires grounded efficacy. For example, imagine yourself as a new school counselor in a school that does not have an established school counseling program. But you have been trained to be a school counselor leader; therefore, it is your belief in yourself that catapults you to design a school counseling program aligned with your school's instructional goals. Think about the questions below and reflect on your level of self-assurance and confidence.

- Do you view yourself as a change agent?
- Have there been opportunities to lead and you chose not to do so because of fear of failure?
- If needed, are you confident you are equipped to design a school counseling program?

Resourceful problem-solving: Often-times, parents enter the school building seeking answers to questions that have nothing to do with school counseling. More times than not, school counselors find solutions or direct parents to appropriate resources relative to the issues. Stakeholders often rely on school counselors to fix problems that run the gamut from simplistic to complicated.

A doer reacts; a leader responds with data-informed options resulting in systemic solutions producing self-regulated behaviors for students. Resolving problems also requires leaders to be goal-oriented. A school counselor leader with acute problem-solving skills operates with annual student outcome goals in mind.

In the context of the Deliver component, a school counselor leader provides services that fill data gaps presenting barriers to student achievement. Similarly, forging a business partnership to sponsor college tours or purchase learning manipulatives for an afterschool tutoring program are examples of integrating resourceful problem-solving strategies.

Consider the day-to-day hiccups school counselors encounter. Ask yourself if you are providing random acts of improvement or resolving problems that provide equitable outcomes for all students.

- Are you leading or reacting?
- When faced with obstacles, what steps do you take to remove barriers?
- Can you identify systemic barriers plaguing students in your school?
- Do you know how to find resources to secure what is needed to improve services for all students?

Systemic collaboration: Meeting the needs of all students does not occur in isolation. Collaboration is not only a mandate for school counselor leaders, it is an imperative for all educators. Imagine working in a school as the sole school counselor. Isolative decision-making does not effect change, nor does it produce organizational effectiveness. Building relationships and partnerships with parents, staff and community members produces sustained outcomes.

For example, collaboration is present in the Manage component; an example is a school counselor leader communicating with the principal to share the school counseling program vision and mission and how they align with the school's mission. Collaboration with teachers, administrators and parents is needed to schedule appropriate services within the Deliver component.

- Do you know the key stakeholders in your school community?
- Do you work with stakeholders to implement school counseling programs?
- Is collaboration encouraged in your building?

Social justice advocacy: School counselor leaders give voice to marginalized students and their families with the aim of producing equitable outcomes for students through transformative methods. Leading from a social justice lens involves public acts that energize others to work toward collaborative multicultural competencies. Leading from an advocacy lens is inclusive of students from unrepresented populations or who may be marginalized. Social justice advocates cannot simply do, they must lead. The impact becomes evident in all of the ASCA National Model components. When leadership, social justice and advocacy are joined the outcome is riveting.

School counselors' day-to-day work should be driven by an explicit emphasis on social justice activities and advocacy. School counselor leaders should be ever-vigilant to produce equity in educational outcomes across all student groups. A social justice advocate recognizes and responds to injustices. For example, challenging and eliminating policies and practices that negatively affect students or parents who might be marginalized due to race, gender, ethnicity or sexual orientation promotes transformative change. Consider your level of competency as a social justice advocate.

- Do you ask for help when needed to advocate on behalf of students and parents?
- When you recognize an inequity, how do you respond?
- Do you challenge status quo to advocate for all students?

The complexity and uncertainty of today's society should not prevent students from creating goals and fulfilling their dreams. The primary role of a school counselor leader is simple: help students reach their maximum potential. If you are doing, aim to lead instead.

Anita Young, Ph.D., is an associate professor at Johns Hopkins University. She can be reached at aayoung@jhu.edu. Reprinted from ASCA School Counselor, November/December 2019

Chapter 1

All examples and resources in the appendix can be found at *www.schoolcounselor.org/MTSS*

MTSS Pyramid of Strategies and Interventions by level (Loudoun County Public Schools)
Elementary school level

Middle school level

High school level

District-level school counseling brochure

District-level MTSS brochure (English)

District-level MTSS brochure (Spanish)

ASCA Position Statement: The School Counselor and MTSS:
www.schoolcounselor.org/positionstatements

Chapter 2

All examples and resources in the appendix can be found at *www.schoolcounselor.org/MTSS*

Article: The Case for Universal Mental Health Screening in Schools (Goodman-Scott, Donohue, & Betters-Bubon, 2019)

Chapter 3

Risk ratio calculator

Chapter 4

All examples and resources in the appendix can be found at *www.schoolcounselor.org/MTSS*

Schoolwide expectations (Mustang Elementary School Illinois):
QR code links with a corresponding video on YouTube, which models the expected behavior

Elementary school, behavioral matrix (Loudoun County Public Schools)

Middle school, schoolwide expectations (Loudoun County Public Schools)

Middle school, behavioral matrix (Capistrano Unified)

Sample lesson: teaching schoolwide expectations (Milwaukee Public Schools): At the start of the school years, classroom teachers conduct lessons, teaching students how to behave in specific settings (bathroom, fire drill, cafeteria, etc.), rooted in the schoolwide expectations. To note, these lessons are typically created by members of the MTSS team and delivered by teachers during morning meetings, advisory or at the start of the day of a class period. Here is an example of one lesson for the bathroom:

Documents to provide suggestions for classroom routines and procedures (Sugar Creek Elementary School): Teachers use documents, such as this checklist, to remind them of classroom procedures and practices, thus ensuring greater consistency in their practices. Such documents are often created by the MTSS team.

Unified Mental Health Teams, by Dr. Tracy Jackson
www.schoolcounselor.org/magazine

Chapter 6

All examples and resources in the appendix can be found at *www.schoolcounselor.org/MTSS*

Sample Functional Behavioral Assessment (Milwaukee Public Schools)

Wraparound Integrity Tool (Milwaukee Public Schools):
https://mps.milwaukee.k12.wi.us/en/Families/Family-Services/Intervention---PBIS/Educational-Wraparound.htm

Acknowledgements

Thank you to ASCA, including the ASCA staff. Thanks for decades of work serving the school counseling profession, advocating for our role through creating position and role statements, national and state-level advocacy, grants, *Professional School Counseling* journal, leadership training, education and professional development, and so many other important resources and efforts. And a special appreciation for collaborating with us on this book and for seeing the importance of aligning school counseling and MTSS. We appreciate using this alignment as a strategy to continue strengthening and advocating for the profession so we can best serve our students and schools through school counseling programs.

Thanks to the National Technical Assistance Center on PBIS. The center (a) provides the technical assistance to encourage large-scale implementation of PBIS; (b) provides the organizational models, demonstrations, dissemination and evaluation tools needed to implement PBIS with greater depth and fidelity across an extended array of contexts; and (c) extends the lessons learned from PBIS implementation to the broader agenda of educational reform. The center, along with senior advisors Robert Horner and George Sugai, and Bob Algozzine have laid the foundation for what has become PBIS as we know it today. We also thank current center co-directors Heather George, Tim Lewis, Kent McIntosh and Brandi Simonsen for continuing to improve capacity, scale up and sustain PBIS through the center's work.

Many thanks to the researchers who have investigated school counselors' work within MTSS, with a special thanks to Chris Sink and Melissa Ockerman, who edited a special issue on the topic in *The Professional Counselor* journal (2016).

We continue to have appreciation and admiration for the community of school counseling MTSS scholars and experts who wrote "The School Counselor's Guide to MTSS" with us, including (in order of chapter): George Sugai, Adam Feinberg, Tamika P. La Salle, Susannah Everett, Emily Goodman-Scott, Melissa S. Ockerman, Christopher Sink, Erin Mason, Caroline Lopez-Perry, Jacob Olsen, Jolie Ziomek-Daigle, Alexandra Huguelet,

Brent Henderson, Jennifer Diaz, Jason Cavin, Peg Donohue, Blaire Cholewa, Kathleen C. Laundy, Julia V. Taylor, Melanie Burgess, Melissa Mariani, Summer Perhay Kuba, Jennifer Betters-Bubon, Stephanie Smith-Durkin and Holly Kortemeier.

Thanks to Brett Zyromski, Carey Dimmitt and the Evidence-Based School Counseling Conference Advisory Board for their promotion of evidence-based school counseling within school counseling and MTSS implementation. Thanks to Trish Hatch and colleagues for their work with ASCA National Model and MTSS alignment. We appreciate Damien Sweeney providing his assistance and expertise toward this book, and we also appreciate the conversations and collaboration regarding culturally sustaining practices from others: thank you Natalie Edirmanasinghe, Rebecca Pianta, and Tim Grothaus.

Last, thanks to our loved ones for their encouragement and patience as we spend time on this school counseling/MTSS scholarly work. Many a conference call or writing session was spent with a small child or family pet on our lap or playing nearby. Your love and support keep us going.

About the Authors

Emily Goodman-Scott, Ph.D., is an associate professor, assistant department chair, graduate program director and school counseling coordinator at Old Dominion University in Virginia. She's a former elementary school counselor, as well as a special education teacher and also worked in multiple mental health settings counseling youth. Goodman-Scott is passionate about researching school counseling topics and has published extensively regarding MTSS, preparation, practices and counseling children with exceptionalities. She is the lead editor of the book "A School Counselor's Guide to MTSS." Goodman-Scott is the 2019–2020 chair of the Virginia School Counselor Association Board. She co-coordinates the ACES School Counseling Interest Network and is on the editorial review board for *Professional School Counseling* journal and the *Journal of Child and Adolescent Counseling*. She is a recipient of the 2020 American Counseling Association Research Award, the 2018 Insiders Business: Top 40 Under 40 recognition, as well as the 2017 Southern Association for Counselor Education and Supervision Outstanding Pre-Tenure Counselor Educator Award. She earned her doctorate and master's from Virginia Tech and her bachelor's degree from James Madison University. Goodman-Scott is a licensed school counselor, a licensed professional counselor, a Nationally Certified Counselor and School Counselor and an approved clinical supervisor. Follow her on Twitter @e_goodmanscott.

Jennifer Betters-Bubon, Ph.D., is an associate professor and program coordinator (school and clinical mental health counseling) at the University of Wisconsin – Whitewater. She teaches both clinical and school counseling courses to master's students. She has received multiple grants to ensure students gain relevant experience in diverse schools throughout their training. Prior to her role in academia, Betters-Bubon spent 11 years working as a school counselor and one year as a special education teacher. Her active research agenda focuses on the role of the school counselor within multitiered system of supports as well as trauma-informed schools. She is co-editor of "The School Counselor's Guide to MTSS" and has published in numerous peer-reviewed journals. She is active in the Wisconsin School Counselor Association, serving on the board for six years and receiving the 2017 research/writing award. She currently serves on the editorial review board for the *Professional School Counseling* and was recently awarded a three-year Telfer Fellowship through the University of Wisconsin – Whitewater. Betters-Bubon earned her doctorate from the

University of Wisconsin, her master's from Boston University and her bachelor's from the University of Wisconsin – Madison. Betters-Bubon is a licensed school counselor and licensed professional counselor. You can follow her on Twitter: @jjbetters

Jacob Olsen, Ph.D., is an assistant professor and school counseling coordinator at California State University – Long Beach. Prior to becoming a counselor educator in 2016, Olsen spent several years as a school counselor with Highline Public Schools outside Seattle, Wash. As a school counselor, Olsen implemented a school counseling program aligned with the ASCA National Model. In addition, Olsen was part of a district leadership team that supported the development and implementation of a multitiered system of supports (MTSS) framework across the district. This work included training and technical support for aligning school counseling programs with MTSS. Olsen's research agenda is focused on school counseling program and MTSS alignment, school counselor's role in the MTSS Tier 2 process and the implementation of school counseling programs aligned with the ASCA National Model. Olsen has published in a variety of peer-reviewed journals and is the author of "Tier 2: Providing Supports for Students with Elevated Needs," a chapter in "The School Counselor's Guide to MTSS." Olsen has also delivered several presentations and conducted district-level trainings across multiple states and is on the Board of the California Technical Assistance Center for Positive Behavioral Interventions and Supports.

Peg Donohue, Ph.D., is an associate professor and school counseling program coordinator at Central Connecticut State University. She is a former school counselor as well as a former teacher in comprehensive and alternative settings. Donohue earned her doctorate from the University of Connecticut, her master's from Harvard Graduate School of Education and her bachelor's from Georgetown University. Her primary research interests include aligning school counseling programs to effective multitiered system of supports, universal screening for mental health concerns in schools, the impact of school counselor ratios on student outcomes and the implementation of evidence-based social/emotional learning interventions. She is co-editor of "The School Counselor's Guide to MTSS." Donohue is a research fellow with the Center for School Counseling Outcome Research and Evaluation and is past president of the Connecticut Association for Counselor Educators and Supervisors and serves on the board of the Connecticut School Counselor Association. Follow her on Twitter @DonohuePeg.

Collectively the above authors publish and contribute to research on MTSS. With shared interest in how aligning school counseling programs with PBIS/MTSS programs creates stronger systems of support for students, families and schools, this collective group is committed to helping move the field of education and, specifically, school counseling forward. Learn more at *www.schoolcounselors4mtss.org*. Facebook: @SchCouns4MTSS and Twitter: @SchCouns4MTSS.